STRICT

A true story of life a

letters, diaries and journals

Roy Douglas

'When love beckons to you, follow him,
Though his ways are hard and steep.
And when his wings enfold you yield to him,
Though the sword hidden among his pinions may wound you.
And when he speaks to you believe in him,
Though his voice may shatter your dreams as the north wind lays waste
the garden'

On Love from The Prophet
Kahlil Gibran

Dedicated to Steffe

Part One

The Affair

PROLOGUE

April 1976

It was a dull and miserable morning, though dry. Looking out of our back window, Bath looked drab and weary. It reflected my mood. Things were not going well between us, she was distant and was away so much. I had grown increasingly resentful of this. Right now, she was about to leave for her weekly four day stint at the drug hostel in London where she worked. These stints could straddle weekends and she worked over our first Christmas together.

She had packed her green velvet bag that had a zip at the top. I heard her go into the bathroom and I turned round to face the room. Her bag was in the middle of the floor and wide open. I immediately saw that her dutch cap was on top. It was such a shock for it meant only one thing. I gave myself no time to think, it was beyond my capability as a surge of pain, disbelief and anger surged within me. I violently opened the door, stepped into the small hallway and looked through the open door of the bathroom where she was looking in the mirror.

'Jesus Christ, Steffe,' I shouted, 'What the fuck's going on?'

She turned her face to look at me. Her eyes were cold and unresponsive. She came out of the bathroom, brushed past me and entered our room. I followed. She said nothing other than 'I have to catch my train and get to work'. I lost it. I grabbed hold of her, pushed her against a wall and put my hands around her neck. I screamed 'How could you do it?' I had never touched her or any other woman in anger before. It was momentary. I dropped my hands, defeated. She looked at me but still said nothing. She simply walked to her bag, zipped it up and walked out.

It took less than 5 minutes. I sat on our bed, dazed, broken. What had happened to our love, a once so passionate and intense love that had defied the odds for so long? Now coldness, hardness, a refusal to engage. Why couldn't she just stay, explain, pay at least some recognition to the fact that we had been the closest of lovers, recognise my inevitable pain and at least show some warmth and sensitivity?

Later I reckoned the open bag was deliberate, it had to be. A way of telling me without having to explain. How could things have come to this?

I didn't see her again for more than 5 years.

ONE

October 1971

The nights were drawing in rapidly and it was approaching twilight when we stepped through the gateway to Trinity Hall, one of Cambridge's oldest and smallest colleges, and into the porters' lodge.

My parents stood behind me as I spoke to a porter who stood behind a high dark wood counter. He checked the register and then said 'follow me, sir'. As we left, he pointed to a wall of pigeon holes. 'You will find yours there. It's where we put notes, messages and mail'. Little did I realise that 16 months later, it would become our dead letter box. We stepped back out of the lodge and into the front court; it was stunning, peaceful and beautiful.

The black-suited porter immediately turned right and headed for an opening in a corner giving on to a worn wooden staircase that spiraled up to the floors above. We followed him as he ascended and as he walked to a door which he opened and then ushered us through. Passing a bathroom on my left, I entered a substantially sized sitting room with two large paned windows looking out onto the front court below, the chapel to the left, and the dining hall straight ahead. Two doors led off into separate bedrooms.

The porter left and my mother began to fuss. I insisted that I wanted to sort my stuff out myself and practically pushed them out the door and back home. In truth, I had found them embarrassing for the last 3 years. Very cruel, really. They had scrimped and saved to privately educate me at prep school and then at a Quaker public school. In a real sense, it was because of them that I was now at Cambridge. But that very privilege and education had alienated me from them. They were aspiring middle class but with little formal education and no interest in culture, contemporary or otherwise. They were very conservative socially and politically.

I looked out onto the front court as the light faded. I wanted to explore so I left my rooms, made my way down the staircase and crossed the front court towards some double doors into what can best be described as a thoroughfare and hallway. To my left was the wood-paneled dining hall with the High Table at the far end, raised above the long dark dining tables with matching benches that stretched the length of the hall. On the walls hung large oil paintings of eminent Hall men.

I pushed through another set of doors and stepped into the rear court. It took my breath away. It was so tranquil and beautiful. I glanced to my right and through lead-paned windows cut into ancient stone I saw the bar. To my left was the Master's Lodge. Even now, deep into the autumn, flowers bloomed in the beds lining all the buildings. In front of me rose a huge tree that in summer cast cool shade onto the grass below. Behind it I saw a raised terrace surrounded by a wall, steps at the front. I walked towards it, passing a gateway to my right, with massive double doors, leading to a side lane. I climbed the two or three steps onto the terrace, ambled towards the rear wall and then I saw the river, flowing gently by. To my right was a hump backed bridge connecting the side lane to the acres of green beyond. It was so quiet, so still and quite magical.

As I stood there, I heard footsteps behind me. I turned and saw through the gloaming a young man with long brown hair, parted at the middle, falling on each side of his face. His eyes were dark as were the rings underneath. He wore a long old RAF coat which he clutched about himself as he stepped onto the terrace and across to the wall. Little, if anything, was said but I was excited to see him. He did not look straight at all, definitely alternative and a bit debauched.

I returned to my rooms and within minutes the door opened. In stepped the man who had joined me by the river. He was my room-mate for my first year, Ian. Perfect. Ian and I became life-long friends.

*

10

The first time I saw John was from behind. He was walking a few feet in front, heading in the same direction as me. Grey tight cords around slim legs, grey sports jacket, long thinning hair flowing back, broad long sideburns. It was a lovely late Cambridge autumn day, a clear blue sky, crispness in the air.

It appeared we were going to the same place, a meeting of the Cambridge University Labour Club. I remember little of the meeting but I kept my eyes on him. He was different, older for a start, more mature. And radical. He had dark eyebrows and quite intense brown eyes. He spoke out, even at that, his first meeting. Because it turned out it was his first meeting too.

We found ourselves walking back together.

'So what did you think of that?' he asked.

'Pretty tedious and unimpressive. I liked what you were saying.'

'Well, I'm a socialist. The Labour party needs radicalising.'

'I totally agree. I'm a socialist too. I guess my big two influences have been Marx and the Quakers.'

'The Quakers?'

'Yes. It was through them that at school I sort of gained a moral and political focus. Quakers have always struggled for justice. It's inspired me. I occupied Michael Foot's study!'

'Really?'

'Absolutely! And my history teacher, who had only just come down from here, he was only in his mid-20's, was a Marxist and opened my intellectual mind in so many ways.'

'So what are you doing here?', he asked.

'Just arrived to study law. At Trinity Hall. And you?

'Research fellow in law at Sidney Sussex. Like you, I've just arrived.'

'Researching?'

'Working conditions on oil rigs, trade union rights, safety law, that sort of area.'

Despite being some years older than me, we enjoyed talking. As we returned to the centre, he suggested I go back to his flat for a coffee. I agreed.

We passed over the bridge by my college and down to Trinity Lane. We turned right, past my college entrance, and then up the passage by the Old Schools (wherein lay the law school) and crossed the top end of King's Parade and entered Market Square. We immediately turned left into Rose Crescent, for foot passengers only. After about thirty feet, John pushed a door to our right, next to a Berni Inn. We climbed three or four flights of stairs and came out onto a flat roof area upon which small flats had been built. His was the first one on the left.

He opened up the front door and we stepped into a small living room. A wide window looked across to other flats on the rooftop. Underneath was an impressive looking turntable, sound system and a collection of records. Along the left-hand side wall was a mattress with cushions scattered on it and a bean bag. To my right was a small desk with a typewriter and a chair in front. There was a counter towards the rear, stretching half way across the room. Behind it was a tiny kitchen area. There was a woman standing there. She turned round. She had long dark brown hair, dark brown eyes, an angular face, full and well-shaped lips and a look of shyness.

'Steffe, this is Roy. Roy, Steffe'.

She glanced at me briefly, said 'Hi' and turned back to the sink to fill a kettle. John and I sat down and talked. She then brought us mugs of tea and retreated to the rear and what I later found out to be the bedroom.

He had studied law at Durham university which was where he first met Steffe. They got together later when they were living in London and had both come up to Cambridge that summer so he could take up his fellowship. It was only later I found out she was working as a nursing auxiliary at Addenbrooke's hospital.

We became real friends. We bonded over politics and he was extremely bright and energetic. It was nice to form a friendship with an older man and one outside my college and undergraduate life. We began to plan to take over the Labour Club. We wanted to change its name to the Socialist

Labour Club (why did we keep the ridiculous word Club, instead of Society?). We wanted to promote real socialism, with ideas like workers' control. We began to identify and link up with fellow thinkers.

But also I found him good company and so I began to call round at his flat unannounced, aiming for when he was likely to be around. In time, I would occasionally go in the evening and then we would smoke dope and listen to music, Jefferson Airplane, It's a Beautiful Day, Dylan, mainly American stuff. Steffe would join us then but she really didn't say anything. But I could tell she liked getting stoned and listening to music.

*

Through John, I met a wider range of people, beyond my college. It was only towards the end of my first year I found there those kindred spirits who became my close friends over my final two years. My friendship with Ian developed but he too was to finding his feet.

*

Meanwhile, I was working reasonably conscientiously at my legal studies, going to lectures, seminars and tutorials. Looking around the lecture hall, I felt so different, and even then alienated, from the great mass of them. Virtually all of them were men, the majority visibly conservative. Indeed, lawyers dominated the Cambridge University Conservative Club, as I was later to find out. The actual study of law proved to be dry, narrow and understanding its link to society was forbidden territory. I was not alone in being frankly bored. There proved to be a small but significant number of Hall law students who were similarly disengaged. We naturally came together.

My recollection is that there were just five women law students. They would tend to sit together and my friends and I were the only ones who would join them. One became a friend of mine, a fiercely intelligent woman from a left wing legal academic background and a socialist

February 1972

The miners' strike. A state of emergency announced. Its only discernible effect on Cambridge was a surge of enthusiasm from the far left. I came to share it. And just then, a dispute between the radical Cambridge Students Union and the university came to a dramatic head. The demand was for a reform of the exam system and student representation on course content committees . It was refused. What followed was a 48 hour sit-in at the Old Schools, where the law library and lecture rooms are, an emblematic building next to King's College chapel at the head of King's Parade. Just round the corner from my college.

I had not followed the issues, in a sense I was being opportunistic, but I liked their ideas and I decided to join in. Ian came too. I remember stepping through the front doors, smiling at the rebels gathered there and climbing a long stone staircase up to the main lecture theatre. There were no chairs – they had been cleared away. Instead, the floor was covered with hundreds of mainly freaks. I felt so excited. I realised that this was what I had hoped to experience.

As day turned to night, a band set up on a make-shift stage and blasted us with rock. Ian and I smoked joint after joint lying on the floor listening to the sounds. Which suddenly included the smashing of wood on wood. We staggered down the stairs to the front doors to find we were under attack. Occupying students were barricading the doors with chairs and anything they could find. I glanced out of the window and saw the attackers were right-wingers from colleges like Magdalene . The attack was repulsed and it felt so liberating. I later wandered out onto the front lawn and met 4 striking miners. How the hell were they there? Something like Paris 1968, students and workers coming together?

Oh how splendid it felt. Inside, all was permitted.

I continued to see John regularly and then one day he said he and Steffe were getting married and I was invited, along with some mutual friends.

May 1972

14

The reception was at Steffe's parents' home, a large detached elegant house of the late 20's. A circular drive curved in front of steps leading up to a front porch. My friend and I parked up and entered. The place was abuzz and it took time for us to find people we recognised. Most people were smoking and I sat down and joined them. Then I spotted John and stood up. He smiled warmly.

'Congratulations! All went well at the register office?'

'Yes, all cool'.

'I must congratulate Steffe. Where is she?'

'Just there, see?'

I saw her across the room. She was wearing a long white dress, beautifully cut, with boxes of gold material at each corner of the square neckline . She had a silver clasp around her neck, with a large oval green stone at the centre and a matching ring on her right hand. Her hair hung as usual each side of her face. She looked happy. I went up to her and she turned away from the person she had been speaking to.

'Steffe. You look wonderful. Many congratulations. Dominic and I have bought you a ridiculous present. Sorry. It's a large white teddy bear'.

She laughed. 'Well, at least we don't have one already!'

'Is it cool to smoke a joint in the garden?'

'Sure'.

'Do you want to join me?'

She did. It was a lovely garden and we sat in the shade of an old oak tree. I rolled up, lit up, had a drag and passed it to Steffe.

'So how does it feel to be Mrs Martin?'

'I'm not really sure. Strange thing to say on my wedding day.'

'Is it being Mrs Martin or is it being married?'

'To be honest a bit of both.'

'So why have you married?'

'Well, there's been a lot of family pressure. You know, since we live together, we should be married and so on. And things haven't been all that easy between us. So it's a sort of statement of intent, to try to make it work. I do love John. He's a lovely man.'

'I agree. We've become good friends.'

'He said to me recently that you are his best friend.'

'Really?' That surprised me. I could think of no more to say.

'You know, even today I was thinking to myself that I can always divorce him if things don't work out. Not that I'm intending to. That's a strange thought to have on my wedding day, isn't it?'

There was a brief silence. I was rather taken aback and also a bit flattered that she had shared such an intimacy with me.

'So are you joining us this evening?' she asked, 'We're going up to Battersea Fun Fair, smoke lots of joints and take to the sky.'

'I couldn't say no.' I smiled.

Just then, some people came out of the house and approached us.

'Look, Steffe, telegrams! You must read them out,' someone cried.

I walked slowly back inside. What a strange conversation, I thought to myself. Unconventional, honest, and her voice was so beautiful. Soft, reflective, gentle.

It was only much later that I found out that a night or two before the wedding, John had got it on with one of Steffe's oldest friends in a room next to where she was 'sleeping'. She said she had lain there absolutely shaking. But still she married him. Why? A statement of the time? Was it that having thrown off the shackles of the sexual repression of our parents' generation, the opposite extreme became the norm in the 'alternative' culture? Freedom, no more possessiveness, follow your instincts, see jealousy as a bourgeois concept designed to imprison. It became a licence for men to screw and for women to go along with it, not to show any sign of repression. That is not to say the culture did not empower women sexually – it did. But later, we both agreed a lot of people got very hurt.

It was great fun at the Fun Fair. We took so many screamingly hilarious rides. And then it was time for Steffe and John to leave. As they waved goodbye and walked off, I was surprised to be hit by feelings of real jealousy and envy.

The summer term passed but it was a time of change.

I began to find and connect with the small Hall freak community whose members I came to be so close to. A few were lawyers but others were studying English, philosophy and even maths. My style of dress changed and my hair had not been cut for over a year. I took to wearing loons of various colours but typically denims, shirt and neckerchief. I also changed my glasses to round ones like John Lennon. I began to walk the streets differently, feeling I represented something new, challenging. I liked feeling I was getting into people's faces. I felt myself changing gear.

But I was still active in the Labour Club, working with John and others to wrestle control. In the summer elections, we won some seats on the committee for the following term. I had the most lowly role of being in charge of the food for our regular lunchtime meetings.

And at last I lost my virginity! I was invited to a party at Girton College, one of only a couple of women's colleges at the time. I went with others and we found ourselves smoking joints in this woman's room. She was a 3rd year and about to leave. I realised I quite fancied her and she clocked me. We managed to shift the bodies on the floor out of the room. The love we made was very sweet and sensual and drifting in and out of sleep with her afterwards was glorious. I was very lucky. When morning came, she confronted me with the problem of getting out. Men are most definitely not allowed overnight. So it was a question of slightly opening the door, checking the corridor and quietly creeping down the staircase. It was wooden so each step I took creaked loudly around the generous hallway. I anxiously glanced around as I reached the bottom, checking that no one was coming from behind. I moved smoothly towards the door, praying it would open. I pulled the handle but it was locked. Think. Simple. Just pull the lever above. And I was out, walking down the drive to the road. As I strode back to college, I exalted in feeling that now I was a man.

I wasn't aware about it at the time but my life was beginning to change path.

TWO

October 1972

It was a joy to return to Cambridge to start my second year. I was staying in lodgings in Bateman Street about a mile from the centre. They were in a terraced Victorian house. Ian was lodging more or less opposite as was Christian, who came to be a very important friend. Another friend lodged just down the road so it was a nice little community.

We took to talking through the night, maybe just Christian and I , maybe others too. Dope had now become a daily essential and it was a habit more or less all of us shared.

In the meantime, I was carrying out my Labour Club duties and regularly popping round to see John and sometimes spend evenings with the two of them. One day I called round and only Steffe was at home. She made us tea and for the first time we began to properly talk.

'So you knew John at Durham?'

'Yes, but only casually. He was not really part of our scene.'

'Which was?'

'My happiest memories are living in this house in Durham with an amazing group of people. One guy, very charismatic, was a great musician. He also had such interesting ideas. I learnt a lot there.'

'So give me more of a picture.'

'Well, there was a lot of dope, of course. But also such wonderful discussions plus plenty of nights wiped out by music. It was amazing. That was when I first properly fell in love. I was in awe of the guy. When he dumped me, I was in such pain. He went off with Mo Mowlam! We actually got back together for a while but I did get over him.'

'So what were you studying?'

'Spanish and Russian. Not a good idea. I got chucked out at the end of my second year.'

'Ah. But you had a good time, it sounds?'

'Yes, I did. But it also makes me feel a bit of a failure.'

'So tell me what happened then?'

'Oh, I moved to London, had some good friends, worked in publishing and at the Family Planning Association, met John again and here I am. In fact, I've just started a 3 year degree course on social policy at the LSE so I will be splitting my time between London and Cambridge.'

I found myself returning and finding her alone and us chatting. We began to open up to each other and I felt there was a real friendship developing. No, that's wrong. I felt something more than that.

One night, Christian and I were talking in my room. Sometimes we would talk until sunrise and then he would go back to his room opposite and we would open our windows and talk across the road, everything silent save the dawn chorus. This night he told me about his great love. In his gap year, he had gone to work on a development project in Africa. There was a married woman working there, a beautiful fair haired woman and Christian fell in love with her. The feeling was mutual though she specified that there could be no final consummation. He said she captured his soul. A great love lost.

'That's how I feel about Steffe,' I said. I had not even said this to myself before. 'There is something about her. A depth, an intensity, I don't know. And I find her indescribably beautiful and desirable. But it's hopeless. I know it.'

November 1972

I fell ill with flu. It was pretty ghastly being confined to my room, which was very dull and plain and had little furniture. I had done little to it.

One afternoon Christian called round. I had been in a slightly delirious state and had been dreaming of Steffe. I felt very strange and found myself telling him that I absolutely had to see Steffe. Unbelievably, he

20

immediately said he would zoom round on his motor bike and fetch her. In a state of some confusion and anxiety, I gave him the address. Off he went.

I lay there wondering what on earth I had done. I must look terrible. It was all so weird.

In what seemed no time at all, the door opened. Christian walked in followed by Steffe – and then John. I was lost for words. They stayed only briefly but throughout my eyes kept creeping back to Steffe.

After they left, I lay there quite perplexed. Such a mad request but they had come, Steffe had come.

*

As the term passed, the left in the Labour Club prepared for the committee elections that took place in late November. John was a leading light in the group and it was suggested that I should stand to be chair. Flattered, though unconvinced that I was necessarily the right person, I agreed.

What an insight this election proved to be. We had a left 'slate' with a view to taking all positions on the committee. Hitherto, it had been packed with right wing would-be careerists. This group was centred around an oily toad of a man who liked nothing more than playing games, particularly if they were dirty. One story that was put about was that I had been going around Girton College, offering free membership of the Labour Club plus some unspecified other, if students voted for me and the left slate! We did nothing of the sort, of course, merely set out our agenda and political thinking.

We won, taking over complete control of the Labour Club. We celebrated in the Baron of Beef. I got increasingly drunk. John came with Steffe. Again and again I sat down next to her. I was finding her irresistible. John even complained about it (apparently). Bicycling home truly drunk, I drove into one of Cambridge's ludicrously huge gutters, right outside Addenbrookes Hospital. I was unconscious for a short while. The following day I suffered from concussion. I felt I was going a bit mad, was depressed and confused. Somehow I felt it summed up what was happening to me. The straight me had just achieved political office (not infrequently helpful for would-be MP's) but what I was feeling was that now the real me was saying 'I don't want that anymore. I want to be free'.

You see, all this was happening just as I was properly and profoundly discovering drugs and at last finding the hedonistic alternative people I had been longing to meet since arriving. And I was beginning to spiral away... And Steffe just stuck in my head. I realised I really, really wanted her.

December 1972

Going down back to the truly hideous new town of Bracknell at the end of the autumn term was grim. I yearned to be back in Cambridge instead of which I felt trapped at my parents' house. And I needed to see Steffe. So I wrote to her, falsely claiming that I was going to be in London shopping and maybe we could meet up since she was at the LSE. She replied.

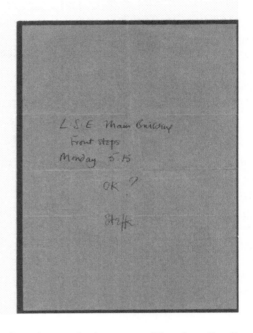

I couldn't quite believe her reply. Its composition, brevity, directness, and most of all her agreement to meet me. I was so excited but also so nervous as I took the train from Bracknell to Waterloo. I had an A to Z and worked out which tubes to take. Emerging from Holborn station, I was greeted by winter sunshine. I strolled down towards Aldwych and, after a bit of searching, found the front steps to the main building. I was early and so leaned on a nearby fence and smoked a cigarette. I kept glancing up at the steps and, dead on the dot of 5.15, she came out. She was wearing pale denim jeans, lace up boots, a long dark navy coat, scarf and a subdued crimson woollen hat, pushed back so her hair fell over her brow as well as down her face. I got up and approached her. She saw me and gave me her wonderful smile. As I approached, also smiling widely, I could not help but look at her beautiful deep brown eyes, accentuated as always by her delicately applied black eyeliner on both her upper and lower eyelids.

'Steffe, really lovely to see you.'

'You too. But you don't seem to have much shopping!'

'Well, it all proved a bit of a disaster so I don't have any. But I've enjoyed wandering around. So what shall we do? You're the expert. My last train from Waterloo is 10.30, by the way. But I'd like to eat.'

'I suggest we go to this little Italian restaurant that isn't far away but would you like to walk for a bit?'

'That would be great. I really don't know London.'

We wandered round this lovely part of London, Chancery Lane and Lincoln's Inn nearby. Conversation came very easily. I asked about her course at the LSE. She once again referred back to her being required to leave Durham University and her feeling of being a failure. She told me how she had managed to gain entry to the LSE to study what really interested her, social policy. It was a three year course and she would be spending her time between London and Cambridge.

She asked about my course.

'It's awful. I can't stand it. It's so narrow and desiccated. All it does is concentrate on pure black letter law which means just knowing and understanding the rules. I really did expect that there would be some discussion of what these rules are achieving, how they affect society, why they exist. There's none of that. I've practically given up on going to lectures now. I went to one on jurisprudence given by an eminent professor of jurisprudence, Professor Dias. I found myself standing up and challenging his ridiculously narrow view of the philosophy of law. I based my arguments on basic Marxism and said that his lecture was so detached and in a sense irrelevant. Did he not think about how law reinforced class oppression, how it enshrined the primacy of property, how law protected the interests of the rich, ruling elite? It didn't go down well. So I'm done with them.'

'Wow, that was impressive!' she smiled, 'So why did you choose law?'

'Good question. I guess I felt, for various reasons, that I needed to take a degree in something that led to a profession. Actually, what I had really wanted to do was to become a doctor. I had always been fascinated by human biology and was knowledgeable. I had genuinely enjoyed dissecting animals and examining their life systems. And it seemed an unequivocally good thing to be. The trouble was I just couldn't meaningfully grasp chemistry, and physics was not my thing either. In truth, I loved history and English. So that door was not open to me. But I was good at, and really enjoyed, public speaking, debate and argument. So law seemed a possibility but, Marxist as I was, I really didn't want to become just any old lawyer. When looking at universities, I was mainly drawn to Warwick which ran a very enlightened law course. LSE as well, in fact. But my headmaster, my teachers, were telling me I should apply for Oxbridge. It was rather an irresistible force. So that's how I ended up at Cambridge. Not that I regret it. It's a magical place, and I am now meeting some amazing people. But the course is becoming a bit irrelevant.'

We decided to eat. She led us through the streets to a little side alley at the top of which was the restaurant. It was not busy. It was still early evening. We were shown to a small table by the window, quite secluded, with a red squared tablecloth and an old wine bottle, a candle on top, with thick candle wax dripping down its sides. We were brought the menu and drinks list.

'Shall we get some wine first? How about an Italian red?'

She agreed and we called the waiter. Then we looked at our menus until the wine arrived and then ordered our food.

'So tell me more about you. Your childhood, that sort of thing.' I asked, wanting to get to know her.

'OK, if you won't be bored.'

'I won't.' I said, quite honestly.

'I was born by the sea, in Brighton. I loved it there. It was a terrible wrench when we moved to Reading. My father is a bank manager so we had to go where the job took him. We had a flat above the bank right by the Thames.'

'I know Reading well. I went to school there – Leighton Park, you know, the Quaker school?'

'Yes, I do know it. It was not far from my school, the Abbey.'

'The Abbey! You went there? That's where my first girlfriend went. There were dancing classes arranged at my school with Abbey girls attending. Very few boys joined and not many girls either. But that's how I met Sarah. I always rated Abbey girls. So, sorry, go on.' I was amazed at this connection.

'I loved my time at the Abbey. It was a liberal place with some good teachers. I look back on those days with pleasure. Rather a contrast to my next school. We often took a boat on to the Thames and though we only lived in a flat, there was always the river. But then my father was moved again – this time to Chobham.'

'I know Chobham. Near Guildford. It's a very pretty and expensive-looking village, isn't it?'

'That's true. I did have some fun there but I was sent to Guildford High School for Girls. It was just ghastly. The teachers were hard-nosed spinsters who knew nothing about what education should be. And they hated me. I've never really understood why but they called me selfish and that hit home horribly. I had some good friends but school overall became something of an ordeal.'

'What about life outside school?'

'I had a social life, quite county but some fun people. When I was older, I had a Vespa scooter and Mum let me drive her Ford Prefect so that was liberating. But I was quite shy and constantly having my heart broken.'

I laughed at that.

'But I didn't get the A level results I needed. Honestly, it was such a bad education. I was never taught to actually think for myself. I felt a failure and went to a tutorial college in London for A level retakes. And I did well enough. So I got into Durham University.'

'Why Durham?'

'I could say because it put me a long distance away from home! I'm not sure. Not long before, I had travelled up to Scotland with my brother

Lindsay in his Morris Minor and we had stopped in Durham and it is a beautiful small city. So there I went. What I didn't realise is that it gets seriously cold. I ended up sharing this house with some guys and girls. It's where I began to get educated. Everybody was embracing the alternative, dressing wildly, growing their hair, making music, talking. I had no fixed world view so I just slipped into a new and wonderful way of being. As I've told you, I fell in love. He was a great guy but he broke my heart. I all but stopped working so it wasn't really a surprise when I failed my second year exams and got chucked out. Failed again!'

'So you said you came to London.'

'Fortunately I had friends, including Durham ones, there. I managed to get work. For a time, I worked for a publishing company and then the Family Planning Association. I enjoyed myself and then I hooked up with John. What about you?'

'Me? So I have always been the blue-eyed boy, the apple of my mother's eye. My parents wanted me to succeed and so I had a very privileged education but I don't come from a rich family. I became the big hope. So at school, I always felt the pressure to excel. And I did. Head boy and now Cambridge. At school because I was head boy, or rather senior prefect, I had to meet the headmaster in his study every morning before assembly and we would talk about the temperature of the school. But I sat there as a Marxist with dreams of change. So I was aware of the rebel in me. But, you know, what's happening now is that I feel I am beginning to find the real me, beyond the constructed me. Does that make sense?

'You need to explain more.'

'Dope plays an important part. It's helped me see things differently, experience things more intensely. Music now touches me like never before. I've always loved music and listened constantly to the pirate radio stations back in the day, Radio Caroline and Radio London. But now I hear it at times almost physically. And my mind. My friends and I often gather and talk deep into the night. New ideas flash around the room. But the thinking is different. I feel the chains of my past are dropping from me. Oh God, you must think me pretentious.'

She looked me in the eye. Her face was warm and still. Her hand reached across the table and rested on mine. Her eyes looked straight into mine. They had such depth.

'No, I don't,' she said in her soft, quiet, rich, quite gorgeous voice. 'I really don't.'

We were staggered to see that not far short of three hours had passed.

'I better go,' I said, 'I can't miss the last train.'

And so we left. We briefly kissed each other's cheek and went our separate ways.

As I took my seat by a window on the last, very uncrowded, train back to Bracknell, I realised I was smitten. I saw her face reflected in the window, a face that had a beauty that I had never seen before. And that beauty exuded the authenticity, the depth, the soul life, that I had glimpsed that night. I could hear her voice, so gentle, warming, suggesting understanding, real communication.

But what did I realistically think was possible? She was married to a good friend of mine, she was significantly older than me, I didn't think I was handsome or particularly attractive, she was beautiful, she was clearly very sexually experienced, I was one step away from being a virgin.

Next day, I borrowed my father's car and drove to Finchampstead Ridges. As I looked over the rhododendron shrubs towards some misted low hills across the shallow valley, I felt the pain of not being with her. But I resolved to do everything I could to get closer to her.

I longed to be back in Cambridge. I felt really excited, alive. And simultaneously sad.

THREE

January 1973

I was back. My priority was to pop round to their flat. I remember one evening in particular.

It was a Saturday night and I was pretty sure I would find both of them in. They were. We sat around for a while smoking grass when I suddenly took it into my head to play Steffe this amazing debut album I was totally into – Roxy Music. So I roared back to Bateman Street on my bike to borrow Ian's copy and then roared back again.

'Right, guys,' I said as I re-entered, 'this is something else. Just sit or lie back and listen to this extraordinary music. Roxy, take over!'

Steffe was lying on the mattress with cushions behind her head. John was sitting on the upright chair in front of the desk. I went across to the sound system, lifted the lid, and laid side one onto the record player. I lifted the needle and gently laid it onto track one.

I lay against the counter on a bean cushion close to Steffe.

'*Remake/Re-model*': The sound of a party, voices speaking, glasses chinking, then piano, drumming and Bryan Ferry's crooning voice, frantic guitar, wild saxophone, and a weird synthesiser curling sound. All about falling for a gorgeous woman that you cannot get. Five minutes of something completely new, ending ecstatically after what felt like a long journey.

'And that's just the first track,' I quietly said. Steffe lay still, eyes shut.

Then *Ladytron*: A plea to connect with an adorable woman and a statement of intent. Crazy, almost extreme at times, thrashing guitar, insane sax, addictive drumming, stretched sound.

And then the ultimate – *If There is Something*: Basically a song of absolute devotion. And poignant. Soaring saxophone, almost orgasmic. And Ferry's deeply emotional, smooth, and often just slightly off-key voice. 7 minutes of pure ecstasy. The song that became our song.

2 HB: Two romantic people, a song incorporating Bogart's line – here's looking at you kid. Is this the future or the past? Or just dream land?

Chance meeting: Nerve and emotion-stretching synthesiser, mapping the pain of lost love. What's life been like? Seems such a short time ago since seeing you for the first time. True love is so rare. Strangely prescient.

Sea Breezes – another 7 minute epic: The loneliness of lost love. How to find a way out? A relationship crashing and not seeing how to put it right. And then when it's over, the pain. Guitar grating through the waves of emotion. What brilliant lyrics. Genius.

And finally *Bitters End*: The title speaks for itself.

A truly romantic and revolutionary album. When it finished, I looked across at her. Her eyes remained closed and she didn't move.

'Well?' I asked, turning towards her, not a word having passed throughout.

She looked at me, a gentle smile on her face, eyes almost glowing, and said, 'Just amazing.'

At that moment, I felt so close to her, so thrilled that she loved the album, aware that there was a message in the lyrics that I hadn't previously recognised. Silence followed, only broken by John saying he didn't like the album. It felt like a little victory.

Roxy became a central part of our relationship, endlessly listened to, endlessly made love to. This was a breakthrough experience. It touched something very deep in us.

*

February arrived. I had an invitation to a party, an unusual event in those days. It was across the river in a newly built block near the University library. Not the best setting, perhaps, but there were lots of people there and the music and lights were good. I spotted Steffe and

John across the room and went up to them. I then drifted off. I was standing still for a while, talking to no one in particular, when I felt a finger slide its delicate yet firm way up from the base of my spine to its top, and this delicious, now so familiar voice, whisper 'I'm crazy about you'. I turned around and looking at her, replied, not altogether poetically, 'the feeling is mutual'. I couldn't really believe it. Her eyes said that it was true. I almost melted on the spot. We said nothing more and she walked away.

I stood motionless, stunned.

I made sure I left when they did. We were joined by others. I was quite reckless. I couldn't help joking with her, having fleeting physical contact with her. I laughed and looned around. We parted near my college.

I was in a world of my own but I needed to be with others, to prolong this night of pure joy. So I found company in some drug-filled room and finally made my way back home.

I realised my life had changed profoundly. My instinctive connection with her was reciprocal. I couldn't really believe it – it was the realisation of my dreams. How could it be true? Me? It felt unreal and absolutely gorgeous.

I wanted her so badly.

*

There were of course no mobile phones and I didn't have a landline so we had to find a way of communicating quickly. So we thought of my pigeon hole. Make it a dead letter drop. I could leave my messages and she could leave hers. Despite occasional conflicts with the porters who questioned Steffe on what she was doing in a young gentleman's pigeon hole, it worked well.

Her first note said she would pop round to Bateman Street on her way back from London at around 8pm. I sat waiting for her, playing music on my ancient reel to reel tape recorder. I heard her knock and I let her in. As she entered the room, we said nothing, just kissed. It was our first kiss and it seemed to last forever. We sat on my sofa, Santana playing. We

31

talked a bit but couldn't resist kissing again and again. By the time she left, I was in another world.

 We met maybe two more times and then I received this.

Roy,

John is going away from 20ᵗʰ to 22ⁿᵈ.
He thinks he's going out of his mind (literally, very existential) and tells me he needs me. I think I'm going out of mine and I want you.
Do you realise that I'm nearly 5 years older than you?
Have you tried following that thought around?
Here's looking at you kid.

 Good God. It was happening. I felt quite overwhelmed. What she wrote was so sexy, so arousing. I realised that I was experiencing something I had never experienced before. Beautiful love songs by Simon and Garfunkel played in my ears. But I was still the bloody chair of the bloody Socialist Labour Club (as it was now called) and I had no interest at all. I had by now gone beyond the old world, with its old structures, I felt I was on a new path of self-discovery and liberation and the Labour Club hung round my neck like a dead weight.

 But I put such thoughts aside. Then:

Monday
Dear Roy
By now you must be getting very confused.
The fact is I was sitting in a class talking about Utopia and I began to feel really weird so I decided to split.
As it happens I feel better now. Amazing.
J. leaves at the shriek of dawn tomorrow. I suggest you call round when you can (and as early). If milk bottles out with message, J. has gone. OK?

'And as early'. I felt the urgency of her note. Somehow I managed to sleep. Quite amazing given how excited I was, more so than I had ever felt in my life. I set my alarm for 7. I hadn't got up that early for a long while. I bathed, shaved and applied my rather strong after-shave. I chose denims. I was slim and they accentuated this. I went down the stairs, opened the front door and climbed onto my trusty and very old BSA Bantam 125 motorbike, bought for £10 at Christian's insistence.

I drove through empty streets, down to King's Parade and into Market Square. I parked up and walked across to Rose Crescent. Pushing the door of the main entrance open, I hoped I wouldn't bump into John. I climbed the stairs and on getting to the top, I looked nervously out through the window towards their flat. The milk bottles were out. John was gone.

I knocked on the front door and it was immediately opened. I stepped inside and we kissed with both passion and tenderness but also surprising ease. We were like a couple of excited kids embarking on an expedition.

It was a simply beautiful day. How blessed we were, the sky blue , the air crisp and pure.

'Shall we go to the Gog Magogs?' she asked.
I had never been there but knew of them.

'We'll go on my bike, OK?' I said.

We didn't bother to think, we just trotted down to my BSA and headed off. As we left Cambridge behind us, we revelled in the cold air blowing through our hair (no helmet law then) as we drove into the flat countryside until reaching the small risings that were the Gog Magogs. Climbing the final hill was slow – 15 mph. It was an old bike. We laughed so much. Steffe even offered to get out and push.

But we got there and parked the bike up against a fence. We looked around and saw a clump of trees across a field. We decided to head for them. When we got there, we looked out across a wide plain and just took in the view and the quietness. We looked at each other, held each other, kissed. It felt just perfect. We were so happy. We were disturbed by a group of school children walking past nearby and we laughed. Had they spotted us canoodling? We were thirsty, having smoked at least two joints, and Steffe spotted a milk cart that had drawn up at a nearby farm. We headed over a bought some milk. It was heavenly.

We returned to my bike and drove back to Bateman street. I led her to my room and locked the door. We looked at each other intensely.

We went to the bed and began our lovemaking but I held back from its final consummation. 'Why?' she asked. 'Oh, I feel a bit guilty about John.' But that wasn't true. I didn't care about him right then. No, it was because of my fear of failure, the fact that I knew I was all but a virgin and she was obviously so sexually experienced. I didn't want to seem as innocent and inexperienced as I was.

What she said broke the log jam. I wanted her so badly and when we finally came together, it felt so natural, so driven by emotion, so deeply sensual. Magic from the very first time. We were very lucky.

Afterwards, we went to the cinema but all I could think of was making love to her again.

We went back to her flat and her double bed. We took off our clothes and resumed our lovemaking, a lovemaking that lasted for vast passages of time.

After that, we made love again and again. Bed became our playground, our special place, our field of freedom, the place we talked – month after month, year after year. We never bored of each other. We entered a world of fantasy that was entirely our own. That was the ground-rock of our love, indeed our addiction, to each other. Ours was a very horizontal relationship.

Coming to the end of those 2 days felt like coming out of a dream that you just long to return to.

I was now deeply in love.

With a married woman.

A woman married to a friend.

And I was really so very young still.

I was just 20.

She filled my head. Everything else was irrelevant. I missed supervisions, tutorials, even Labour Club meetings. I needed to hear from her. We managed some communication and contact but it was brief. Like this:

Roy my love,
I'd really rather see you in Bateman Street tonight if that's OK - I'll take a taxi there and maybe you could walk back with me. I'll come as soon as J. goes to his meeting - I don't know when it starts, 8 o'clock or so. I hope you didn't get too much of a bummer bumping into J. But I couldn't resist coming to talk to you. I had a really weird dream about you.
See you tonight.
Steffe x

It was intense on both sides. Steffe was constantly looking to engineer time for us to be together. But we managed it. I asked my dear friend Christian if he could find somewhere in London we could stay. He came up trumps – Johnny, an old Etonian friend of his at Trinity, could lend us a flat in Maida Vale. It was so exciting travelling down together and making our way to this unknown flat. We let ourselves in through the very substantial front door and made our way up to the first floor and the flat. As we walked in, we gasped at its splendour. Oak panelled throughout with a bed right in the middle. We held hands as we walked in.

'This is going to be our special world' I said.

'Oh Roy, wow, it's amazing'

Indeed it was. No one knew we were there. We had no connection with the outside world. We could make of this place what we willed.

And we did. We settled in as only we knew how and entered that magical bubble in which our love and desire blossomed.

We left the flat just once. We found a nearby park, bathed in sunlight, where we fooled about, dancing and leaping and just laughing.

Did we ever eat? I really have no memory. We just seemed to float through heaven. There was nothing apart from us. When not making love, we talked endlessly, invariably in bed. Our very isolation , our physical intimacy, meant there were no defences up, we opened our inner selves to each other and found a profound connection. We are both very emotional, sensitive and romantic people and we found we shared a deep synchronicity.

From then on, we met when we could.

We managed another wonderful weekend in the Maida Vale flat. I was totally in love with her and it seemed she was with me too.

We were lying in bed on a Sunday morning. We had made love and I looked at Steffe and asked:

'So where do we go from here, Steffie?'

'What do you mean?'

'Well, you know, John.'

'I'm not saying anything to him. What would be the point? I'm not intending to leave him.'

I guess I had sort of assumed that she would. Remember I was still so young. But it was clear that she did not see it like that. And so began the struggle of coming to terms with being in an affair. But never underestimate or downplay the joys of an affair. Its secrecy, intensity, sexuality, intimacy. These we both loved. And there were the emotions. At this stage, pretty wild on both sides.

She wrote afterwards:

Roy, my love,
Sorry - downer - J. didn't go to London. But I'll do
everything I can to see you as soon as possible.
That was such a beautiful trip we had - I'm sorry I had a
headache and dragged us down to Battersea on all those

tubes but it really didn't matter because I was so happy being with you.
I hope you're still on your feet and having a good time. I'm so bored with working, I can't tell you.
Incidentally, we're going to the King's Event on Tuesday, is it? Are you going?
I'll leave a note or come and look for you whenever I can. Take care, my love, Steffe x

From then on, she began to write to me in earnest, it became a mark of our relationship, how we maintained the intensity of our relationship through the many days apart. I loved it when she used her very special purple-bordered, thick, almost parchment-like, paper. And her writing was beautiful. Both in its form and content.

We snatched an hour or two here or there. There was a desperate passion. I would get a note suggesting I call round while John was at a meeting or something. I remember one evening going there and in no time at all we were naked and slowly making love on the cushion-covered mattress in the front room. We were now becoming quite reckless.

There followed other nights in London. But unbelievably, on one occasion when we were in London, the phone rang in the flat and it was my mother. God knows how she tracked us down. I was completely thrown. I can't remember what I said but I know that somehow I let the cat out of the bag. And it was then that the outside world began to smash into our precious world of beautiful fantasy. I felt embarrassed, her ringing made me feel such a boy.

*

Dear Roy,
This letter may go a bit awry in a moment. I'm waiting for the train to move out.
I'm afraid I haven't been really tackling any problems in any very strictly practical way in London today. Rick was

37

feeling pretty bad so we went to the park with Penny and played Frisbee until we flaked out and then we played this amazing game with pictures that I want to show you. But there is a point where talking gets a bit past its uses. Anyway, it cleared my head a bit and presented another problem - that I wanted you to be there.

But .... there are some things we could do together if you want to. Apparently the Red Buddha at the Roundhouse that they went to see was absolutely incredible - I've not seen people flipping out over something quite as much for a long time. Angie and her bloke are going again next Monday and maybe we could go too. Only I would have to get tickets fast because the word is getting round. Also they might be having dinner on Tuesday or Wednesday which we could think about dropping in on. But that's a pretty haphazard arrangement.

I know I am really evidently evading the issue - in a sense this is part of it (that is, the issue).

I'm going to call in at Bateman St. to see if you're in but I guess you'll be doing your number at the LABOUR CLUB. Mark and Fergie are round at our place - if you could face it, I could certainly face you with ultimate pleasure but I know my wishes pretty often go beyond the limits of sanity. Anyway they'll probably be around until midnight or so. If the milk bottles are out with a message for the milkman, they're gone.

Complex, huh?

I had a look at Cancer. I couldn't really get much out of it at the time. It's a cardinal (active) water sign. Action motivated by emotion. Very, very strong universal womb idea (don't let that freak you out - the Earth Mother can be in anyone). Tenacious, protective. But remember that's

38

*your Sun sign only, which is, if you like, your outer self
and conscious aims. For your inner self you take your
Moon sign.
Incidentally, I went to see if you had left a note this
morning and the porter got very huffy - I told him I had
an arrangement to do so (well, I did think I did only it's
not exactly bearing fruit at the moment ...!). Maybe you
should sort him out, dark, thinnish bloke of
indeterminate middle years, and a bit conscious of his
duty.
I hope you're in when I deliver this.
Love
Steffe x*

Yes, the Labour Club. I was chair but increasingly disinterested. We had
changed the name to the Socialist Labour Club but it suddenly seemed so
irrelevant. What did the Club actually do? It certainly didn't connect with
the community of Cambridge or the wider student body. I came to see it
as simply a means for certain ambitious would-be politicians to learn the
skills of manipulation and self-advancement. I ended up becoming
negligent of my duties. Sometimes I just didn't turn up to meetings.
When term ended, I never went to a meeting again. My politics were
now evolving. I read Marcuse, Leary, Cohn-Bendit. I began to see
personal liberation as political liberation. I saw Parliament as irrelevant.

March 1973

Cambridge terms are remarkably short. Just 8 weeks. So all too soon,
the vac approached.

We met up. We were so carried away, both of us, that we couldn't bear
the prospect of being apart. On top of that, my parents knew about us
and I knew it would be hell back at home.

'So, Steffie, my love, what shall we do? I just can't bear the idea of not being with you'.

'Nor me'.

'So let's be crazy. Let's just go down to London. We'll find people to take us in. I need you Steffie'.

She didn't really hesitate. She said yes. We didn't hang around. We would go today. It was still morning. We agreed to meet back at my place in Bateman Street in the afternoon. What happened back at her flat, I don't know. She turned up with a bag. I picked up the one I had packed and we headed off to the station. We were eloping.

It was almost more than I could take in, it was unreal and absolute bliss. We sat opposite each other on the train down, talking just a little, smiling at each other a lot. I suspect both of us knew it was crazy. But it felt so liberating, so wild. Our emotions were out of control. And so was our desire for each other. I was a twenty year old taking off with a twenty five year old married woman. It is impossible to describe the pure excitement, to quote Roxy *The thrill of it all*'.

We had no real plan but I knew Ian would help out. So we made our way to the bottom end of Ladbroke Grove and found his house. We climbed up the front steps and he came to the door. He was so welcoming as was his father, a truly lovely man, who immediately made us coffee and said we could stay as long as we wished.

Our room was on the top floor and for the three days we were there we made it ours. On our second night, Ian's brother crashed in on us as we made love, checking that we were OK.

It was only later, in a letter, that Steffe told me she had rung John on the morning after our elopement. Whether she had seen him the day before, I don't know, though I suspect not. She seemed too calm when she came to my room that afternoon. Maybe she left a note? But on the phone, John was told the truth. It must have been a profound shock to him. His wife, to whom he had been married for less than a year, down in London with her lover – me. At the time, she said nothing about this call. It was like she was wiping it out of her consciousness.

At the beginning, we didn't bother to think. We just revelled in being together. We were driven by a desperate desire. We indulged in pure hedonistic nirvana, living entirely in the present. We simply didn't think of tomorrow. We moved on to another friend's flat. During the Sunday afternoon of what was to be our last day of our mad freedom, we took a bath together. We talked, we laughed, and we even tried to make love yet again but baths are not comfortable.

That night, in our candlelit room, we spent a long time just looking at each other. The intimacy was almost overwhelming. It was dream land. As we made love once again, she said:

'Who taught you to make love so beautifully?'

'No one. With you, it just comes naturally.' And that was true.

It was the Monday when reality struck. We had no money. We had no accommodation. The magic couldn't cope with that.

So, unbelievably in retrospect, I went back home. Steffe came to Waterloo station and there was such a sadness to our separation. We didn't even sort out our next meeting.

I so needed to hear from her. Did she have a plan? Each morning I listened out for the post and then a week later, a letter arrived. I took it up to my room and carefully opened it.

Lionel's - Monday

Dear Roy,

Well, the decision is made today I am going back to Cambridge. When I left you at Waterloo, it seemed almost inconceivable that this would be the direction I would decide to go in. But a lot has happened, there have been a lot of changes, and they've come from John, which was where they had to come from - and I never believed they would. But my leaving Cambridge had a really cataclysmic effect on him - it really brought home the enormity of what we were into. Especially after I spoke to him on the phone on Friday morning from Ian's. He really plummeted over the weekend - he'd lost his fellowship and he seemed to have lost his wife and for the first time he really felt he had hit the bottom and was forced to take a really good look at himself. And on Monday he wrote me a long, long letter - and the things he wrote were quite remarkable. I think maybe you understood better than I did the way he regarded me before - I couldn't understand it because, well, I rather expect people to treat other people as individuals and not merely as extensions of themselves. But it turns out it was true that he really had absorbed me and taken me for granted and had simply <u>not comprehended</u> that I might have my own ideas about the environment in which I wanted to live and furthermore was prepared to leave him for it. And there were plenty of other things too, like his incredible difficulty in relating to people because if people deviated from the norm he set up he really wasn't interested in finding out why they did, and finding out the way they thought or why they followed different thought processes - he was only interested in telling them the way he thought and trying to convince them that he was right. And so although he had this hang-up because he wanted to get close to people, he always pushed them away.

Recognition of these and other things altogether seem to him like a breakthrough and he wants to work on them. The first thing he wants to do is leave Cambridge - he's sick of being labelled and inhibited by his role and rightly feels that it is simply not going to be possible to break people's image of him. So he wants to live in London - also because he feels that the things he's got into in Cambridge are holding him back. But mainly, perhaps, because he realises he has created an impossible situation for me there. In fact, he said that if I didn't come back he'd stay in Cambridge because otherwise he'd be on top of me in London, most of his friends are mine and also he'd be working at LSE, etc. But if I did want to go back we'd move. And he repeats again and again that I am _free_, that I must have the freedom to live the way I want to...

You know, Roy, that one of my basic hang-ups about John was that he couldn't change - but it struck me that this was pretty arrogant of me. And we are married, and I did love him once, and I think I must now work on the assumption that it is possible for him to alter his view of life and his way of looking at people and that we must try again. And so I am going back with the real intention of making a life with him again. We are getting a room with S.C.H. - the squatters thing in Camden - and should be able to move in soon after Easter. We'll keep the flat in Cambridge - J still has to keep term until June - and give it up in the summer - if things are working.

And now - the people who seem to have been forgotten in this affair - you and me. In a sense we must be forgotten now. If I didn't go back to J. now, determined to try again, it would be because I still love you so much - and that would be all wrong. I would be leaving John solely for you. And I know you understand the really, really heavy implications that would have for us. I'm at a very low ebb at the moment, life is being lived in the 10% level. Nothing has changed in the way I feel about you - except insofar as they were changed by external pressures over time. At first it was so high, the thing we had, and it was possible to feel completely free as long as we isolated ourselves from everything. But things kind of battered their way in on us and became increasingly hard to shake off and love was always accompanied by a really oppressive feeling. The time, Roy, was simply not right.

If I said that it ever could be - I don't know which I more honestly believe. It is quite unbearable to me to say that we must now simply get on with forgetting - but we must. I hope I will have left Cambridge before you come back but anyway I will have left at least during the first couple of weeks of term. So at least we are physically removing the possibility of bumping into each other - and that's the main reason I want to leave now, not wait until next year, because I want to put us both out of danger. I'm not strong-willed enough, I know I would try at least to see you. And it's really important for you at this particular time to be left alone.

Writing this letter I feel that I am in some kind of contact with you and I don't want to stop. I've been desperately anxious to know how you are, and even made devious plans for finding out, via your sister or Ian, but you may be relieved to know that I haven't followed them through. We did rather storm through people's lives, didn't we. If you feel you could write once more, I really would like to hear how you are. But if you feel that <u>now</u> communication must end, I understand.

Roy, my love, please take care of yourself. And take care of other people too. We are both slightly dangerous people - we can hurt and be hurt at a fairly high level of intensity and we have to guard against that. We must only love when we are free to love - and now we have to redirect all that energy and zap off into new things.

My love, Roy, Steffe x

I sat immobile for some minutes, then read the letter again and then again. I felt such sadness and such helplessness. I was not angry or annoyed for she had been so authentic and open and her love flowed through. But I felt bereft. I put on the second Roxy Music album, *For Your Pleasure*, and wrote to her (one letter I wrote out in draft form and so I can share).

My dearest Steffe,

Your letter lies before me – I've read it a thousand times and still the full impact of it has not hit me. Perhaps I should wait before writing to you but I desperately need to make contact with you in the only way which now seems possible.

I understand why you have made the decision you have and I really do wish you both well.

But as for you and me, my love, what can I say? I love you to distraction and find it so hard to imagine a future without you. But that's what I now have to face up to. That will require a strength and determination that I don't feel I have right now. I feel so empty, so sad, and want only to be with you. I will try to be strong, my love. It will be easier when I am back with my friends in Cambridge.

My aim is not to forget, only to cherish the memory of us, to let it enrich my life, to know that it will make me a more complete person. How can I ever forget those moments of unadulterated beauty that we have shared together?

When a relationship comes to a natural end because it's just not working out, maybe it's easier to reconcile oneself to reality. But when the end comes as a result of the time and place being wrong, as a result of the world outside alone, then isn't it so much more difficult to accept? Just tragic regret.

......There is just one thing I must say. Look, Steffe, if things for any reason become difficult or desperate, even if it's a long way in the future, and you want to contact me or see me, then, my love, I will always be available. I may get over the pain of never seeing you again but I will never lose my profound love for you. So, my love, I will stop now. Take care of your precious self and I will be strong and do my best to look after myself.

Oh, my lovely, it's so hard to end ....

Roy x

Her reply just stunned me. It only strengthened my love for her.

My sweet, sweet Roy

Don't be sad. Please don't be sad. You're not alone. There is a bond between us that can't be broken. At this time it is a sad, lonely trip. But while you exist, and I exist, there's a thought stream going across - you can feel it, positively feel it. Gradually it will lose its intensity of loneliness and become a peaceful flow. I know it takes over at times in waves of heart-breaking helplessness. But whenever the music, or a book or any beautiful trip lifts you out of yourself even for a moment, I'll be speaking to you. And although we are now going our separate ways - if something good was really meant to happen between us, Roy, it'll happen. And if it doesn't, we have beautiful memories.

Don't write back, Roy. Leave the communication to thought - it's there.

I do just want to add, though, that I was wrong about the 2nd Roxy, it's really nice.

My love, as always,

Steffe x

FOUR

Summer 1973

I returned to Cambridge. I didn't try to contact her. I had to accept it was over. Every sinew in my body, every thought, every heartbeat, wanted to reach out to her. But I felt I had to respect her decision. Throughout our affair, I realise that was what I repeatedly did. To that extent, our relationship was not properly balanced – or put it another way, the lover in an affair is always dependent on the one who is loved but attached. In a sense, you really are not in control. And then the short times together are extraordinarily intense, making love becoming absolutely central to nearly every meeting. But when she walked back out and into her everyday life with John, invariably I felt such joy but simultaneously such pain. And frequently, that was a pain I partially hid from her. I suppose I just didn't want to tarnish those precious moments we had together. And I never lost the knowledge that was she was so much older than me, so much more mature, and I was rather in awe of her. It was only much later that I came to understand her fully in all her complexity, vulnerability, confusion.

I was down, very down, but I waddled through and gained great comfort from my friends. One day, on checking my pigeon hole, I found a daffodil. Shortly after, on returning to my room, I found it festooned with daffodils. Could it really be Steffe? Was she still in Cambridge?

Then this came.

Nevertheless, communication ....

A refence to the second track on Roxy's *'For Your Pleasure'* album, *'Strictly Confidential'*. An excruciatingly sentimental, painful song. An image of a fragment on the ground far below. Thinking of what once was.

And then she searched me out. She was not leaving Cambridge after all, at least not for now. Once again, we met and loved. It seemed like before, but the innocence and simplicity had gone. Steffe had decided to try to make a go at her marriage but found she couldn't walk away from us. So she was conflicted and confused. We spent an idyllic few days together but immediately after she said she needed to think things through.

She then wrote to me from London.

W2
Sunday night

My dearest Roy,
Well, I've done my thinking and believe it or not I really got somewhere. I think maybe, or I rather hope, that you will have already guessed what I've decided to do. It struck

49

me really forcibly that for nearly two years now I have not really been on my own and it really is about time I should be. For the last few months I've been floundering about, pulled in different directions, acting without thinking and causing a lot of trouble - fucking up J, myself and, which hurts me badly, you. So I think it's time I faced the world by myself for a while, to try and find out where I really am. I've just been on the phone to John and told him what I want to do, and why, and he seems to think that it is perhaps the best thing. So I'm coming back to Cambridge on Tuesday and I'll probably leave again on Wednesday and stay there until the end of term. I'm not quite sure where in fact I shall stay, here at least for this week, and then afterwards I'll have to start doing the rounds of people's floors probably.

Roy, believe me, I don't _want_ to do this. I hate being on my own - even today, although I was with friends, I painfully felt the lack of my usual automatic support that I rely on far too much. John will hate it, of course, I phoned him earlier from Petersfield and he was really burnt up (as he put it). And I know you will hate it - please, please don't feel that I have cheated you. I want to see you a lot, but at the moment there is nothing to be gained by it. I have been wrecking people's lives and it's about time I got a grip on myself and stopped harming people I love. And the shock of having to think for myself (not of myself) for a while will I hope stimulate some kind of self-knowledge that's got very, very lost somewhere along the line.

So please understand that for once I am trying to be strong for long-term good despite short-term unhappiness. I'm sure you will, because like I told you, lots of times, you're stronger than I am, and recognise how weak I am, and will recognise what an effort it is for me to take any form of action which doesn't seem to be for the immediate best. If you'd like to write to me, that would be nice, but you may prefer not to, which might be better. I'll leave that up to you. If you should feel you need to, Angie will pass on any letters addressed here.

As for what I say to John, as things stand (in a limbo), I don't if possible want to say anything about what we have been doing this week. I know it's a lie, but I can't see what at this stage is to be gained from having J. at your throat; in his present mood I think he would hassle you badly, and I think you have enough to cope with at the moment. I'll tell him I saw you, that we went for dinner on Wednesday, but if possible no more. If it does all come tumbling out, I'll let you know at once so you are prepared.

Oh Roy, I hope this isn't going to hurt too much (any of us). I feel such a shit, a real SHIT, and yet, because last week with you was so amazing, really really beautiful, I somehow can't be left with a bad taste in my mouth, because that part is unshatterable, and will always exist in my mind.

Take care of yourself, Roy; I don't know what's going to happen, I can't promise anything, and I don't want you to rely on anything. And look, I'm not inaccessible. If things get bad, and you feel you have to see me, well, I'm here. But I hope that simply knowing that will give you the strength to let us sort ourselves out in isolation.

My love,

Steffe x

I found it really difficult. I was still only 20 and Steffe was my first love. This was so complex and challenging. But her honesty and authenticity which flowed through her writing merely cemented my commitment to her. I wrote, telling her I respected her decision and would wait. But in truth, I hid my despair and loneliness. But it seems she was told of it.

Saturday

Dearest Roy,

I've just been out to buy some milk and I found your letter - I was hoping you would write so that I'd know how you were, in every sense, and I'm really happy that you seem to be handling everything. You know I went up to Cambridge for a day last week and a couple of things that were said really shocked me (things said about you). Dominic was in and out a few times and mentioned about you seeing your tutor, and there were a few words said about how you had been incredibly depressed recently, etc, etc. I'd seen Bill for lunch on Tuesday and he said he was really struck by the change in you since his wedding. But the worst was bumping into Christian - he hardly said anything but an amazingly sharp message came through just one word he said. Look, I don't feel guilty anymore, because the way I've been working things out makes that kind of feeling irrelevant, but I know that I'm responsible and my one concern is to do everything possible to help you get through to the other side.

So I thought one thing I could perhaps do is to really try and honestly get over to you how I see things now, which may take some time. Being apart really has made things clearer - I do believe you when you say that you are already getting somewhere, the reason is, I think you'll agree, that the absolute intensity of what we got into, partly caused by never having any time together until last week and the horrific paranoia because we were both aware of the immensity of what was going on, made thought impossible. Or, I should say, apparent immensity: not because the feelings weren't immense - they were. But the consequences, on reflection, should not have taken on such total dimensions. We were speeding mentally and emotionally and felt that drastic steps had to be taken immediately. Now I'm not so sure about that. Action taken precipitately like we were thinking of would result in us both being landed in a situation which at the time (and now) neither of us would be able to cope with. If you follow through what I'm implying I think you'll perhaps agree. To have decided to leave J. right now (or then) would have left me totally lost and unable to cope with anything and I know would be disastrous. It's one thing to be on your own to think things over calmly; it is another to completely tear up your roots and find yourself in a limbo of insecurity and uncertainty.

And it's precisely this limbo that I don't want you to feel you are in, and this is where the time thing, and the vac, present a problem. I want you to know that you are with me in thought all the time - but it does worry me that if I stay down here until the end of term that leaves you on your own for a long time. Perhaps by the time you have finished reading this letter and thought a bit you will know if you can take it. And here whether or not I can is irrelevant - at least, I think I can assure you I can and will.

Now it's the hardest part - trying to search my mind (and mind is such a drag anyway - perhaps I mean my head) for an explanation of what I feel and felt. Like I've told you lots of times, I discovered in you a piece of my own past, and through you I re-experienced the whole trip I went through a few years ago, and all that knowledge that had been put to the back of my mind was brought to the forefront again, and I had to re-evaluate its importance - no, that's going too fast. More, I re-acknowledged its importance, but didn't know what to do with it. One thing I've realised is that we came upon this knowledge in different ways and that's important. I found it soon after leaving school, when I had no set value system thought out: I simply had never thought about things before, so I was not presented with a conflict because there was nothing to conflict with. I simply formed my values around this knowledge and developed spiritually with it, and found the conflict later through becoming involved with people who didn't have it, and then, because easily influenced, dismissed it to a certain extent - but only very temporarily. And meeting you really brought it out into the open. For you, it was different; most people who know you talk about how amazingly worked-out you were when you arrived in Cambridge. So for you to find out that there were alternative values meant that you had to (have to - are doing? I hope...) resolve the conflict at a much earlier stage. And to approach it from that side must be so much harder. For me, it just confused me a lot at the time, but basically I found it stimulating and beautiful. For you, and for me now I suppose, it kind of pulls the ground from under your feet.

And so I feel with you a strong spiritual affinity, and because of that I love you. But because of the scenes I have been through in the last few years, and because of the fucking ridiculous way society is organised, my capacity to love has been repressed and fucked up and I find it almost impossible to love. In our society, love immediately assumes possession and exclusiveness, and is felt on the wrong level.

And what we must accept is that that is not the kind of love I feel for you - that is the kind of love J has for me and when I say I love him I mean that in some ways I need him for support, companionship, security. And I do. And when I say I love you I don't mean that. That's why I said I don't try and fit you into my life on any practical level. I do not want, Roy, a relationship with you in that sense. To talk with you and make love was beautiful, and both would perhaps be again - surely would. But I don't want to live with you, go out with you - nothing like that - at the moment or probably ever. While I accept that some people can get it together on every level and have a really ideal relationship - it's incredibly rare and I am fairly certain it would not work with us. I also accept that you probably won't accept this - I dread to think of the motives you will impute me. But I can't help that - I believe what I say. I believe that people are not naturally monogamous (and that's no brilliant discovery) but even though it's obvious that you need different people for different things at different times, we are conditioned to think the opposite and unless you really understand this early, it's too late and the damage is done and you are swept into the marriage idea in a totally wrong way. Which is what happened to me, and it's too late for me to break away from now. When people get married, they put each other through an awful lot of shit, because they are the ones who bear the full brunt of the other's problems all the time; all unhappiness, discontent, aggression, etc is released at home, just like we released ours at home when we were kids. So marriage is a really difficult state and it's made that way because society requires that we do limit ourselves to one person.

I know I'm not telling you anything you don't already know, so I'll stop. In fact I think I'll stop altogether because I hope by now you will understand how I feel. It's probably expressed a bit wrong because one-sided conversations aren't a particularly good form of communication. But this is as far as my thinking has got me so far, and now we must simply let things take their natural course for a while. The purpose of being alone now is not for me conscious thought, it's more simply to allow things to follow a progression, without external hassles, and it is really calming me down a lot and giving me a stronger base. Now I just want you to think over what I've said, and then let me know if you'd like to see me - I think if we don't, we'll probably be able to communicate better after a long separation but it's hard for both of us. I shall be staying at Angie's for most of next week I expect.

One thing that is rather heavily ironic, but which I hope you will take as one of those lovely ironies, is that John and I are going to see Red Buddha on Tuesday. He found out that I had tickets because he wanted to come to London last Monday and in my confusion I told him I gave them away but he wanted to take me on my birthday and since it is important to keep him on an even keel, because he seems pretty calm at the moment, I agreed. I'm sorry, Roy. You know I desperately wanted to see it with you - but perhaps we could manage to see it again.

My thoughts are with you, Roy,
My love, Steffe x

It was a hard letter to receive. But once again, I respected her clarity. But it did hurt. We hadn't seen each other for weeks and I felt too crushed to respond. Instead, I finally got down to work because my second year exams were imminent.

June 1973

On the first Saturday of June, in the early afternoon, she turned up at my room. It was a total surprise. Afterwards she wrote:

Dear Roy,
I'm sorry for my total untogetherness when I rushed round to see you on Saturday - although the whole thing was thoroughly premeditated and I had all sorts of things worked out to say to you, I wasn't prepared for the buzz I got out of seeing you again which left me totally inarticulate. In fact what I wanted to do was gauge your reaction to lunatic fantasies that I had (as ever) in my head but inevitably we shied away from any practical issues until I had to go, and my having to go accentuated and brought back all the old problems.
So perhaps it's better if I write a few things down. If you can't discuss things in bed, then discussing them unilaterally on paper is easier than going right into them in frenzied afternoon visits. One place to start may be the insecurity I mentioned I have been feeling, which I think comes from a combination of confronting the possibility which I did last vac of leaving everything familiar & getting back into being on my own again, and also of the concept of moving to London & leaving Cambridge which I have to accept anyway. I've done a lot of moving and I've grown really attached to Cambridge & it makes me sad to have to leave. Obviously everybody comes across that. But it had the effect of making me lean a lot more to J for

support, and because of the way he's altered I've been able to do that. Shit, all these hang-ups about father figures....but in a way that's what he's becoming. Very odd. But nevertheless he can't give me everything, nobody can, we went into this, and there are still things you gave me which are both unique and essential. But I see you, as I've always done (apart from a brief period maybe) as an isolate that I desperately want to return to because of the pure feelings of joy we had, that we could uniquely give each other, if the world would only disappear for those time. But I don't know, apart from everything else, maybe because of everything else, whether we could get into those trips again anyway. Their beauty lay in some senses in their unreality, and because they were ephemeral they were like magic. And maybe now we've let too much of the world in and we've lost it. That, of course, is provable only empirically, which is why I have lunatic fantasies. I'd better get one of these right out front, because I'll never dare say it to your face, which is that when J goes to Trieste in the summer I had this image of spending the time with you ... come on, you must have had fantasies too, please don't make me feel too bad.

And the emotional implications of all this when we have to get back into the world again - for my part I confess that since seeing you on Saturday I've been a lot more intolerant and bad-tempered with J; but what I can't tell is whether this is resentment because he is an obstacle between us and to my escapism or whether it is a general lack of capacity to handle the situation. But the situation could theoretically be tolerable from all sides because it shouldn't pose a threat to anyone, but J's consciousness is in practice very much on the base line in this matter, and

*I'm not sure where ours are. And that's an essential part of
it, because when guilt comes in the whole thing blows. And
when dishonesty is forced upon you, you're bound to feel
guilt. I suppose another lunatic fantasy I nurse is that both
of us could handle it so perfectly that we would overcome
the rest.*

*Have things progressed at all since the vac? If they haven't,
I guess we are condemned to separation. I'm supposed to be
working very hard, I could lose myself in that (to a limited
extent!) but that doesn't remove what I would always feel,
like you said, tragic regret. I just simply wanted just one
more, even if it could only be one more, trip with you. But
if we tried and it failed? But I don't think it would, not
on my side, not if we had long enough to try.*

*Before I talk round in circles any more, I'll stop. The
problem with this unilateral discussion is that it really is
unilateral, and I'm not sure how you can join in. But look
- the election is on Thursday. J will be at the count. I'll leap
on the bike and come ripping round to Bateman Street.
Unless you feel you could say what you have to say in real
words, you could absent yourself soon after 9 and leave me
a letter. That sounds all right to me.*

*I think about you all the time, Roy. It's a Whistle Test night
tonight, lots of dope, lots of dreams.*

Love, Steffe x

... This is a gift we must not lose...

Again from *Strictly Confidential*.

8 June

Roy - you really are an incredible gas. The mood you were in when I arrived has caught up with me - totally blissed-out. I was expecting such a heavy scene or else a heavy letter but instead there was all this happiness. It's so good to see you happy again. See what you can do about Johnny's place for next Thursday/Friday & leave a note in your pigeon hole* (only maybe you could have a word with the porter) or else I'll try and come round.
My love
S xx
*As soon as you can

So off it went again.

We really left normal reality. Few experiences were richer, more glorious, more intense, than making love to David Bowie and *The Rise and Fall of Ziggy Stardust*, and in particular, *Moonage Daydream.* Lyrics capturing the ecstasy of sexual love. Minds touching. Souls embracing. Freaking out in the church of man, Love. Travelling to outer space, the planets and beyond.. And then Mick Ronson's exquisite, soaring, madly sexual and no less than orgasmic guitar. Pure ecstasy.

David Bowie was so important to me. Just like Roxy Music. Revolutionary.

*

Exams came and went. Despite my indolence, I managed to pass although only moderately.

There then followed an inevitable period of debauchery and excess, helped by the weather which was glorious. Drifting down the river on a punt, probably about 8 of us, young men and women, very intoxicated despite it being only late morning, Queen's College on our left. Me suddenly standing up in wild exuberance and in the process capsizing us. Seeing a handbag floating away from us. I had to be helped out of the water and ended up being led back to a friend's room in college. His girlfriend stayed and looked after me. She was very nice to me, I recall. It felt a bit electric. Attending an afternoon garden party in the grounds of a college a little way out from the centre. No sleep the night before. My next memory was coming round in another friend's room at about 10pm. I had no recollection of what had happened in the meantime, how I had found my way to this room. A trifle disturbing.

One fine evening, Christian suggested that we zoom out to the country on his Norton 750. Neither of us wearing crash helmets, I climbed on behind him and off he shot, fast from the very beginning. We hit the country lanes, empty of vehicles, and he opened up the throttle. I leant back and felt so exhilarated – and so terrified. We drew up at a pub, had a drink then returned to Bateman Street, as speedily as we had on our outward journey. Wild and reckless.

One night, I decided to break my psychedelic virginity – and take acid. I was nervous and excited. It was early evening and the beautiful weather continued. A group of us went to an Italian restaurant in Market Square. Afterwards, I found myself walking across to Rose Crescent, finding the entrance to their building and climbing the stairs to their flat. As I ascended, I felt the acid begin to take effect. The stairs became wobbly and gained a life of their own. Coming out through the top doors onto the roof I saw their flat in front of me. I was now not fully rational and was driven only by a need to see her. For a while, I just stood there, hoping that psychic connection would draw her out. When it didn't, I knocked on the door. Steffe answered. I could see John sitting at the desk behind her.

'I just need a quick word with you' I said.

She stepped outside, pulling the door almost to.

'I know it's reckless, I'm sorry. But I've just dropped some acid and I really need to see you. I just had to see your face so I can carry you with me.'

She smiled.

'I just wish you could stay with me.' I said.

'Me too. But I must go back. I'll make up some excuse for you coming round.'

'I love you.'

'And I love you.' And she quickly kissed me.

She went back in and I left. It was coming on strongly now. Reality was changing.

I headed back to Market Square, past the Old Schools, into Trinity Lane, past my college and then over the river. I was on route to a party. As I walked, everything was in a state of flux and change. Trees vibrated with life, lights swam rainbows of colour, the distant sound of traffic echoed across the grass.

I found the party, outside in a large garden. Lights festooned the bushes and trees. I was struck dumb. Music captured me physically – it was like I was living it. I felt I could almost eat the intensity of the moment. This was a new reality. Life could never be the same after this.

I spotted someone who rang a bell of recognition. Long hair, denims. His face was alive with vibrancy and dazzling colour. I approached.

62

'Man, your face is amazing.'

It was only later I learnt I had been speaking to my Director of Studies.

Finally returning to my room, I felt I had crossed a threshold of understanding. I was different now. It was all about liberating myself from the strictures of thought and behaviour I had grown up with.

*

It was inevitable that my politics changed. Phil was a working class gay philosophy student from the north with revolutionary tendencies. He was seeking personal liberation, to feel free to be open about his sexuality when gay sex had only become lawful a few years before. The gay rights movement was in its infancy. I too sought liberation. I had been sexually awakened and felt the oppression of disapproval for this, particularly from my parents. I increasingly felt that the personal was political. Parliamentary rule, political parties, what did they have to do with such an outlook? Phil and I became good friends.

Through him, I discovered the Situationists who had played such a radical role in the Paris uprisings of May 1968. They called themselves the Enrages after the revolutionaries of 1789. I quickly fell in love with their outrageous approach to effect revolutionary change. In 1968, the Situationists called on the students and workers of Paris to "take your desires for reality." This was not a call to mistake wishes for facts, but a call to take in the active sense of the verb : to seize, to grab hold of. The aim was to obliterate the spurious division of "reality" and "ideality" in revolutionary action.

Slogans from those times:

The bourgeoisie has no other pleasure than to degrade all pleasures.

Going through the motions kills the emotions.

63

Struggle against the emotional fixations that paralyze our potentials. (Committee of Women on the Path of Liberation)

Constraints imposed on pleasure incite the pleasure of living without constraints.

The more I make love, the more I want to make revolution. The more I make revolution, the more I want to make love.

I'm coming in the paving stones.

Total orgasm.

Comrades, people are making love in the Poli Sci classrooms, not only in the fields.

Revolutionary women are more beautiful.

Zelda, I love you! Down with work!

The young make love, the old make obscene gestures.

Make love, not war.

Under the paving stones, the beach.

Boredom is counterrevolutionary.

We don't want a world where the guarantee of not dying of starvation brings the risk of dying of boredom.

We want to live.

Don't beg for the right to live — take it.

Already ten days of happiness.

At every moment something is happening.

Live in the moment.

I take my desires for reality because I believe in the reality of my desires.

Desiring reality is great! Realizing your desires is even better!

Be realistic, demand the impossible.

Power to the imagination.

Those who lack imagination cannot imagine what is lacking.

Forget everything you've been taught. Start by dreaming.

Form dream committees.

Revolution is the active passage from dream to reality.

Open the windows of your heart.

To hell with boundaries.

65

You can no longer sleep quietly once you've suddenly opened your eyes.

The future will only contain what we put into it now.

All this fed into my love for Steffe. We were breaking the rules, we both felt this, but we believed in what we had together. I introduced her to the philosophy of the Situationists and she too felt the connection. She was excited by the trajectory of my journey and it brought back to her, in a new way, the spirit of the 60's. This felt like liberation.

'Bliss was it in that dawn to be alive,

But to be young was very heaven,

William Wordsworth

FIVE

The long vacation came. Months away from Cambridge, away from Steffe. I was completely broke, having massively overspent. I had no choice but to return to my parents.

It was a disaster. My mother, a woman of choleric temperament in contrast to my quiet father, asked about my relationship 'with that woman'. I was so angered that I exploded.

'It's got absolutely nothing to do with you. You just don't understand. We love each other. That's it.'

'It's disgusting. She's just lured you in. She's a corrupting dreadful woman.'

'I know what this is about. You just don't understand about sex, do you? You think it's dirty, you have no idea of its magnificence. Well, I am me and this is what I want.'

Things could only get worse from this point. It ended with her saying that they would no longer support me financially at university.

I was so beside myself that I went out into the front hall and smashed my fist through the glass window of the inner front door.

My hand still bleeding, I took myself to my room and immediately wrote to Steffe telling her what had happened.

She replied:

Thursday

Roy - poor, poor Roy. This whole thing is going beyond the limits of sanity - from anyone's definition of it. I got your terrible letter this morning and just felt as if the whole world had been ripped apart and that I have committed an unforgiveable crime against humanity. Obviously I've not had any time for reflection - but my instant reaction is that the situation must be stopped dead - it's too late already to prevent disasters but to continue will only prolong them. Your parents and all that they stand for are winning the game - or this game at least. We haven't got the weapons to fight them with - we can't escape. They have brought into our relationship the horror of guilt and deceit which makes what seemed to us as beautiful ugly. To get that straight, the guilt and deceit exist anyway - we both feel them incredibly strongly. Your parents didn't create them - we did by having loved when we shouldn't - or rather, _I_ shouldn't. The terrible unhappiness that I have created can't be wiped out. My God, if I'd known we were going to have a repeat of last vac.... I really thought we were going to be given some peace and were going to be allowed just a few days of freedom together - but obviously I was being naive, kidding myself. The downfall of hedonism. Dreams shattered. I've been counting off the days until I would see you again - and I know you have. I've planned and dreamed. But now it all seems horrible and corrupt and I can't take it. I've been able to look J straight in the eye and lie to him - easily. Somehow I have been putting him in one world and you in another - my fantasy world - and the two haven't overlapped or collided and there was no problem. I've not been intending to leave him - we're fairly stable and happy at the moment. But I've not demanded much from him as the real, pure bliss that I search for and long for I find with you and I'm content that it should be fleeting and patient to wait. But obviously you can't lie the way I can - you're too honest. It's rather incredible that you should have trusted me when I have shown how dishonest I can be. But I guess you

realise that you can't lie to someone when you get as far
into their head as I have got into yours. But who can you
trust? Your parents haven't proved themselves very
trustworthy either - they promised to leave you alone and
they didn't.

And now you are the one who is left in the worst mess. My
God, how could I wreck the life of someone I love so much?
And what can I do to help now? I can't cope with your
parents. I've just not had to deal emotionally with people
whose ideas were so totally contradictory although also
comprehensible - I've just stayed out of such people's way.
Last vac they defined me as the old hen, old corruption
and even now I find it hard to shake off the paranoia of
growing old - an idea which had not occurred to me
before. The adulteress bit I can take - I can define
marriage in my own terms and J is happier with me since
last vac than he has ever been. But the liar, the cheat - yes,
those definitions go really deep and hurt and damage. I
can't handle them. Purity and love and evil - no, I can't
reconcile them even with my devious reasoning powers. So I
must get out of your life.

Well, you wanted me to write - and I have, but hurriedly
and with instantaneous reactions. I shall not abandon
you, though, Roy. I'll do whatever is in my power and my
realm of action to do. But I won't take on your parents. If
this sounds hard - it's because I am in despair.

I will be in Cambridge on Saturday if you need to contact
me.

I won't send my love because it brings you nothing but
nightmares.

Steffe

Sweet Roy, I just want to hold you and love you and tell you everything will be fine ... and we will wake up ...

What a mess. I was devastated. What to do? So I worked on a building site to raise some money. And decided to go to Morocco with a Cambridge friend. It was a good decision. In the meantime, this:

Cambridge
Wednesday

Dear Roy,

This is the first chance I've had to write to you; I hope it's not too late, that you haven't already left. I'm desperately anxious to find out how you are but I wanted to write before phoning because it would be fairly impossible to tell you what's been going on over the phone and you know I find it a really difficult means of communication. But I will phone you - I'll try tomorrow but you may not have got this by then.
The vac hasn't exactly been an unqualified success so far. Attempts to get back into life with John are just futile. Whatever we're doing, wherever we are, I just have this constant, constant pain in my gut which comes from thinking about you, wanting to be with you - which is just ludicrous. I suppose part of the reason is because, quite simply, I can't see you, and that knowledge really hurts. But what I was supposed to be doing was really trying to get back into things with J and to see how things went between us - without any reference to you. Because when I was in London, although I wanted to see you, I didn't actively miss you, and I could get really involved with other people. What's going on now has really, really taken

me by surprise and I don't like it - Jesus, Roy, I feel totally
inert and disinterested in everything and get intermittent
attacks of nerves in my stomach and it's not exactly
conducive to working things out or getting close to J. I
know the sun and spring always makes me restless -
perhaps that accounts for some of it.
Anyway, what I'd really meant to tell you about is a couple
of fairly interesting things that have happened. After John
had (so secretly) seen you in the Whim, he found
something of yours lying around - some notes with your
name on it - so, rather prematurely, everything came out.
Not exactly in detail and not exactly willingly because I
had wanted things to be calm until after John's lecture on
Friday - but the general idea that I had seen you a couple
of times since what John always refers to as 'that weekend' -
when I told him before - and that, yes, I wanted to see you
again. And so he told me that he too had been sleeping
with a chick in London - unfortunately only a few times
and no, he wasn't particularly bothered if he didn't see her
again. This accounts for why he told me before that he
would rather I was dishonest unless it threatened the
marriage because he didn't want to tell me. What the loon
didn't understand was that it was the dishonesty which
was in itself and in its consequences threatening us.
My first reaction was to have a really good laugh - partly
because I was surprised and partly because it seemed
briefly to put things on a less heavy footing. But much later
in the evening I suddenly got really angry because it
dawned on me that there we were, creeping about in a
state of total guilt and paranoia, while John was calmly
bombing off to London with evidently very few worries. OK,
so I realised fast that the comparison wasn't very good,

71

considering who you are etc, etc. but it's impossible to say what would have happened if I had felt the same freedom. But anyway in the heat of the moment I told him what had really happened the other weekend with your parents, and that I was the sole cause of everything, including the fairly horrific prospect of the vac for you and losing your grant. And so John said that (he was fairly horrified by the last thing) he'd write you a letter that you could show your parents saying how he's also been unfaithful and how I'd led you on ("because you did, didn't you") and that you weren't to be blamed but had just got caught up in a bad situation, etc.

Well, Roy, I guess that would be a perfect resolution of the whole problem. It would surely ease things between you and your parents - and, as of course, the letter would be written on the understanding that you and I completely stopped seeing each other (John is trying to arrange to move to London next year anyway) it ~~might perhaps~~ (!) would put a pretty forcible stop to you and me. What do you think?

The problem is that, unless you really have made up your mind not to see me anyway, I know that whether or not you think it's a good idea depends on whether I think it's a good idea. That would be a fairly good reason for ending the letter there, but there are a couple of things I want to say.

One is that I feel, as you know, really, really bad at causing this hassle with your parents. I'm really sad that we hurt your mother so badly and, whatever you say, I feel totally responsible for the financial bit as well, and I'm determined to help you if John's pleas or whatever don't work. I know that's a joke because I don't have a grant *either but I do have some savings which are more trouble than they are worth because having so much capital in my name stops me getting social security benefits so I might as well use it while it's losing value.*

Anyway, that's pretty boring.

The other thing is that I now fully understand and accept is that we can't contemplate any repeat performances of secret and intermittent meetings. John has his fellowship interview on Tuesday - this may sound specious but this is his annual ordeal and I really, really want to keep things cool until after that. I'm really pleased because everything else is going really well for him at the moment & Cardiff was very successful and he's been asked to do another seminar in Munich in September & they're going to pay him £140 + fare + expenses!! Amazing. And we've had a long talk about his career and things so apart from me life is treating him pretty well. The thing is John knows I'm unhappy and restless, but he doesn't really know why - at least he hasn't mentioned it specifically and I don't want to at least until after Tuesday or maybe never. Roy, I'm being really stupid, I'm trying to say things and yet not say them and I think I'd better stop before they come out.

Look, I'll phone tomorrow morning, O.K? About 11 or so.

My love

Steffe x

Ah yes, my meeting with John. He had asked me to see him. I was inevitably apprehensive. He arrived before me and I made my way to his table. We ordered tea.

'So, John, you wanted to meet me'

'This isn't easy. The fact is it's clear Steffe still has a thing for you.'

I couldn't answer so I waited for him to continue.

'Look, I love her. I don't want to lose her. So I want to ask you this. Will you please say you won't see her again?'

I was a coward and a liar. How could I not see her again? But I couldn't tell John the truth.

'OK. I won't. I understand.'

He was visibly relieved. We then talked about other things.

As I left, I didn't feel guilty about my lying. But equally, I didn't feel comfortable about it. I never did.

It must have been quite humiliating for John to have to plead with me.

*

Morocco was amazing. It seemed to form part of my journey. In those days, there were very few tourists, mainly just hippies. I was stoned the whole time and it led me to seek out secret journeys in the ancient cities of Fez and Marrakesh. I would wander on my own for hours, completely lost. One magical morning, I was sitting down having a mint tea deep in the maze that is the casbah of Fez, not a single tourist around, and I heard the sound of Santana playing from a nearby window, my favourite Santana album, one we used to listen to endlessly, '*Caravanserai*', with its glorious cover showing a camel walking through the desert, with a huge orange sun behind. Both sides were played. It was the only time I ever heard a western album playing whilst I was in Morocco. How extraordinary.

I later learnt that over the summer, my parents rang both Steffe and John. They rang Steffe at her place of work, the FPA (I've no idea how they found out she was there). Steffe was buzzed and told there was a Mr Brown on the phone (Mr Brown!). When Steffe took the call, it was my mother. My father had obediently followed orders pretending to be Mr Brown. I don't know what was said other than that my mother characterised Steffe as 'Mrs Corruption'. They also rang John. When I heard about this, my animosity towards my parents inevitably only grew.

I was drawn to R. D. Laing and his theory of the family as an oppressive, norm-demanding tyranny.

SIX

October 1973

Back to Cambridge for my final year. I had new lodgings in the centre near to the river. I liked them.

I had had no contact with Steffe for many weeks and felt unable to contact her. But she was always in my mind. Every time I walked the streets, Trinity Street, Senate House Passage, St Mary's Street, I was looking out for her. But I never saw her.

One time around midnight, I found myself walking towards Rose Crescent. I pushed through the doors accessing the stairs to the roof where the flats were. I carefully opened the door at the top and stepped out. Their flat was immediately in front of me. There were no lights in the front room. I crept past the front door, round the side of the flat until I reached the rear. I looked down into a well at the bottom of which was the back of the Berni Inn. There were metal fire-stairs leading down. To my left was a narrow passageway that accessed the back of their flat. This was where the bedroom was, the one I knew and had slept in.

I took a few steps and stood near to the window. I just wanted to be physically close to Steffe. She was but feet away. I stayed for maybe five minutes. As I walked away, choosing to use the fire-stairs, I felt so sad. I wanted to be where John was lying. I never told her I did this.

*

It was early afternoon when I entered the porters' lodge to check my pigeon hole. There was a letter poking out. I knew it was from Steffe from the colour of the envelope. It felt quite thick. I held it in my hand anxious to read it as soon as possible but wanting to be alone. I made my way across front court and out into the rear court. No one was around. I

75

walked to the terrace and sat on a bench. Should I get a drink first? No, I couldn't wait.

It was some pages long. As I read it, my heart melted. I felt her by me, sitting watching me holding her parchment-coloured, purple bordered, writing paper. When I got to the end, I rose from my seat and lent over the wall, looking at the trees swaying gently, weeping willows brushing the surface of the river. I felt pure joy.

It didn't cross my mind for a second not to contact her, not to see her. I turned around and breathed in the beauty of the college. Its smallness gave it an intimate quality. There were no grand courts like at Trinity, almost intimidating in their size. Instead, an extraordinary peace and calm. I wandered to the beech tree that rose above the rear court, lent against it, and read the letter again, and again. I wanted to stretch this moment of joy for as long as I could, to luxuriate in the love she had for me and I had for her.

Dear Roy,

I've hesitated in writing to you because possibly our long separation has given you a chance to turn things over in your mind and I didn't want to precipitate you into action as soon as you are back in Cambridge. I got the impression from Dominic that you found Morocco fairly amazing, and I also heard you met Ian and Christian on their way back from Thailand. So hopefully that lifted you out from the fairly debilitated mental state you were in when I last saw you - and maybe this is where I should make my exit. Between us, your mother and I fairly wrecked you - and I want to make it clear that I am not interested in seeing you unhappy, I would infinitely rather not see you and suppose/know/hope you were happy. I'm sending you a letter I wrote to you about a month ago on a very strange, slightly drunk, very stoned night when I felt uncannily close to you. That was a kind of crescendo, since when your physical return to Cambridge has been drawing nearer, arrived, passed - and I seem to have almost totally internalised my longing for you so that now I feel prepared not to see you. Certainly it would hurt. But I know you will agree that the pain would be duller than if we had seen each other recently.

So I want to leave it entirely up to you whether you contact me or not. If we were to see each other again, it would be very sporadically as I seem to have got more busy and John less. We spend a lot of time in London now. But if you want to, you can phone me on Wednesday evening after about 4.15 (make sure it's me who answers) and before 5.30. If this doesn't give you the time to decide, probably the following Wednesday would also be OK. And if you want fate to decide, well, I am at the LSE for the next 2 years...... But this is the last first move I shall make because basically I want to give you a chance to have a good life, and I can offer you so little.

My love, however, remains the same,
Steffe x

Roy, oh Roy, I have to write to you, the decision no longer seems to be in my hands, but a momentum has begun, gathered pace and taken over. Roy, I seem to be going literally crazy about you, over you, because of you. You wrote once......'how we can communicate with one another every minute of every day' but I do that with you, every second, until you take on a presence which begins to dominate my life. You are taking on the role of "the other" in my existence, I imagine I am with you all the time, tell you things, enjoy things with you, try to look pretty for you, as if you were there. I have begun to be able to form a clear image of you which I can call into my mind any time I like, so that I feel I hallucinate you into physical existence. At night I can go to sleep happy, confident I will be with you during the night because I know I will dream about you because I do, every night. I have even got over the pain of waking up and having you taken away from me by reality, as it hurts less when I know you will be back again, as the being which I am but suppress to the waking world meets you again. So you see it's (or, I suppose, you're) getting to dominate my life (or me) - and while I enjoy it and in a (very full) sense live for it, it frightens me. But it is somehow divorced from reality, and this is reinforced by the fact that I don't tell anyone, no one knows, and therefore the confirmation of it in real terms doesn't come, and it's all there, locked in my head and .... I'm not sure if I like the way this letter is writing itself, a note of paranoia, or something less definable than paranoia, more like withdrawal, is coming through. But it's nice to withdraw into your own head if what's going on there is more interesting than what's going on outside. But that doesn't imply that things outside haven't been interesting. On one level things have been really nice in Cambridge, I've met lots of interesting people and had some weird trips with them, and the weather has been amazing so I've been out in the Meadows a lot, and it's so quiet down there now. Just sun, some amazing Pink Floyd cows and the occasional punt passes silently by. No, this is funny, the other day a kid was fooling about in a punt by the bank where I was lying and its mother said 'Be quiet, there are people trying to sleep' ... Also the odd freak comes by in a canoe, his woman looking like some kind of an Indian squaw. The river, I was amazed to discover, is quite full of

fishes. And frogs, beetles, dragonflies. The peace of it is
astounding, mesmeric. I've also come across the guy who
does the translation of Vaneigem but I haven't yet
managed to get hold of any of the books. But you're still
there. Always.
I'll make no attempt now to come down and try to look at
it objectively - working out what it all means and where
it's taking me is a down-trip. I sometimes think Fulbourn
(see 1 below)... *I could just sit there, flip out from reality and*
dream forever, doesn't sound so bad. But I know there is a
mental clock somewhere in a very real sense ticking up the
days until the beginning of term, and the agony of
knowing you are around, in the real world, will begin
again. And I know that then it will be harder simply
(simply?) to feel your presence, because I will be aware
that it could appear, tangibly .... and I shall be looking,
imagining, instead of just being with you. Amazing
thought, the meeting of the ethereal and tangible, I
wonder which I will take for reality. I have fallen so far
into the Enrages' dictum (see 2 below). *So many things may*
have changed, or so little may have changed that reality
might not be preferable. But there's one totally imaginary
picture that I am able to hallucinate that shows me that I
am possessive..... in so far as I find an affirmation of
myself, and the most fundamental, important one to me,
in your love.
But I love you, Roy, and I live for, in, our world.

    (1)   Fulbourn was the local mental hospital.
    (2)   The Enrages' dictum – 'Take your desires for reality'

I replied immediately. I was so touched, so moved, so overcome by her words of love. I said how over the months we had been apart, she had always filled my head, warmed my heart, made me sad. I gave her my address and said she could leave a message there and avoid the ever-vigilant eyes of the porters who were always rather disturbed by this woman going to my pigeon hole.

She dropped in a note the following morning saying she could come round for an hour at 3pm. The room was much more attractive than the one I had in Bateman Street. It was on the top floor, with a sloping roof, into which was cut a window overlooking the street below. It had real character and lovely light. I had begun to make it mine.

As 3pm approached, I lay on my bed listening to music quietly. The front door to the house was not locked so it was a tapping on my door that told me she was here. She entered and we briefly just looked at each other, both smiling each other. Then we came together and kissed intimately, slowly, sensitively. We felt our souls touching. We parted.

'Steffie'

'Roy'

'I've missed you so much,' I said, 'I think about you every day.'

'That's true for me too.'

But quickly we tipped back into ordinary conversation, exchanging news, me talking about Morocco, she about the LSE and the summer. We avoided the big questions. I didn't tell her about the loneliness I had felt, the challenge our relationship was, my deeply disguised jealousy of John. Nor did she address her own issues. We needed time for that, we needed to properly reconnect. And then, as was the case so many times before and after, she had to go and her leaving brought out all the complexity and pain of the tangle we were in.

'Look,' she said 'I'll sort something out. I want to be with you as much as you do. I'll make up some story.'

'I can't bear for you to go.'

'I'll be with you again soon. I promise. You are so precious to me.'

She rose to leave. I took hold of her, held her, looked into her eyes and then we kissed.

It was very hard seeing her walk out the door. But also exciting.

I went to my pigeon hole to collect my mail and found an envelope, sent internally, the handwriting on which I did not recognise. I opened it. What a strange surprise.

The notepaper was luxurious, with a bold green heading saying 'The Asparagus Club' and with a small illustration of two sprigs of asparagus lying one on top of the other, in a cross formation.

'I have the privilege of offering you the dubious pleasure of joining the Club'. The writer humorously outlined how the Club met at termly 'eatings' to celebrate the glory of the asparagus plant. Enclosed was a small booklet setting out the rules.

I did not know the writer, I did not know about the Asparagus Club. Why on earth was I being invited to join an invitation-only dining club which, I later found out, was the only college dining club there was? I asked around and discovered that Ian and Christian had also been invited. What to do?

Money was an issue. 'Eatings' were expensive, black tie was obligatory. And how did this fit with my revolutionary thinking? But I had also become very hedonistic. Indeed, I saw hedonism as a key element in my personal liberation. And I was only going to be at Cambridge once. And Ian and Christian were joining. So I accepted.

I later found out that I had been invited because I was 'an interesting character'.

*

My lodgings were no more than five minutes' walk from her flat. It made it easy for her to pop round, often unexpectedly. It was how she got to know some of my friends for on occasion she would enter a room filled with collapsed bodies and smoke. Of course they knew about her already. It was lovely her beginning to experience a bit of my world. But normally, we were alone.

Since we were snatching just moments together, at best a couple of hours or so, we rarely wasted time on idle chit-chat. Typically we would first make love, very slowly, very sensually, very intensely. We would always be playing music which fed into our union. Only afterwards would we talk. But we normally avoided talking about the difficulties our relationship brought to both of us albeit in different ways. Instead we lay in bed and shared thoughts and feelings from deep within ourselves. We felt such intimacy. It was like we were leaving the ordinary world behind and instead inhabiting a magical world of our own creation. We wanted to keep the outside world out. This had always been a crucial characteristic of our relationship.

But watching her leave each time was so difficult. Bitter-sweet. She was returning to her everyday life with John, eating with him, socialising with him, sleeping with him.

I did feel sexual jealousy even though I knew that was absurd given that I knew in reality I was Steffe's sexual partner. But more it was jealousy of John simply being with the woman I wanted. When she told me of things they had been doing, when she constantly said 'we', that was when I felt pain. It made me feel lonely. I hid it, though Steffe being so perceptive and intuitive, no doubt sensed it.

I grappled endlessly with my feelings of jealousy. I felt they were illegitimate. That in the new consciousness of love and sexuality, jealousy was just a manifestation of possessiveness and that was wrong. I had learnt from Steffe about her own sexual past. She had come of age at the very time the sexual revolution exploded in the late 60's. She was always a very sexual woman, a woman who liked men more than women, and she had slept and had scenes with many guys. I felt I too had to embrace this freedom. It led me, even though I was absolutely committed to Steffe, to expand my own sexual experience. Women at Cambridge were few in number, men outnumbering women by 10 to 1. So the women I met were my friends' girlfriends (unusually for Cambridge at that time, my friends tended to have girlfriends) and it was with them I was from time to time adventurous. Did I feel guilty towards my friends? I didn't. It was almost as if, having broken a fundamental social rule by embarking on an affair, falling totally in love with a friend's wife, certain moral barriers had been broken down so I did play around. And I convinced myself this was what liberation was about.

Meanwhile, my other life was becoming ever more extreme. I had not been to a single lecture for more than a year. My attendances at supervisions were sporadic and lacked any preparation. On one occasion, a particularly odious lecturer in another college, his exciting area of specialism being land law, violently threw Megarry's Law of Property at me – a very substantial and heavy tome. I never attended one of his supervisions again. I was not alone among the surprisingly renegade minority of law students at Trinity Hall (traditionally cited as THE law college) who were similarly indolent. Strangely we were rather indulged by our tutor, an eccentric and profoundly interesting man (who had a vitriolic hatred of the Tory party) and a love of beer and wine. He seemed to be attracted by, albeit also frustrated by, our hedonistic abandon. I suspect very strongly that our year was to prove to be a unique year in that respect.

My time was spent mainly with friends who had become close now. Typically we got up no earlier than lunchtime. We might meet up for coffee in the Whim and then drift off, with no determined plan in mind. We never ate dinner in Hall but may meet one or two guys in the college bar.

A word on money. The college had its own money, in a booklet of tabs, as in raffle tickets. This money could buy you drink in the bar and everything in the buttery which sold cigarettes and bottles of wine and spirits. To obtain a booklet of money, you simply signed for one in the porters lodge and it would be added to 'the gentleman's bill'. No wonder I left with a substantial debt.

But the best part of every day was night-time when we would gather in a room, smoke dope, listen to music and endlessly talk. This was where I found my real intellectual stimulation, amongst these incredibly bright, exciting minds probing fundamental questions. We acquired the label 'the freaks' which I quite liked. To some extent, that was accurate. We were carrying forward the counter-culture of the late 60's, a culture of self-exploration, a renewed interest in philosophy and beliefs, a commitment to personal liberation, an embracing of pleasure and hedonism, a throwing off of restrictive sexual mores – and lots of drugs.

Steffe was an important part of this. I shared my thoughts with her and she responded with total understanding. She led me to a whole range of writers who profoundly influenced me, none more than Hermann Hesse. On her recommendation, I started with Steppenwolf. As I read it, I felt that just as the central character is shattered, so in a sense was I. I felt I was so many different people. So who was I really? Reading Narziss and Goldmund afterwards was a great consolation.

But we longed for proper time together. I had also got it into my mind that I wanted to drop acid with her. Steffe said she thought that John would be going away and we began to get excited but then he changed his plans. But a reprieve....

Dear Roy,
Situation salvaged - hang on to your hat (and your acid)
- Freedom Week begins Monday November 26th 1973.
This is guaranteed *
I'll come round on Thursday evening next week after 6 to go over the minor details.
Does this sound O.K?
I realise this doesn't get to the fundamentals but I think it helps.
Take care,
My love
*Steffe x   * Subject to Acts of God*

It happened. But the acid proved to be a bad idea. We dropped it in my room, probably too quickly, before we had properly managed to connect. I had imagined that we would make love whilst tripping to the stars but in reality we felt disconnected, both too lost in our personal psychedelic worlds to be able to communicate. We both regretted wasting the time, spending time apart. We recovered but it left something of a grey cloud that we could never quite dissipate at the time.

*

I had to prepare for the first 'eating' of the Asparagus Club. That meant getting some sort of black tie outfit. Fortunately my financial position had been improved by Christian advancing me a large lump of cash but I needed an authorised overdraft with my bank. So I made an appointment and then to the bank I went.

I sat somewhat nervously in the waiting area until the manager invited me in.

'So, Mr Douglas, how can I help? Looking at your account, you seem to be finding it hard to budget.'

'Well, the problem is my parents aren't willing to make up my maintenance grant and so I am rather struggling'

'Ah, and why is that?'

I was at a loss as to what to say and remained silent.

'So tell me' he nervously said 'is it anything to do with drugs?'

I guess he looked at me, sitting there in my tight jeans, denim jacket, linen shirt, neckerchief, long hair and Lennon glasses and thought 'drugs'.

'Oh no, nothing like that.'

'So, it's personal?'

'You could put it that way.'

I got the distinct impression that he thought it was because I was gay. He seemed relieved.

'So how can I help?'

'I would really appreciate a proper overdraft. I'm studying law. I'll be able to sort it.'

'By proper, you mean how much?'

'I've been thinking £500.'

'£500? Um. Well, OK. I have to trust you Mr Douglas'

'Indeed.'

I stepped out of the bank with a spring in my step.

I didn't want just any old dinner jacket so I went to the best men's clothier's in the city and found a delightful dark red/crimson velvet dinner suit. I was slim and putting it on I loved the way it shaped my body. So I bought it, together with a modest dress shirt and matching velvet bow tie.

The night came. I climbed the old wooden stairs up to an exquisitely oak panelled room, flickering in candle light. A long dark dining table with high chairs placed each side dominated the room. The members stood around, holding glasses of red wine. A white-jacketed waiter approached me holding out a glass. They were all jolly and welcoming and soon Ian and Christian arrived too. I began to relax. This was all very strange.

We were called to the table. All but one of us took our seats. One remained standing and placed a chef's hat on his head.

'Gentlemen, the asparagus'.

It was borne to the table and we were served. Five courses followed, each accompanied by fine wine. Joints were lit as the port was passed around. This was not the Bullingdon Club though all were undoubtedly privately educated. The conversation was lively, there was a lot of humour, but it remained civilised and restrained. I enjoyed myself.

How peculiar. I felt I was beginning to spin out on new experience. There was danger in it.

*

Some of the Asparagus Club, Roy front centre

I told Steffe about it. It must have seemed so strange to her. But I felt that she also loved my search for adventure. She shared that enthusiasm. We were both hedonists at heart.

But all too soon the vac came. So back to my parents I had to go. Steffe wrote:

Friday morning

Roy my love,
I had wanted to write to you last night when I was alone
and had an opportunity to let my mind wander off on a
piece of paper - and then the headache came pounding
in.....in fact it was unbelievably a neckache, more of the
kind when it hurts to move in any direction. As I have, for
the first time in ages, got caught in a cycle of insomnia, I
was really was beginning to feel that you were

transmitting so hard to me that the physical trips were coming through....

Though for some reason I don't feel as though any kind of buzzes are coming through from Bracknell. Maybe it's because I am in too dead a state myself to receive them - maybe you are not sending them. It really doesn't matter if that's the case: it's only a temporary state. I half wanted to wait until I had aa letter from you to find out; naturally enough no clues came from our polite telephone call. But I know you would be wondering why I wasn't writing.

Actually I will be on my own again on Monday night, John is going to see one of his 'friends' in London. It's odd; I am an insanely jealous person - I really mean that, it's one of my worst hang-ups and certainly the one I loathe most because of all its implications. But I can't summon up any about J's friends - I'm just rather curious about them. One of them is in my class at LSE and I'm simply intrigued by her. This fact is one of the few <u>certainties</u> in this whole scene.

Roy, my sweet love (something I never dare call you to your face - I find that kind of thing in our relationship really mind-blowing but I <u>like</u> it - the distances and the fencing) in a sense I am missing you; but in another sense I feel very removed from life, as I am so caught up in a part of what might also be called life, although that thought is horrifying - but I don't want to think in those terms at the moment because the abyss of reasonless is a bit near - and I feel we couldn't offer each other too much.

I'll hope to write to you on Monday - I really enjoy doing it when I have the chance to get into it, but planning a trip like that is hopeless. I'll go round to see if you you've

written on Monday, too. It would be nice if you had -
nice? It would make my heart melt.
Take care of yourself and your mind.
Love
Steffe x

I didn't know she felt she was a jealous person. Her revealing this helped in a small way to make me feel less bad about my own jealousy. But amongst 'alternative' people, it was seen as a weakness, showing possessiveness, a left-over from the pre sexual revolution. I really struggled with this. Also, now 21, I was experiencing and seeing at first hand, in a sense was a part of, the complexity of an unconventional marriage in those days of sexual liberation. It was challenging.

I wrote to her, addressing my letters to a friend who was staying in Cambridge. Another letter arrived at the beginning of January.

Sunday

Dear Roy,
When I didn't find a letter from you on Saturday I realised there had been a fundamental misunderstanding - that I was waiting for your reply to my letter before writing again and presumably you were waiting to hear whether I was in fact picking up your letters before writing again - so if that was so, I'm sorry I didn't write before. I did eventually get the first 2 letters last Thursday morning by leaving lots of messages .....
Your weekend with your sisters sounded very peaceful - although I suspect that the periods in between the ones you described probably weren't so much .....But sitting on empty beaches watching the waves is very absorbing and dreamlike - it can't fail to be with all those elemental rhythms. When we moved from Brighton to Caversham I

couldn't conceive of how people could live without the sea -
I would like to live near it again.

I'm feeling a bit odd today as last night we had to go (J had
been elected as a local Labour councillor the previous May) to a truly
extraordinary Labour dance at Alex Wood Hall to
celebrate the passing of the old etc - I couldn't believe it
when I walked in, the place was transformed. There were
little tables in rows with chairs round them, and candles,
and all the decorations from the Co-Op Club; there was an
old '50s group playing kind of BBC Northern Dance
Orchestra music, and the average age of the people there
must have been 93. They had a raffle, and sentimental
speeches, and a folk singer - and paste sandwiches and
swiss-roll! But it got incredibly hot and we were standing
talking to someone, dead sober and everything, and
suddenly, very unexpectedly, everything started to go fuzzy
and dark and I passed out on the spot. It's such a weird
feeling, I can never get over it, the coming round - usually
it's really nice, like being in Heaven. But this time I seemed
to be speeding back to consciousness, everything was going
too fast, it was intolerable. I tried to walk to the car but
blacked out again and I had to be carried into the car. I
think it must have been the atmosphere, but anyway I still
feel strange today................

...If you are coming back on Wednesday, I'll come and see
you on Thursday morning. Meanwhile I will keep going
round to look for letters, and I'll see you very soon.

My love, Steffe x

SEVEN

January 1974

It felt wonderful to be back for what was my penultimate term at Cambridge. The very next morning she came. After a break or separation, both of us were initially quite shy, needing time to get close. But we did come together and our love seemed undiminished. But, as usual, when it came for her to go, we had to face the same old practical difficulties. I never tried to persuade her to leave John because I knew she wasn't going to and what could I offer? I was a penniless, soon to be ex-student, with no clear idea about what I was going to do. But there was an urgency about trying to work out when we might meet again. I always felt a bit desperate as she rose to finally leave, especially if it had not been possible to fix a time and a date.

Steffe knew the pain I felt and was always kind to me in response.

'Roy, my love, I want to see you, be with you, as much as you do. I'll do everything I can to sort something out. It's really difficult managing a night with you but trust me I will come round absolutely as much as I can.'

*

I now had no connection with my course. Instead, I spent my time talking, reading, endlessly listening to music and on occasion writing long letters to Steffe.

It proved to be a term of extremes. I was feeling increasingly unanchored and simply went where my head took me. No longer were my thoughts all golden and exciting, a darkness was slowly creeping in. I had gone through the madness of The Electric Kool Aid Acid Test, travelled with Carlos Castaneda, and now I was finding existentialism. I found it unnerving and over time it tripped me up.

Like in Steppenwolf, I felt there were so many different parts of me that needed to be found and that this could only be done by throwing away my outer character and seeking out new experiences. Steffe was central to this. But I also felt myself fragmenting. Who was I? I was not alone in pushing the boundaries. It was true of some of my friends too, though perhaps not to the same degree as me.

From 1 January until 7 March, there was the Three Day Week. The miners were on strike again, action having been initiated in the immediate aftermath of a surprise attack on Israel by Arab States in October 1973 which led to oil prices rocketing. There had already been power cuts. Now commercial users of electricity were limited to three specified consecutive days' consumption each week and prohibited from working longer hours on those days. Services deemed essential (e.g. hospitals, supermarkets and newspaper printing presses) were exempt. Television companies were required to cease broadcasting at 10.30 pm during the crisis to conserve electricity. And the power cuts continued.

My friends and I spent many an evening sitting in centuries-old College rooms talking by candlelight through the evening. All was so peaceful. Somehow it changed and deepened the tone of our conversation.

Steffe came round when she could, sometimes for hours at a time. As I shared my thoughts, she seemed to really understand. They were not conventionally rational ones, instead they grew from my heart and soul as much as my brain. I believed in intuitive thinking. This Steffe really connected with. She told me about her own experiences at Durham, travelling across America getting jobs here and there, taking mescaline in California, encountering new ideas and new ways of thinking. It felt to me like we were travelling together. It was exciting.

I wrote many letters to her. One night I remember in particular. I was alone in my room, the gas fire alight, just one low light on, candles burning, music playing. I had a bottle of red wine and a 10mg tablet of Valium, a bluey. And spliffs. I wrote her an immensely long letter, and it felt like I was speaking directly to her. It was a wonderful journey, slowly sorting out my thoughts, finding the right words, opening up completely.

Once she wrote:

Dear Roy,
You fairly blew my mind yesterday evening for an
amazingly speedy and pretty paranoid visit - you were

putting out thoughts that really seemed to be coming from my own head. The people I've talked with who go through the same kind of reality/unreality or whatever it is don't usually seem to be bothered where they fit into the socially constructive scene because as they don't fit in, norms are simply rejected - as are the other people who accept the norms. It's trying to keep the two together which creates the problems of validity and relative success and failure - I suppose.

There doesn't seem much prospect of seeing you at the moment. Tomorrow in London I'm going to try and find out what's going on down there - I want to see Rick if possible because I generally manage to get things clearer in my mind through talking to him. But it may not be possible because he is also pretty fucked up at the moment because the woman he loves is getting married on Saturday - but maybe we can do a bit of mutual sorting out.

News is filtering in from the sit-in - it sounds like there is a modicum of direct action going on - e.g. Ian crashing out stoned on the floor - keep it up.

What can I say? See you around?

Steffe x

Yes, there was a second sit-in though it had none of the character of the first. It was a modern building that was occupied and the main room was a tiered lecture hall, in stark contrast to the massive room in the Old Schools. It was more narrowly political, less cultural and fizzled away.

We were still addicted to Roxy Music, now on to their third album. But Brian Eno had left the band and had just released his first solo album *Here Come The Warm Jets*. I loved it. The art work of the cover struck me as peculiarly beautiful. I was entranced by the reflection of his made-up face in a mirror, the ash-tray loaded with butts, the dried flowers, the hair dryer, the pack of naughty cards, the colour. The lyrics, the music itself, excited me. And the gorgeous beauty of the final track.

Steffe was never a particular Eno fan but she joined me and other friends when he performed in Cambridge, one of very few concerts he ever did.

As we approached the building where it was all happening, we realised we were late. No matter. Eno was performing in a very austere modern lecture theatre.   There were not many there. I spotted my friends near the front and we joined them.

I was transfixed. Eno looked so amazing. Shortly afterwards, there was a tap on my shoulder. I turned round and it was Thomas. He came up a year after me, a smiley, generous-hearted guy, with extraordinarily long hair. He held up a large brown bottle.

'Ether?'

This was new to me. I took it from him, inhaled and held it out to Steffe who also breathed in deeply. My head swam, reality felt molten, but the feeling swiftly went. It all felt very strange.

How delightful it was to walk back, arms around each other. We had never previously been together as a couple and in plain sight out in the world of Cambridge. We crossed the bridge over the Cam, my college on our right, into Garret Hostel Lane and then through the passageways and streets of the city.

Shortly after, we managed another night out. A dance with live music was being held in college. Many of my friends were going. They were no longer strangers to her. Could she come? Yes!

Inevitably, what was going on outside the concert venue was the most interesting. We took speed, not a favoured drug for us, but in many ways it was splendid. We both recall mad scenes – did they really happen? A friend, a gay compulsive alcoholic, came up to us dressed as a bishop in magnificent cloth and head gear. He rather shakily bowed his head, his skin so pale and emaciated, and blessed us. It was so lovely to have Steffe with me amongst my bonkers friends. But she couldn't stay the night – she had to go back to the flat – so I walked her back to Rose Crescent.

3 days later, Steffe wrote:

Dear Roy,

Having got up at 7.30 this morning and done 8 solid hours of statistics today - I'm feeling worse than I did on Saturday morning. Although in fact I picked up amazingly on Saturday and worked all day and went to the flicks in the evening - to see The Sting which is a zappy film, guaranteed to lift anyone out of the worst state. At 11 o'clock I crashed into bed.

With further distancing on Friday night it all appears to have got back into the original perspective - that it was a real gas. I'm still not sure if some of the things I saw were true - and I'm still embarrassed about what I might have been up to - but then that always bothers me when I've been drunk anyway. But I still think the come-down from that fucking drug is so heavy - it outweighs the pleasure really. So much pressure on the solar plexus. And too much of a crutch - the music and the action should stimulate release.

Roy - I'm really feeling too rushed/jumpy/tense to get into writing properly - it's hopeless trying to write in London - there's nowhere to retreat to in LSE. I'll be back tomorrow evening - I'll come and look for you the first possible moment - if all else fails then I'll see you on Wednesday night.

Please forgive me for being so abrupt - I do hate this whole mess so much sometimes. I feel I have boulders in my stomach whenever I think about it - so I just cancel out and try to avoid it. The vac is going to be hell - I only hope - desperately - that some happiness for everyone can be salvaged in the end.

See you soon, my love,

Steffe x

'This whole mess'. The fact is that both of us found the whole situation extremely difficult. I constantly missed her, frequently felt lonely and was always dependent on her carving out little segments of time for us to meet. Steffe felt guilty, she knew that I wanted to be with her openly and all the time and realised what pain I often felt, and she knew how John had been so upset when he knew about us before. And she was constantly lying to him now. But she was as addicted to me, as in love with me, as I was to her. Simultaneously, she loved John, more as a friend and support than a husband.

So our affair continued pretty much unchanged. Though we increasingly talked about us and our relationship. We managed to get a night or two away from time to time and they were always like magic. But one day whilst at home in her flat with John, it appears Steffe's feelings towards me burst out and she revealed that she 'had seen me a few times'. Then, one Sunday morning, she wrote this:

Roy,
Incredibly fucking hurried note while I'm meant to be buying newspapers.
Everything cool (except me, gently smouldering). I may have overdone the story a bit because I was feeling a bit over exuberant but it goes something like : You don't want to get involved in the situation in any way, too heavy etc, not wanting to spoil friendship with J etc. I get a distinct feeling we won't make it to the party, we will if I can organise it. Maybe a good move would be you moving in on another chick ... ? I may miss the train on Tuesday in which case I'll be around at 4 instead.
I keep looking over my shoulder ... amazing paranoia.
I need to see you really badly...
Oh yes - I, having got the dreadful secret off my mind, am now recovering from my aberration.
J is threatening to take me to Brussels with him ...S x

Oh yes, the party. There was a bit of me that was a touch Brideshead when at Cambridge. The thrill of it all.

Three (rich) friends, including Ian and Christian, and I decided to hold an afternoon party in college. Or rather they decided and talked me into it. It would be expensive but, like an addict for any experience, I went along with the idea. The cost would only be put on my bill.

It was held in the wood panelled room where the Asparagus Club had its 'eatings'. There was no food but large quantities of Trinity Hall punch, extremely innocuous tasting but quite lethal. People began to arrive sometime after 2 pm and soon it took off. Waiters in white coats kept guests topped up. The drink began to hit and the atmosphere became increasingly noisy and merry. I kept glancing at the door hoping, but not really expecting, that they would come. And then they did. By this time, I was well on the way to intoxication. But that notwithstanding, I somehow restrained myself and endeavoured to treat them as just friends. But again and again, Steffe and I caught each other's eyes. She gave me such knowing and amused smiles. Were we enjoying the deceit? Or was it just that she was amused by what she saw? It all felt a bit decadent and outrageous. I loved her being there.

*

The vac was almost upon us.

One morning just before going down, I was lying in bed having just woken up. It was 10.30. There was a gentle knock on the door. On my calling out, Steffe walked in.

'Wow, Steffie.'

'I am at the launderette. So I thought I would pop round whilst the washing machine is doing its job.'

She was wearing an overcoat over jeans and a sweater. Her hair hung softly round her gently smiling face. I lay there and our eyes engaged. There was that incredible recognition and understanding. We didn't speak. She slid off her coat, took off her boots and socks, and standing right by the bed unbuckled her belt, lowered her jeans, raised her arms to take off her sweater and finally took off her knickers. She climbed into bed and there followed an hour of pure lovemaking.

'I must go.' She said, ' The cycle will have finished.'

She gave me a kiss and then put on her clothes and by the time she left she looked no different from when she came in.   It was glorious, an unexpected surprise but I felt emotionally raw and exposed as I lay there watching the clock tick towards midday when I was supposed to have a supervisio

March 1974

Back to my parents for the Easter vac. I hated the vacs – I always felt so lonely.

Monday night

Dear Roy,

Now I am really missing you. Life has become so quiet - I haven't been out of Cambridge since I last saw you, which to me seems a long time, I'm so used to moving - and seeing you. In fact I've hardly been out of the flat - except for a weird Matthias party on Friday. And in a sense it's really good. Staying still and being on my own a lot has made me feel very calm, and at least my mind has stopped churning in the dominant kind of way it has been over the last few months. And I've rediscovered the pleasure of being alone without feeling lonely. I guess I'm not alone as I'm surrounded by cats - but I find them very beautiful company - when they aren't freaked out by activity around them, they are very peaceful animals.

So I feel that everything is slowing down and also I've been able once again to withdraw into my head and the only external event, the party on Friday, was another of those unreal experiences that doesn't conflict with one's own reality. We went with a girl from London and her boyfriend who has come to work at the Fitzwilliam. As usual there was the strangest mixture of people - the middle-ageing academics trying to keep their wives under control (if only they could lose it), RB getting heavily and aggressively and self-pityingly drunk, his wife

98

intermittently sulking dramatically and insinuating
herself on a very heavy teacher from the tech - also pissed
out of his head but totally in control, John deep in
aesthetics with equally ashen-faced bearded cheerful poets,
us in the middle of the floor passing joints around with the
au pair girl, and the lovely perfect Diana being the hostess
and wondering whether it was polite to pass the joint to
one of these demure academic spouses or in fact politer not
to ... the au pair girl told me about one of the children's
games, which was called 'Sad Doctors' (these kids are 3
and 6) where they get their dolls out and then one by one
accuse them of crimes - like being a 'stolener' or of 'trying
to kill a bad man' - there's America for you. I also had a
really good talk to John Matthias about his poetry - you
remember how I was knocked out by his reading? He said
he had a buzz for a week off that reading, because he was
able to totally lose himself in the poems knowing everyone
was with him and all he had to do was to keep them with
him, and reassure them that it was O.K. to follow him down
into the poem. He said he read his poems as he heard them
in his head when he was writing them - so it's a totally
cerebral transmission. He said lots of other things - but I
thought they were interesting - he said his impersonal and
personal poems were two ways of looking at the same thing
- the impersonal ones are about witchcraft and alchemy
and he's into the Middle Ages because the spirit and energy
of that time hadn't yet been subjected to rationalisation ...
I'm sorry to maybe go on a bit long about that - but
nothing else has happened to tell you about. The kittens
have all got fleas and I'm itching everywhere. I was woken
out of a beautiful dream last night but I can't remember
it.
Roy, what do you think is going to happen? What's going to
happen to us all - can I decide the pattern of my life? Or

has it been decided? I'm frightened of myself - sometimes, well, a lot of the time I'm frightened of the effect we have on each other - we spiral up and down so easily - does either of us have a power to resist when we go down? That is what frightens me fundamentally. Because sometimes I think we need catalysts - but then we sacrifice the up-trips. It's like a kind of bargaining process, also a gambling process.

But it's not really possible to go into this in a letter either, not at least when I can't see you to talk about it because there are too many dangers of misinterpretation. I love you Roy, and at the moment you are essential to my happiness, if disruptive of my peace. But I feel also the peace would have no possibility without you. And I know that to give you real happiness would be like letting a bird that's already out of its cage out of the window - but do we know how to use freedom? And does anything last.....

Write to me soon, My love,

Steffe x

P.S. This letter has long pauses in it.

My reactions were mixed. In part It made me feel so young, so immature. There was 26 year old Steffe mixing in this interesting, disparate, in part bohemian, group of much older people. She always carried with her a sophistication that at times made me feel so unsophisticated. Strange that. I realised early on that she came from a cultured family. Her brother went to Oxford, her sister to the Courtauld Institute of Art, her mother read, went to the theatre, the ballet. And Steffe was, in the old phrase, very 'well-spoken'. Her manner was full of grace and inherent gentleness. I did not come from such a family. They were aspiring bourgeoisie. I should be fair. My dad came from a poor working class background. He grew up in a dark brick-built terrace, a worker's home, in the back streets of Reading. Two up, two down, with a tiny walled backyard. He left school at fourteen but went to night school and became a professional, a Fellow of the Royal Institute of Chartered

Surveyors. He was a very bright man, with extraordinary mathematical abilities. But his childhood had no books, no music, no culture – just pure grind. In another time, he would have gone to university and become the man he should have been but never was. As for my mother, she was all emotion and very little head – not that she wasn't bright, she was. But she, like my dad, was a person of her time and background. Mum's dad had been a violent alcoholic who drank and gambled away what money the family had (and it was a lot, I am told). She carried the pain of that childhood of witnessing abuse. My family had dreadful rows, shouting matches, items thrown. I felt my background was lesser than Steffe's. Only later did I learn about the dysfunctionality of her family and come to appreciate some real positives my family, and in particular my mother, had given me.

And on top of that, I felt marginalised. I was no part of this aspect of Steffe's life. It did pain me. But this I never felt I could tell her.

On the other hand, she wrote so beautifully and interestingly. I was touched that she shared her experiences so vividly with me. And her love for me flowed through. Her letters were always read and reread.

But the questions she raised about how we could so profoundly affect each other…. I didn't want to acknowledge it but it was true – we touched each other's soul so profoundly, we engaged emotionally so strongly, that nuances of feeling on either side could tip the other over. For my part, I wasn't finding the relationship at all easy and so when we met inevitably that could not but impinge at times, just as Steffe's own confusion and occasional despair about things also came alive.

And during the vac, I became ill. Also for months now I had been suffering from an extremely painful neck ache on an all but daily basis.

April 1974

I returned for my final term at Cambridge with some considerable trepidation, not least because I had Finals coming up and I had done very little work all year.

But I couldn't wait to see Steffe. She came as soon as she could – another pretty flying visit. We caught up, I shared my work anxieties. She

101

then told me that she was going to be in hospital in London for a couple of weeks. She reacted badly to the sun and she, and others, were going to be 'investigated'. We had one or two more meetings, even a night together, before she was admitted. We talked about the future.

'What's going to happen Steffe, after the exams, after I leave Cambridge?'

'After your exams and mine are over, I promise we'll have proper time together. But what are you aiming to do on leaving? I know we've talked about this but what do you want?'

'Oh God. I'm so confused. I just feel so alienated from the straight world. I look at my fellow law students and think – do I want to join them? Is that where my personal revolution gets me? I want to be creative, I want to be free. But it all feels fraudulent. I try to write but it's crap. I just feel rudderless. And worse than that, I don't know, but what felt so colourful and wonderful before is now confusing me. Is it, was it, all just fantasy? A mirage? Sometimes I feel despair. And then I miss you even more'

'Sometimes, you frighten me a bit – or rather it frightens me, what you are saying now. I'm not the strong person you think I am. That's what I was getting at, I guess, in my letter'

'But I see you as strong.'

'I'm really not'.

'Steffie, you have always been so clear with me, so authentic, so honest. I reckon that's strong. I can honestly say I've never respected anyone more than you. Really. You laugh but it's true. And I feel you are completely open with me – I trust you. But trust in me too. I'm young. I've been through quite a journey. I need time to sort myself out - it's all a bit a fight with the devil at times, at present.'

'I believe you do have strength but I can see how you are struggling at the moment. I want to help you, support you, but I really am not strong. I am endlessly confused and uncertain. And I get afraid about what may happen when we both feel uncertain. I need security – stability. That's what I feel John gives me. Don't look so down. You are the one who gives me life, who gives me the magic of what we have, the love we share. But don't think I don't recognise how difficult it is for you. I love you, Roy, and I hate to see you down.'

So things were left hanging. We saw little of each other for weeks on end. It was inevitable. I, like a number of my fellow law students at the college, finally dedicated ourselves to trying to make up for all our missed work and actually prepare for our Finals. We managed to persuade a star student, a very kind guy, to lend us all his lecture notes which we copied. He also let us copy other crucial notes. We then sat around, 2 or 3 of us at a time, and worked our way through the syllabus, making notes and ramming case names into our heads. It was exhausting and tedious but at last we put in a huge effort. Meanwhile, Steffe was admitted to St John's hospital.

Hostel Ward Unit,
St John's Hospital,
London
Monday

Dear Roy,

As I'm already feeling thoroughly institutionalised and desperately in need of a cigarette, I doubt if this will add up to much of a letter - I have the time to write, that's for sure. The decision to give up smoking was an over-hasty one and a bit irreversible since I purposely didn't bring any fags with me. Being in hospital when you are well is like being in prison. I'm reading a book at the moment by Erving Goffman on Total Institutions - places like monasteries, prisons and mental homes where all the inmates are stripped of their personalities and work, sleep and play in big batches, strictly regimented. Boarding schools are also total institutions - and hospitals get uncomfortably close to being so as well, especially when you realise you've come in without all the necessities of life like alternative food, cigarettes - and writing paper - and this is such a forgotten little dump, it's a question of coercing nurses to buy them in their lunch hour.

The reason I want writing paper is that I was looking at the ads in the Sunday Times for cottages in Scotland - there seemed a few possibilities although the most attractive one was a stone cottage by the river for 2 from May - September in Wales for £8 pw - not bad ..... And I could have written for details but they might turn their Celtic noses up at my Maxipad writing block. There's also a problem of where they should send these amazing details as J does not know yet what's afoot .... I am very wary of letting him know at the moment because he might possibly freak out and pay you an untimely call and I thought I should let your exams pass first too. But there's still time and I would quite like to see if Student travel have any suggestions.

I hope your work and head are both under control at the moment .....

Lionel's party on Saturday was a real laugh - lots of old friends, including from Durham were there. There was loads of booze and most people were into that, which meant all the more j's for us...I was sitting cross-eyed with P and A in Lionel's room smoking about my fourteenth joint - there were so many and people were drifting off to dance and things so we were kind of left there with a large one each - and then this lunatic came in and we offered one to him, he said he hadn't before but he would try etc - and then he started asking us how many we had smoked and to describe our feelings - Jesus it was so painful, he really had caught us at the wrong moment and we could only laugh helplessly - and he wouldn't go away and every time I bumped into him he asked if I was still smoking - he probably wasn't a bad guy, just having his own private put-on - but I wish people wouldn't do it.

The hospital scene is entirely ludicrous. I swear to God they're not interested in a cure, they just want to find out what's wrong for their own research. Every day we have to sit in front of this machine that they have built and have rays of the sun shone in little circles on our backs and then

104

they spend the afternoon 'reading' our backs, i.e. seeing if any spots come up. There is a weird game-like quality to the whole proceeding, like the ritual games I used to make up as a kid, when you're fascinated by charts and figures and bureaucratic procedures so you design secret and meaningless documents and stamp them and sign them and all that. This machine they've made, it's all junky and made out of hardboard and the room it's in looks somehow like one of those rooms where little boys (and my step-father-in-law) play model railways or making radios. There are three of them who play this game together and I think they're all mad. We're not really part of the hospital, we are in a little unit with double rooms which is the only redeeming feature of it but it's very boring and the food is sickening so like I said we have to send out for iron rations. And there's something about the other patients which makes you want to scratch all the time.
...... I think I am let out on Friday. I'm hoping you have time to write - I would like to write again but they will be very empty letters about lights and spots - but I will write. Meanwhile, take care
My love
Steffe x
PTO

Tuesday

Poor Roy, I've just been given your letter - it really doesn't seem fair that you are ill again, especially now just before your exams. You are, of course, crazy to worry that I might have caught it - to start with, I haven't, and anyway what better place to be ill than in hospital. I did in fact have a sore throat on Saturday and my glands are also apparently up as the doctor did remark on it but I'm not

feeling ill. However, it does occur to me that you do always push yourself physically to extremes - not sleeping enough, etc - so I guess you invite reactions like this……..I'm really sorry about this - you must be going crazy - but remember things always feel worse when you are ill….But I honestly think you should get more sleep anyway - I always feel wrecked after a night or two with you even when you say you've had comparatively lots of sleep! Please don't be annoyed by this - I care about you and I can't help wanting to look after you a bit …We're going to be let out for the afternoon so I'm going to the park and I can get the things I need to buy which is an amazing relief - I'll write some letters to Scotland. I'll write again tonight. Try not to worry, my love -
Steffe x

Yes, I was ill. The timing was disastrous and I was beside myself with worry. I was thinking of getting a doctor's note to allow me to miss them. Thank God, I recovered quickly. I would take them. Often in company with Ian and sometimes another friend, I worked literally all day, day after day.

Hostel Ward Unit, etc. Thursday

I'm really glad you've recovered and also that your tutor has seen you - I hope by now things are straightening out and you're feeling better about things. And as you say, in a fortnight it will be over - and at least then you won't feel, like I did, that you allowed yourself to be conned into wasting literally months sweating over it all. Although I appreciate very well that you've really done bugger all work, I have great faith in your intelligence to do quite well in spite of that - some people do, you seemed to pull it off last time, I always think it's grossly unfair. But now you've decided to do them, you must stick at it solidly -

106

otherwise you'll have done neither one thing nor the other and it will truly be a waste of time.

In some ways this stay in hospital has been quite a gas. We are able to spend every afternoon out, and we've been lying around and walking in Victoria Park which isn't far from here and is really beautiful - it's big, there are boating ponds and a lake with an island, and a strange Victorian monument and lots of huge chestnut trees and not many people. And despite the fact that we are all in here for allergies to the sun, we sprawl out and sunbathe to the absolute horror of the doctors, but none of us can cook up a decent rash. I think probably it's not hot enough yet because I am definitely allergic to ultra-violet rays as the tests show this. But I feel less depressed about it than I used to, because I have some kind of faith that it _will_ go away sometime, and anyway some way I shall find someone to give me calcium even if illegally. The reason they won't give it to me here is partly because it isn't actually statistically _proved_ that it helps (in the same logic that it isn't actually _proved_ that smoking causes lung cancer) and so they don't think it's scientifically justified - they are such prize bureaucrats in their own way - and also because too much calcium may be bad for you - but I'm afraid my philosophy is far too much present-orientated to give a shit about that. My aim is to enjoy life _now_ , not to live until I am a hundred and ten. I find life meaningless enough, so if you can't function fully, why function at all? That's not meant to convey despair or anything like that - it's simply my own hedonism.

I've been writing to the places in Scotland. God knows what'll happen when the replies arrive at our flat but I'll deal with that contingency when it arises. I can't promise anything Roy - money is quite an acute problem at the moment and if you have to pay off your overdraft we

107

*shouldn't spend my savings too rashly. But we'll see if we
can come up with something cheap - but it must be nice.
Otherwise, I'll make sure that we are able to enjoy plenty of
the June orgies together. Everything is in the melting pot at
the moment but I promise you it's not staying there much
longer.*

*Anyway, I'll come and see you as soon as your exams are
over and I'll write to you as often as possible - I'm afraid I
can't get into anything except a straight information-type
letter here. I'm sure you understand why; because
otherwise I really enjoy getting stoned and trying to
translate what's going on in my head into words - or at
least having the right setting to really get into writing.
Please look after yourself and keep your end up - my love,
Steffe x*

'Everything is in the melting pot.' Pre-occupied as I was with my work, I didn't ponder on this phrase. But what did it mean? In truth, things had been in the melting pot to some extent or another throughout our relationship.

Her letters were an essential part of our relationship. They filled the gaps in our contact, they became in themselves part of our intimacy (I wrote many letters to her), we learnt a lot about each other through our correspondence.

Just before the exams began, I returned to my room to find a letter and a card:

*Dear Roy,
I have a feeling that you must be around somewhere -
there's a look about the room which says it hasn't been left
for long - but as I promised <u>not</u> to come and visit you I
won't search the place. I only wanted to see how you are -
in a state of acute disorganisation by the looks of things, if
not suffering from congestion of the lungs. I've found an*

amazing card to send you, but I don't know if I should as it would probably freak you out - depending on your state of mind - oh, but it's so perfect, especially as I sit here and view the scene. I don't know if I will be able to resist it. There have been a lot of changes going on since I came out of hospital which I will tell you about when I see you after the exams. On Friday night, Penny cooked a meal as compensation for hospital food and the evening started at a really high point as everyone was trying to get Richard up before he managed to bring us down, he's in a really black state at the moment - but inevitably he won and the evening was a singular disaster and provided a true confrontation with reality for J. and me - but things are amazingly cool, we are considering a very friendly separation, also a gradual one - but as I said I will explain things when I see you and they are not fully worked out yet.

.... Incidentally, the possibility of a holiday away is fading although not gone entirely - but J. has promised to go away for a while, probably right at the beginning of June, and if I have the car we can do things like go to the sea.....
I still don't know whether to send you the card - if I do, just look at the picture and disregard the innuendoes.

Take care - my love

Steffe x

Take it easy, but not too easy!
My love
Steffe xxx

The room had definite similarities to my own. And I found the image very funny – and apposite.

EIGHT

I took all the exams, bashing out case names forgotten straight afterwards. And then they were over.

All I wanted was to see and be with Steffe. But things didn't work out. We neither got away nor did J go off. We had all but no contact. So instead I staggered from one June event to another, normally extremely intoxicated. The future in every way was uncertain.

It was then the traumatic event occurred. Larry was a very strange man. Always dressed in a droopy colourful t-shirt with contrasting loons. Beard with long dark hair. Never stood still – always moved his legs in only a mildly rhythmic way. Played music constantly. Said very little. Smiled a lot. He took acid every day. Even when he took his finals. He was a mathematician. He left every exam early. He got a first…. He shared a large 3 or 4 storey Victorian house on Hills Road, a little way out from the city centre. They were holding a final party. It was on a Saturday.

I arrived with Ian. By the time I met Larry at the bottom of the stairs, I was quite drunk. He stood there, moving his legs all the time as always, and asked if I wanted a tab of acid. Ian quickly joined me.

'Why not?' I said without thinking.

'I might as well too', drawled Ian in his laid-back, open-to-everything way.

I dropped it. It came on extraordinarily quickly. I guess it was strong.

I found myself up in the attic room. 5 or 6 people were sitting around listening to Astral Weeks by Van Morrison. The lighting was warm and red. I felt thirsty and found I had a mug in my hand. It was empty but I visualised water and there it was. I drank it. A rug lay on the floor. As I looked at it, I saw the history of man's time on earth evolve in three dimensional figures and landscapes, marching across the floor. I saw fields of knights crashing their swords against shields and armour. I saw the Napoleonic Wars fought out before me, cannons and charges, blood and death. I saw the trenches of the First World War.

Then I spotted a ladder leading up to a skylight. I rose and started to climb.

'Guys, I'm going to fly.'

I really said it. I felt omnipotent. I guess it was then they started to really worry about me. They saw I was absolutely gone. So I was brought back down.

The next thing I can recall was coming out of the front door of the house with Ian. It was then things became very dark. At the end of the front path, we turned right. It was a long straight road, with yellow sodium lights all the way down. Lights like in Bracknell. Cold lights. Unfriendly lights. We began to walk, no talking. Then, like something from a horror movie, I saw a fluorescent shady yellow face rise above the end of the road, a face of evil, the face of the devil – and it was laughing. I turned in horror. I wanted Steffe. I needed her. I was so scared. But I didn't feel able to call out for her. So I strode back. I was in search of warmth and comfort. I took a left turn and saw a bay-windowed house. There will be a warm fire and a sofa there, I thought. That's what I needed. And all was possible, so I threw myself at the front window knowing I could pass through it to the comfort beyond. There was the sound of smashing glass. Ian ran to me and pulled me away. I was dripping blood from a severe cut to my right wrist. I just cried as he quickly led me back to the house. Shock greeted our entry. An ambulance was called. It was then pure hell arrived.

I was in this confined space, bright, cold lights bearing down on me, strange people in yellow jackets moving around. I was lying down. We were in motion. I glanced at my bleeding wrist that was being held. Time stopped briefly and then we were going round in a circle again and again. It went on forever. We stopped and doors opened. I was led to a large building and again there were the dreadful lights. Where was I? A nurse behind a desk said 'He took LSD, he must take the consequences'. Or did she? They were capturing me. I saw the door and ran through it. I felt myself running on grass, away from the strip lighting of the monster building. Arms wrapped themselves around me. I was being held. They dragged me back. I could not escape.

I found myself in a large room, like an operating theatre. The lights were brilliant white. I looked at my wrist and saw it was being stitched and unstitched repeatedly. I spotted a clock and read its hands. It said 4.11 and the second hand rested on 20. It didn't move. I stared and still it didn't move. I then realised I had reached complete enlightenment – about this particular moment. And it was horrific. Having reached total understanding, I knew I was going to be stuck in this moment forever. That was my life over. The stitching and unstitching would last an eternity. And then I saw the second hand move and I was released. I began to return to myself but felt so profoundly damaged. Then 2 police officers arrived. They (sympathetically) asked me about taking LSD. God knows how but I managed to come up with a story.

'I've no idea how I came to take it. My drink must have been spiked'.
I followed up by seeking to gain their sympathy.

'I'm a law student at Trinity Hall. This is awful. How could someone have done this to me?'

Unbelievably, it worked. They wished me well and that was the end of any police involvement. Somehow, they never put 2 and 2 together and worked out that my cut wrist and the smashed front window of the house near to the party were linked.

I have no recollection of how I got back from the hospital. It was shortly after 6am when I sat down in the dining room of the house where the party had been. There were a few people still around, Larry, the guy who had given me the acid, Ian, two or three others. The atmosphere was sombre. I felt shame at having wrecked everything. And I was afraid – really afraid. I knew I had damaged my psyche badly. I felt shame, stupidity, loss, isolation.

To top it all, I had an interview the next day in London for articles in the most radical and political defence firm in the country. Yes, despite all my disillusionment with the law, I had applied for this job. I knew I had blown it. (I did attend the interview, my wrist in a bandage, but of course I didn't excel, I wasn't able to be me, I never got an offer. Wonder how different my life might have been had I succeeded?)

*

I needed Steffe that night. I was without the warmth of love just when I needed it most. Later, she told me that of course I or someone on my behalf should have contacted her. She would have come. But I was so locked into the realities of our relationship being an affair, I simply hadn't felt able to do what I should have done. Instead, I was scared of seeing her again. I felt I had lost my lustre, my fire, and instead was drifting into existential despair.

Events conspired against us and our planned post-exam time together simply didn't happen. I indulged in drunken and drugged days and nights but I was ever more aware that I was about to leave the city I had come to love, and without any plan for the future.

I didn't see her until after my results were out, displayed on a board outside the Old Schools. Results were published very quickly.

Roy! You brilliant kid! I was so relieved when I saw the list. Jesus, some of us have to work on these things - you're so lucky to be able to play the game and have plenty of time for other things.

I'm missing you desperately. Everything at the moment seems super-empty. It seems at times that I only feel truly alive when I'm with you.

I wanted to say that my job is only until the end of July. I could maybe extend it - but alternatively we could have a really long time together - in Cambridge maybe. We still have the flat there. Think about it.

Get in touch with me as soon as you can.

Take care of yourself,

My love Steffe x

We met but I played down the trauma of my nightmare trip. Instead, I buried myself in the unique sensuality that we shared with such intensity. But surely she picked up on a neediness that I can't believe I didn't exude. The new Bowie album, Diamond Dogs, came out in May. It encapsulated my feelings in so many ways. Love and alienation. Nightmare visions, drugs, desperation but also love.

Term was about to end. Graduation and then goodbye Cambridge. So bitter-sweet. Saying farewell to such beautiful buildings, gardens, passageways, main courts. Would life ever be so rich again? Christian once said back in our second year when just the two of us were talking into the night and dawn was about to break 'We'll look back on these times and know they will never be repeated'. I was so acutely aware of this now. And I was scared.

I had no meaningful plans so ended back in Bracknell.
Steffe was working in London. But we had definite plans to get away. I explained that my mother was being intrusive and cross-questioning me. She wrote 'Poor Roy, it's all so horribly complicated and devious for you …… Whatever happens, you must not let your parents know what's happening, it would cause a holocaust'. Yes, my parents saw Steffe as the devil incarnate, and me not far behind.

NINE

The planned, gradual separation from John never seemed to materialise. Nor did the long time together. Steffe was working in London and I was in Bracknell. But I knew I couldn't stay there and made plans to move to London. But I needed a job to do that. Through my elder sister, I was able to find employment in the advertising department of Thames Television, where she was a senior sales executive. I managed to rent a small room in a shared flat near Swiss Cottage. In fact, all that was shared was the kitchen. Everybody essentially led separate lives and there was no communal experience. But it suited for now.

Funny looking back on that job. I was in the chart room. There were about 12 of us. We sat around a large table. Behind us were wall charts, with little plastic pockets representing every advert break. Our job was to go through order sheets, read them and ensure tabs were placed in the relevant pocket to reserve the advert slot. We then filed the order sheets. We were like human computers. It was a tedious job, only made lighter by the fact that the 'chartists' were a very varied, quite amusing bunch. I managed to get a job for a mate of mine from Cambridge, similarly drifting. But it was a dead-end job and I found it ultimately depressing.

I managed a weekend back in Cambridge but the city had lost its allure. Not that I found London particularly to my taste. Such friends as I had (from Cambridge) were some distance away and it was often difficult to catch them on the phone to sort out a meeting. So I was often lonely, rather aimless and I rarely saw Steffe, although we got to a Roxy Music concert. But even that failed to meet our expectations and hopes.

We met a few more times, Steffe staying overnight at my flat, but then she said that we had to stop seeing each other, that she had to work on her marriage. She said she was so sorry, that she loved me as always but that things couldn't go on as they were. Back on the roller-coaster. I felt even more depressed though, as so often before, I tried to put on a brave face. But still I couldn't bring myself to accept that there was no future. I was addicted to her.

A few weeks later, out of the blue, she rang me. Soon after she wrote.

Dear Roy,

It was really nice to talk to you last week - although it was unfair of me to call on you to get me out of a period of gloom, which was what I was doing. I think it was unfair because surely you must have also needed scraping off the floor at times, which possibly I could have done, but you probably resisted that route whereas I didn't. Anyway, talking to you did set off a revival and I've been going up ever since. All I hope is that it didn't upset you too much. Inevitably I painted a much worse picture than really exists. It is true that for some reason(s) which I can't really explain I started to get depressed in London. Without going into it in detail, I seemed to lose confidence and get very insecure. It has something to do with the fact that I'm both very dependent and very intolerant of people. I got pissed off with so many of my old friends in London and started to put an exaggerated importance on a few people I had faith in. At the same time the weekends in Cambridge were getting heavier and I couldn't account for it at the time. Now I know part of the reason - John was getting involved with a chick up here who he didn't tell me about, and was getting very confused about whether he wanted me back or not - but as he didn't put it in those terms, I just got the effect of his confusion, which were extreme irritability, distance, general heaviness - and of course I started to feel more insecure, more unsure of myself, etc, etc. Which pervaded everything including my dissertation - I felt I couldn't face interviewing people. In that sort of mood, everything becomes paranoiac - I began to feel totally inadequate and frightened of being with people. It all got pretty horrific - and on Wednesday morning, before I rang you, J. was driving me back to Cambridge with all my stuff, and he kept stopping by the side of the road because he couldn't decide whether he wanted me to come back, or whether to turn round and take me back to London.

Since then things have gradually been sorting themselves out........J. and I are trying to sort things out. That guy is so confused and incapable of making decisions - pathologically incapable - it's pathetic. But basically we are both determined to make a final effort at making things work between us. This may seem absurd to you, but the point you must understand is that we have both been fighting for so long to work out a relationship we both want and can cope with, and we have both been through so many hassles together, that it seems as absurd to us to abandon it now. As we both want an open marriage, but are both reasonably jealous/insecure at the same time, it's not easy to work out, and we would certainly have the same problems with other people. Also there's obviously a pretty strong bond between us to carry us through all out troubles and of course over three years our lives have become very interconnected and any split will be extremely complicated. The fact that J. has now found a girl in Cambridge is also interesting - if only because he is now realising what restrictions he put on you and me. I vacillate between boiling with rage at the fact that he didn't realise it at the time and being vastly amused by the irony of it. But again that's the sort of thing that can only be worked out over time.

I feel this is another highly unsatisfactory letter. Very non-sequitur-ish. Splitting with you has left a gaping hole in my life - obviously I feel it more acutely now I'm back in Cambridge. But it's something I cannot get onto paper adequately. I just know you played an incredibly important role which I am tempted to say was/is indispensable. But now - while I would dearly love to see you and have a long talk with you, I have explained to you the situation between J. and me, although probably badly. The point is that as things stand, J. and I want to stay together; whether or not you want to see me in these circumstances I don't know. I'll be coming to London in the next couple of weeks - I would like to see you then. But if you would rather not, perhaps we could leave it until next term or, maybe, indefinitely. I must resign myself to the fact that you may be left with a bad taste in your mouth because I have explained things wrong. If you want to write or phone, do.

You showed enormous strength when we split up a few weeks ago. This letter is a bit hard in tone because I don't want you to be under any misconceptions - and things are less clear in my mind than I would like and at the moment I would rather err on the side of being too definitive. I don't want to undermine the strength you have built up regarding me.

Take the greatest care of yourself, Roy

Love

Steffe xx

So of course, we resumed our relationship. I was never capable of walking away. I was now 22 years old.

TEN

Wednesday

Dear Roy,

I have been turning over in my mind whether or not I should write to you; I have decided that if I write to you now, and see you on Friday, you will have at least a short time in which to think over what I have to say.

Which is, briefly, that in July I am going away to the States, for at least a year. I found this out for certain a few days before Christmas, after I last saw you. To an extent it accounts for why I was feeling strangely depressed at the time. My horizons had suddenly been drastically altered, and I was trying to assimilate the change. Although of course I'm excited about it, otherwise I wouldn't be going, you know and I know what it implies.

In a sense I hope this will come as a relief to you. We are caught up in a relationship which is too valuable to each of us to want to end, and at the same time I've refused to take the step which would make it a totally satisfying relationship for you. And I have (fairly) consistently been convinced that there was no reason, apart from your loneliness between my visits and your rigorously repressed jealousy, to end it either. At least now there is a definite limit to it. What I have been trying to get used to over the last week or two is the idea that when you find out, you'll decide it's better to finish now rather than carry on until I go. Which is partly why I'm writing to you - so that you

120

*have a chance to collect your ideas, but not too long so
that things start to fester in your mind.*

*I've missed you a lot these last couple of weeks. We both
depend on each other - to an extent which for my part I
don't like to admit. You are, and always have been, my
lifeline. I hope you will forgive me for going away. Please
try to remember the wealth we have given each other, and
don't always regret what you think might have been. It
might <u>not</u> remember.*

*It'll be difficult seeing you on Friday. Please be close to me
- unless you want to punish me. I want to be able to talk to
you about everything - at least, not about my trip exactly,
but about the implications of it.*

Until then, I love you as always. Steffe x

What a shock it was to come home from work on the Thursday and read
this letter. I knew it was carefully written, was honest and loving. But it
was such a blow. I knew I wasn't going to punish her the next evening but
beyond that I had no clarity.

She arrived about 7. I was terribly on edge as she entered my room. But
she did the best thing she could do, she simply took me in her arms, held
me and kissed me. I had no reason to doubt her love or concern. Yet I felt
so raw.

'Oh, Steffe, I can't bear the idea of you going. I can't hide it. It's so out of
the blue. You have never even hinted at the possibility'.

'Oh love, I'm so sorry. John applied for a job at Stanford University in
California and he's been offered it. I saw no point in telling you when it
was merely a possibility. I didn't want to hurt you. And I think I was
avoiding thinking about it until it became a certainty'.

'But do you really want to go, leaving behind your friends, leaving
behind me?'

'No, I'm not clear but it is an exciting prospect and, as I said in my letter, however much I love you, and I really do, perhaps it's a way of bringing things to a head. I am so sorry, Roy'.

'I really don't know what to say. But I am devastated. Just devastated'.

'Oh, sweetie, I hate to hurt you'.

'But you are hurting me'.

I didn't have it in me to say much more. Instead, we sunk into love-making, the only balm that could be of any help.

The morning came.

'Do you want us to end now?'

'I just don't know, Steffe'.

'Look, have a think. I can come again next Thursday. If you don't want me to, just let me know'.

She left, saying 'Please take care of yourself. Never forget I love you'.

We did meet the next Thursday. It was horrible. In the end, I said we should just split and say goodbye to each other. Afterwards, she wrote:

> *Saturday*
>
> *Dear Roy,*
>
> *I'm only writing because I'm terribly worried that there might be a misunderstanding between us. I want to make sure that we both realise that I'm not abandoning you at this moment of time - although by going away in July I shall be abandoning you then. But the decision not to see me now is yours, done for your own sake. It's up to you to decide whether it's better to make the break now. That's all. I want to make sure you know that I still want you and still love you as before. But neither is this a plea for you to ask me to come back. If I can't make you happy, at least I want to make you the least unhappy.*
>
> *I apologise for being so vile during Thursday night. I was trying to hurt myself more than you.*

Don't despair, my sweet Roy. I know that ultimately your life will be good and happy, as you want it. Believe me.

My love
Steffe x

But I was in despair. Weeks passed. Then she wrote:

Dear Roy,
I've been trying to clear a space to write to you - I don't know if the Eve of Saint Valentine will prove to be an auspicious time to choose. I thought during the week that there were some things I wanted to tell you about; now I come to think of them again, they seem to have lost their dynamic intensity and be the same old trips wheeled out again. I've been very lonely during the last couple of weeks. Coming down to London has become a real drag. I've had plenty to do but I'm not getting into it. Last week I got into reading a lot of Laing. Reading anything on psychoanalysis, psychiatry, you can't resist taking it subjectively, I mean you take it in at a level you can't possibly control. By Friday, I was really out of it.. So possibly that didn't help. But I do feel isolated now in my thoughts. J. and I are the greatest friends but we appreciate (I hope) that we work on different levels and need different stimuli. And now that you've gone, Cambridge has become more painful than ever - we had such very good times. And although you've got to have change, and there other kinds of treats ahead, some things are unrepeatable - everything's unrepeatable but sometimes different situations can call up the same feelings, and those feelings, associated with some of the things that happened

with us in Cambridge, have been felt I fear for the last time. And as they used to awaken earlier, similar feelings, it's regrettable.

I suppose that ultimately your armour didn't shine enough, Roy. That is more a confession than an accusation. I can't think about the future. I don't want to be in a situation where I have to. Where I have to face up to everything myself, taking care of myself and taking care of others. I don't mind anything as long as I have some escape route - in a sense, someone to hide behind, but that conveys all the wrong images. But more the knowledge that if I want to say, I think I'll stay out this round, I can do it. And I think you may have these tendencies too. That may be unfair, but think very, very honestly about it. And I know that with you only I would have to become much more responsible and realistic and I don't want to. This hasn't anything to do with jobs or anything. But it does have to do with living from day to day, with plenty of dreams and ideals, which makes tomorrow totally idealistic - the way I want tomorrow to be in fact - but makes today too precarious. I have lost my taste for adventure in some ways. This need for a protective shield against the severe practical imperatives of life places an enormous constraint on me and produces a lot of conflict. I want freedom without ultimate responsibility. If I could find someone who perceived the way I do, but at the same time took life very much in their stride, I could be happy with them. But possibly such an individual can't exist. Although, as I said, I've been finding the everyday world a bit distanced over the last couple of weeks, I've been doing a lot of thinking. And I think that at last I have worked something out - an analysis that comprehends all the

previously rather confused ideas I had about the nature of
society, and its process and direction. I don't suppose it's
original, it certainly has a lot to do with reading Marcuse
and Laing, because both are the first people I have read
who I feel wouldn't just pour scorn and derision on the way
I feel about things. But it's my discovery and that is
important. It has to do with Man and Nature but I don't
feel confident enough to express it publicly....
It's a shame we can't wring the last drop of blood out of
our relationship, Roy. But this letter should be conveying
the message that whatever you decide, there's a lot to
support that decision. I don't see further than arriving in
Stanford ....
I would maybe like to write to you again. Maybe you would
like to reply. I hope you're well again - in mind and body.
My love
Steffe x

I recognised the honesty and the openness of what she said. But it hurt me so much. 'Your armour didn't shine enough'. That hit really hard. It left me feeling helpless whilst simultaneously realising that she was such an exceptional woman, the way she opened her heart to me.

I mentally ran away. I returned to the Kensington Flat of Iniquity, the centre for upper class degenerates in search of heavy drugs and pure hedonism, a flat where the lampshades had specks of blood on them, from temporarily discarded needles. I (just) avoided shooting up but the impulse was there.

And I chucked my job. I couldn't stand it another day. So I went on the dole.

I didn't contact Steffe. I was lost. It was all too much. This was a dark time.

She wrote on 21 February:

*Please write, Roy, just to say how you are, or even just to say
that you're not going to write. Simply that would do, to
break this awful silence. I don't even know if you're alive.*

I couldn't ignore this. That would have been cruel. So I wrote to her – at
excessive length. I guess I was trying to convince her that I had reconciled
my conflicts between the radical world of new values and everyday
reality. It was a long plea to her to reconsider her decision.
She replied:

Dear Roy,
*Thank you for writing to me at such length. I suppose I
ought to be pondering over your letter which I only read
tonight but firstly I feel I do so much daily thinking and
reflecting and I've not had any contact with you for so
long that there seems no reason to delay further, and
secondly that parts of your letter made me feel so sad, and
any pondering was simply turning to weeping. I'm not sure
if there's much point in writing, though; my first reaction
was that I wanted to see you. Not for anything in
particular, but just to see you. Perhaps it's as well that you
weren't in when I rang you just now...Actually, I rang Ian
but he didn't know where you were.*
*I feel isolated. If I think, I cry and I can't think of anyone
I want to talk to. That's not a very good reaction to your
letter, is it? I just want to talk to you - and, as always in
our hopeless relationship, you're not there. So what will
happen, as always, is that I will force myself out of this
weak mood and into the wrong kind of strength, hard and
bitter. I wish I had some way of climbing out of these
moods that didn't need communication with other people
because I don't really want to force a change like that. I
wish I could play music or paint. I could probably do*

126

either but my inhibition prevents me. The guy in the next room here has a whole range of instruments, very easy to play he tells me, but I bet I would feel a fool if I picked one up. I know I feel too self-important, terrified of damaging my image.

Your letter.
You expressed what you have been going through very clearly. And clearly it's easier for me to comprehend the disunity between your mind and your nature - and harder to accept the re-unity (which is what it is - they were once united). Harder to accept because at that point for me it becomes just words - one can only understand what one is capable of experiencing oneself, and if you don't understand in that full sense you can't imagine it, and if you can't imagine it, how can you tell if someone else has found it or not - it's certainly not recognisable in words. At the point of creation there is unity between man and nature, because man is part of nature and therefore nature is within man. Only man calls it human nature - and as man dehumanises himself he quickly forgets what that nature really is; having forgotten the truth of it, he is also embarrassed and ashamed at it, because having forgotten he's part of nature, he's been trying to dominate it - then the term human nature begins to have a pejorative ring to it, which is in fact justified because the human part of nature, man having become dehumanised, begins to be an insult to nature itself. The further man travels from the point of creation, the more he civilises the world for himself and his children, the more nature is cast off from himself, seen in opposition to himself, something to be afraid of because of its immense power and which

127

therefore must be overpowered. And man thrusts the knowledge on his children and they quickly learn to fear and fight nature, both outside and within them.

Nature would not have excited this response if it weren't so powerful and overawing. Nature is strong and enduring. It has endured centuries of man's fear which has expressed itself in domination and destruction......The battle is reaching its climax. Nature takes a terrible revenge on man - repeatedly nature is forced to surge up and fight and show its power - it refuses to feed man or it sweeps him in his thousands into the sea. And it's the same within man. He thinks he has succeeded in the battle to control, dominate and deny his nature and again it surges up and shows its power - and drives him mad? If it doesn't get that far it tortures and nags and makes him reach out more desperately for further justifications for the logic of his inhumanity......

I think that what happens next must depend on man's rediscovery and respect for his own nature. Through this rediscovery he will remember that what is within him is only part of what is outside him.....

..... That'll do for now. Obviously, obviously I haven't come to any decisions...... But I wish I could see you. My term ends soon and then I'll be chained to my desk in Cambridge again and it's all exams and horror. So it's urgent I should see you soon. At least writing this has cheered me up!

Steffe x

So meet again we did – and again and again.

Friday evening

My darling Roy,

This isn't to be a long letter – I just happen to be feeling
particularly close to you and there are one or two things I
thought I would let you know. Incidentally, Monday is
fine, that'll be today as you read this; I would like another
evening in – but if you violently object then we can argue
about it...... I've just staved off the most appalling sick
headache – my period started yesterday, a fact which, I
can now say, was beginning to get nightmares going in
my brain last week. However the less said.....

There have, in fact, been so many things I've not been able
to talk to you about because of the nature of the situation I
am in, because they hurt you too much. Yet I do feel so
badly that I want to be able to talk about them with you,
as there is no-one else I can talk to who would not feel (I
feel) that I was being a bit absurd. Like you, I feel an
outsider, even in relation to friends I am otherwise quite
close to. And sometimes I begin to resent the fact that on-
one will take my worries seriously. Sometimes I project my
thoughts into the future and try and see myself in different
roles. I have fantasies people (including you probably)
would find absurd. I know that's not unusual – but I keep
feeling, I have only one life, it's passing all too quickly as it
is, and I do want to find true happiness and harmony and
if I don't, I will not lose the feeling of life wasted.

Some of my fantasies as fairly orthodox – some of these
more realisable than others. Some involve you. Let's try out
a few. Me as a straight social worker in London, living with
you in a fair amount of poverty – and strain – which I
won't elaborate on now. I think you know why. It's not one
of my favourite fantasies. Me as a tremendously hip

129

community worker in some far-out, radical group in sunny California. (a) fairly unlikely, given my lack of confidence; (b) my heart is not quite in it. Me living in totally natural surroundings, isolated, away from the world, with you, and lots of babies, growing our own food. For me - my heart is in it - I believe that is my strongest wish, to be in harmony with nature. For me with you - I always see us as outsiders in a sense, my natural feelings are that I want to be alone with you, because that way we don't have to struggle with the (un)civilised world. For you - I know it's not what you want from life at all - it's me forcing a role on you that in my heart I know doesn't fit - perhaps it's a fantasy-you. I do have fantasies about unknown, shadowy figures I suppose - anyway, next projection: sometimes I feel so powerless to achieve anything on my own, and so hopeless about finding the perfect mate that will help me achieve what I want, and feel so desperately on the outside, not wanting to have anything to do with society at all, that I do see myself joining a religious or spiritual group and hoping to find peace and harmony within that. Finally - me as John's wife, reasonably contented with life, safe, secure, children I will love very much I am sure when they are born, knowing he will be a good father, and feeling - well, really I'm lucky, I shouldn't expect more. The most realistic fantasy of them all.

The way my mind works: I can't cut myself away from my security now and drift with Roy in his uncertainty. It only compounds my fear of life. I can only be security for him as long as I feel secure myself. Together, in the present state of things, we fall. That was why (as I'm sure you knew) I was so hoping you'd get (and take) the job at Birnbergs. Not _that_ - for heaven's sake - you getting a job = getting me too. So many interpretations possible in a letter - it's a good thing we can discuss this soon. But I project my need for security, for moorings, on to you and thus grasp at anything that offers it to you, not fully knowing quite what it means to you. I feel so insecure, I want everyone around me to be secure. But I still vaguely hope that one day I will find the secure outsider - someone I can relate to, someone who wants the things I want, but who feels sure of himself - feels they have found what they are looking for. Or that one day I will feel sure of myself, sure enough to support someone else's uncertainty, without feeling that one step and I shall be in the abyss.

I must stop now. I hope you understand that this letter was written in a good mood - it's not meant to be read as an unhappy one, only a frank one. I feel that at the moment I must make the effort to find my own level so that I can be independent. I want to, because I love feeling responsible and on top of things; I know what that feels like and I enjoy it. I wonder if I will find it in America.

I'll see you tonight,

Love

Steffe xx

I am rather puzzled that I never responded to her fantasy about the two of us living 'away from the world', deep in nature, alone together. At the time, nothing could have been more attractive. Strange that Steffe thought I wouldn't want this. Was it that I just couldn't see how it could happen, was it that I didn't have the inner fire to try to make it happen? Or was it that I was overcome by her lack of belief in me, and I simply took her decision to go to America as final?

*

It seemed as if the approach of July brought us closer together. For a while, I almost felt happy but it remained a rocky ride.

Monday evening

My darling Roy,
I'm so sorry you are feeling a bit down at the moment -
you've been so happy and buzzy recently, it was lovely to see
you like that. Now I want to make you feel happy again - I
couldn't on the telephone, I wanted to ring again but I
feel that everything I think of that might cheer you up will
misfire. If you can work out what is bothering you at the
moment, so that you can tell me on Friday, even if (as I
hope) the mood has passed, I'm sure it would do us both
good. The trouble is, as soon as I hear you are unhappy, I
feel I am the cause of some of it, so doing anything about
it gets so much harder. I don't want to hurt you because I
love you; I so badly want things to go right for you. Last
week with you was terrific - everything was perfect, it was a
real trip for me. You bring me so much happiness, Roy. We
are lucky in that way - we can give so much and accept so
much from each other; and given that we each cause each
other tremendous problems for the other, we can contain a
tremendous amount of tension without damaging our
feelings for each other. But if things don't go well for you,
and the tension builds up, please tell me openly and we'll
try and cope with it.
Only I would ask you not to resent me working. Other
things you can legitimately resent, I know, and
acknowledge......
You'll get this on Wednesday and I'll be phoning in the
evening. If you should want me to come then, I will.

Otherwise Friday: I miss you terribly Roy. When I'm with
you I try to be aware of every second, knowing it doesn't
last long. Saying goodbye last time was harder than it has
been for ages, My life would be bleak without you, without
looking forward to seeing you. Can we try to keep things
together as they are until June? I want you to tell me all
the things that trouble you but not to make heavy
demands at the moment. I want to be close to you, not for
us to be driven apart. Do you understand? I'm afraid I'm
getting intense and confusing myself.
Take care; remember that I'm always thinking about you
and caring for you, always hoping you will be happy. Steffe
xxx

So how could we possibly part? I was in a sense in denial about us
parting for what would in reality be forever, and also I hadn't given up
hope of persuading her to change her mind. We felt so close, it seemed
almost inconceivable that we should part. We kept on writing

Sunday - which turned into Wednesday morning

Dear Roy,
I've just received your letter - it was so lovely, it really
brought my mood right up. I've been feeling desperate - I
really do want to see you very badly. I had a strange week
last week - Wednesday was not so good. I had a slight
accident at Apex corner on the A1 - an articulated lorry
ran into me with its rear end. Didn't so much damage but
shook me to pieces. I don't seem to have recovered properly;
had another of those awful High Table experiences on
Thursday - was grabbed by the Fellow (bloke) presiding
and made to sit next to him and he was worse than T. God,

133

they are so incompetent, these morons who call themselves academics. So stiff and inhibited. I feel very sorry for them - but I felt sorrier for myself at the time. What was worse was that this idiot got me and made me go up to the Dining Table with him, and I was thinking 'Jesus, I must escape' so as soon as we got in, I shot around to the other side of the table. Everyone stopped and he said really severely 'THIS side, Mrs Martin- you sit HERE'. It was all somewhat of a fiasco. Dick B had come as our guest - he's nice but as sycophantic as the rest when it comes down to it.

But what's really pissing me off is that after the exams I just want to see you - that would be the kind of treat that would keep me going during the ordeal. But it's not going to be like that - John is aiming to finish on the same day so that we can celebrate together - you'll never guess the treat _he_ had in store for me: a visit to Lincoln to see that odious girl I can't stand. She's just had another baby. With her in post-natal depression and me in a post-exam depression, you can imagine what a disaster that would be. However, I refused so I don't know what we are doing - nothing probably. I want to see you so badly. John keeps asking what I want to do - I don't want to do anything except spend some time with you.

But we must be stoical..... One thing certainly - will you meet me after my exam on Friday (30th) - at lunchtime? That would be something. Otherwise I feel I must come down for a real flying visit one night this week - arrive late and leave early etc - please understand I _want_ to see you as much as you probably do, if not more. May you write BY RETURN and let me know which nights would be best......
..... Back on the mogs, not sleeping.

Thank you for your sweet letter, for making me remember
life does have warm spots -
Love,
Steffe xx

We carried on meeting when we could. But one time, I was freaked when it seemed that time that had finally been agreed for us to spend together after her exams disintegrated...

Roy, my love -
I'm sorry that future shock erupted this morning - after we
had such an amazingly good and seemingly
understanding time together - and when I had to rush off
as usual. I feel terrible making you so upset - especially as I
feel it was avoidable, if I had been more explicit and if we
had both recognised the implications of what each was
planning for the other - by talking about staying in
London (me) and travelling (you). I've definitely got my
time switches wrong and hadn't worked out the
implications chronologically.
Please Roy, <u>don't worry</u>; just give me until next Tuesday to
recover my sensibility. I have been steamrollering for too
long - I recognise it, I'm sorry for it, I hope I'll learn from
it. The trouble is, I react too violently to past experiences -
if I feel I made a mistake in the past, I tend to do the
complete opposite without really weighing up what I'm
really into.
Another thing I haven't paid enough attention to is the
differences in our ages - which seem irrelevant except in a
kind of romantic image way most of the time. But I feel
sure the way we each feel is a function of our ages - I also
used to love with a kind of <u>total</u> intensity - my love was my
life and there was no life without my love. But then

135

inevitably you get kicked in the teeth and you're forced to accept that life does go on - and the totality is exchanged for relativity; I mean that I can still get as high as you on our love - but I know it is a moment I am experiencing which had a before and will most surely have an after. So I can go through a series of highs with you and they are not spoiled because they don't last forever. I just feel grateful that they exist at all - they are rare and we have reached some peaks.

So I feel I haven't been careful enough in what I've said, and more importantly, not said, to you. I hope by now you're putting the puzzle together - and the bits that now don't fit we will talk about properly later.

Please forgive me, Roy, for my selfishness. I love you, and you are so easy to hurt, and it's the last thing I want to do, and I do it all the time.

Take heart, my love -

Steffe xxx

'The trouble is, I react too violently to past experiences — if I feel I made a mistake in the past, I tend to do the complete opposite without really weighing up what I'm really into'. I wish I had taken this on board. I didn't. If I had, maybe things would have turned out differently.

Yes, I guess Steffe was selfish, but her frankness, her openness, her commitment to the truth, and her unswerving love, always overcame any negative feelings I might have.

   And then in June, after her exams, we managed a long weekend away. We went to Bath, where an old Cambridge friend and his partner lived. They had a spare room which we were able to use.

   We travelled down together and made our way to the flat. It was on the first floor of a magnificent Georgian house in Camden Crescent. Walking through the splendour of Bath, climbing our way up along uneven pavements to the heights of the Crescent, filled our hearts. The city had the beauty and tranquillity of Cambridge. As we entered the Crescent itself, we looked to our right, the city below us, the hills beyond, upon which the setting sun cast a red glow. We put our arms around each other as we approached the door of number 8.

The sun shone through the window as we awoke the next day. We felt full of excitement. Reality seemed so far away. We were blessed by the weather, warm but not hot, fresh, not humid, still but for an occasional light breeze.

We wandered about Bath's streets. It was a very different city from what it is now. It was shabby and in parts quite run-down. Walcott Street was the hippy area, a succession of poorly maintained buildings, containing a few alternative enterprises. It had a lovely, laid-back atmosphere. The splendour of the Royal Crescent, the Circus, Lansdown Crescent, Milsom Street, was not then disturbed by hordes of tourists but was instead enhanced by the eccentric locals who wove their way through these exquisite streets to their various destinations.

We walked in the countryside nearby, discovering the beauty of St Catherine's valley and its inestimable peace. And as we walked, we became as if one. We looked into each other's eyes and knew we had to talk.

'Sweetheart,' I said, 'I feel we cannot end what we have. It would be so brutal, so painful – for both of us'.

'I am so confused, Roy, I too feel like you. Why can't I just see the way ahead?'

'This is the way ahead. Don't you feel this place, this stunning city, is where we can come together and move forward?'

'But I am so scared'.

'But you don't need to be. This place energises me. I will find my path, of that I am sure. But I want, I need , you beside me'.

'We would be starting from nothing'.

'So? It means everything is possible. Please, my love, say you'll stay with me. How have you felt this weekend? Haven't you felt things have been magical? We've been together for more than two years and you know we

137

just can't separate, however many times we have tried. I really believe you are the love of my life, I could never have reached the places I've been to with you with anyone else. Please, my love, please. Let's make this happen.'

The next day, she said she had decided. She would leave John and live with me. I could hardly believe what she said. But there was a big but.

'But I will have to go with John at the beginning. When we travel across America and he arrives in California. He will want me to. It's only fair. And I want to go too.'

I was really thrown by this but felt I had at that time no option but to accept it.

Later, I formulated arguments against it. Most significantly, that I feared a separation of this sort would mean that we would lose the intimate closeness we had attained. My fear of this was to prove all too right. What we didn't do, what we had no time to do, was think through the way ahead. Such a huge mistake.

The time came for her to leave. It was only five weeks, I told myself, and in the meantime I would be able to build something for us in Bath. But even as she left, I felt a foreboding.

TWELVE

My first task was to move to Bath. My friends with whom we had stayed said we could rent a room in their flat. So, soon after Steffe left for America, I arrived in Bath and my new life. Shortly before leaving London, I received Steffe's first letter from America.

Dear Roy,
This will be a rather rushed letter - I don't get much time on my own at the moment.
Firstly, I miss you, I think about you. I don't exactly wish you were here, because I'm not exactly sure if I wish I were here. First impressions of New York - a crazy, crazy city. An urban nuthouse of immense proportions. Huge, speedy, hard. Covered in garbage. Seedy. Stimulating I suppose but in such a tense, intense way. We're staying with ....in the East Village. It used to be a Jewish area, loads of Jewish delis etc but since the late 60's when a lot of hippies came here, it's also full of junk shops, boutiques, leather shops and all that. But decayed. The woman we are staying with is terrific but I'm finding myself antagonistic towards some of her friends. Last night, they took us to eat in Chinatown and we had a strange, strange time - like they seemed to feel they must perform in front of us, really do a New York City number all the time, impress. I couldn't take it. I was exhausted and suffering from jet lag and I just wanted them to talk normally, treat me as a person. At the end of the evening, there was a terrific storm - rain like you see at the movies - after half an hour the streets, which are full of potholes, were inches deep, rivers. And terrific lightening constantly and terrifying thunder. And at

night I couldn't sleep, my head was too confused by all these people. When I eventually slept, I had one nightmare after another, woke crying several times, really crying from the depths of my being. I find it so disturbing. You wouldn't believe the people - they operate on such a ridiculously speedy level. They can't calm down. All into highly individualist trips, hustling constantly. But some are nice. The buzz of what it was like least time I came, came back to me very strongly. And I don't think I like it so much this time. There's something overwhelming and sickly about it, cloying. Too hip, too heavy.

I hope either I adapt soon or when we leave New York things will calm down. We're having difficulty getting a drive-away car, so will have to stay over the weekend. It's been raining most of the time. It's very hot and sticky. I hope things are going OK for you, my love. I hope and hope something will work out by the time I get back. You must let me know where to write to you. I miss you badly, I miss England (already). Look after yourself. Write. I love you. When I have time I'll write at less speed. But I just wanted to get a letter off to you quickly.

My love,
Steffe xxx

It was a warm and loving letter but I was already missing her dreadfully and was jealous of the fact that she and John were together all the time, that she constantly talked about 'we'.

I wrote to her. She replied.

31ˢᵗ July

Dear Roy,
We arrived in South Bend a couple of nights ago and your letter came yesterday. I'm really sorry to hear that you

were so fed up after I left and I hope so much things are going better now that you are (presumably) in Bath. It's hard to get privacy to write to you properly.

I guess you may have been a bit worried after getting my first letter. I was a bit freaked out on first arriving because of the jet lag and the heat and the strange memories that came flooding back. New York is a weird place - it's incredibly heterogeneous in a way you never find in England - so many ethnic groups, Jews, Puerto Ricans, Blacks, Chinese - who all live in large enough groups to maintain their separate identities. Which means that general criteria of 'normality' are non-existent - anything goes, it has to. Which is amazingly confusing - nothing is predictable and it's really hard to place people. You just have to accept everything as it comes. When you're stoned, it becomes even weirder. Everyone seems to be playing games - but they're not really, they are just being themselves. Once I got used to all that, life became easier. Apart from the people, the city is also crazy. Some parts are really beautiful - the architecture of the skyscrapers in mid-town Manhattan (5th Avenue and all that) and in Wall Street is so diverse - some are intricate in the style of French Chateaux, some are Art Deco, others ultra, ultra-modern with black glass - but the key note is elegance. Then other parts, like where we were and Harlem etc are so poor and falling apart and heaped with rubbish because the garbage collectors are on strike.

We drove a car over here - we did the journey fast because there's not much to see until you start getting further west. John and Diana have a beautiful house in woodlands - but Jesus it's hot. It's hard to hold the pen, I'm so sticky......we probably won't be in California until mid-August.

I know you must be feeling envious of this trip - I knew you were feeling that even though you concealed the feeling when I was with you. The sad part is that I know you would enjoy it far more than I am doing - or that we would enjoy it more together maybe. I feel very much this is second time around - and basically America is not a country I like. First time it blew my mind - the size, the absence of history, the vulgarity, the diversity. This time it really disgusts me overall. Of course there are nice people here. But the general feeling is so heavy. I see so clearly now that this is the country of individualism (meaning fuck the rest), hustling, business, productivity - exciting perhaps but I don't tune in with it - I want peace, quietness, people I can trust. I am stimulated by it - I'm glad I'm having a break - but so far I'm looking forward to returning to England and you, my sweet love.

But I'm really worried about you. One thing I've found is that the prevailing way of life (that if individualism, business, etc) does equip people better if they want to break away from the mainstream. For example, the people we stayed with in the East Village are all around their late twenties and over and went through the 60's thing so don't want to have regular jobs, etc but run a trucking business moving furniture etc - and know how to get it together, make plenty of bread with minimal hassle (this is such a <u>rich</u> country), run big motor bikes and generally enjoy life in a very casual way. The English don't seem to be able to achieve this so easily.

Roy my love, please don't miss me too much. I miss you -

but of course it's different when everything's new. I don't
have much time to think. Don't be too envious - one day
we'll go somewhere together that suits us better - I'd love to
take a trip to Ireland for example. Take care,
My love to you
Steffe xxx

In so many ways it was a lovely letter but I <u>did</u> feel envious and I <u>did</u> really miss her and, for all the letter's warmth, I felt her going away from me, geographically and emotionally.

I began to explore Bath. Once again, I was struck by its beauty and tranquillity. One morning, whilst wandering down Milsom Street, I came across a café/restaurant called Parsenn Sally. I looked through the window and saw that it was of great length, with elegant tables and chairs, a dark wooden bar halfway down on the left and palms and other exotic plants everywhere. I went inside and had a coffee. There was a collection of newspapers to read. The staff seemed different, alternative. I could also work out that an owner or two were by the bar. Calming classical music played. I really liked it and returned the next day. I took a table near the front windows and again ordered coffee. I saw a tall, slim, smartly dressed man in, I reckoned, his late 30's, talking to the barman. He was clearly an owner. So I got up, approached the bar and spoke to him. I asked if there was a job for a waiter. We talked a bit, he asking if I had experience, me lying that I had. And I was offered a job! I later found out that selection of staff was an undefined science. If you were female and attractive, you were in. If a man, at least OK looking, a bit stylish and, in my case without a doubt, possessing an educated accent, you were also in. It was a wonderful entry into a hip side of Bath. The place was open from morning until late at night. I took to waiting very quickly. It appealed to the extrovert in me. I brought character to the role. I wore jeans tucked into cowboy boots with assertive heels that clip-clopped as I walked on the wooden floor. On top, a shirt and over it all a Buckingham green apron.

The wages were quite reasonable, but the best source of income was the tips, all of which we kept.

It proved to be more than I thought. It was new enterprise that had only just been set up by a group of wealthy neo-hippies who had acquired a farmhouse in nearby Wiltshire which they sought to run as a commune. The music changed during the day, merging into laid back rock from the likes of Steely Span from lunchtime into the afternoon, evolving into more challenging music as day turned into night. What nights there were. One Saturday night, the place was really rocking. UV lights had been turned on. With no forethought, Marc, the barman who turned out to be my best friend, and I leapt onto the top of the bar and danced together, to the boisterous acclaim of the customers. Often, as the last customers left, the doors would be locked and the staff and directors would drink, taking bottle after bottle from behind the bar, take drugs, listen to music, talk. I began to make some interesting friendships.

It all became crazy when one of the directors, Roddy Llewelyn, formed a liaison with Princess Margaret. She took to coming down to the farm, putting on her boots and helping Roddy tend his vegetables. And she came to Parsenn Sally. The press got onto it, and suddenly it was all in the tabloids. My new friend, Pete, who also worked there, a gay Bowie lookalike, said 'What a hoot!'

But I hadn't heard from Steffe. Then I received a postcard.

9.8.75

My love – I'm so sorry I've not been able to write you a letter – I'm now nearing the end of the Great Journey – through the most phenomenal scenery it's possible to imagine – real cowboy country, the Wild West. Went to visit the remains of Wounded Knee which is in the middle of semi-desert temperatures of 120f – everywhere there are plastic forts, wigwams – it's amazing that these people have the nerve to first massacre and then exploit just that part of their history. But the Indians have torn down their museums etc

144

*- seems that now they refuse to be a tourist attraction. I'm
pretty exhausted. I think of you constantly. Will write in
California. My love - Steffe x*

I was so glad to hear from her but I still envied her, was jealous, and
missing her. But it wasn't long to go.

*La Cresta Drive
Los Altos Hills
California 94022
Wednesday 13ᵗʰ August*

*Roy my love,
I've been really silly; I've been waiting and waiting for a
letter from you since we arrived on Monday - and I've
remembered now that you may have written Post Restante
and I had forgotten and was looking for post at the Law
School. So I'll write now and then go to Stanford tomorrow
and see if there's a letter at the Post Office and if there is
I'll write again in reply.
You must have been anxious not hearing from me; I hope
all I've managed to write so far has arrived - 2 letters and
a postcard I think. From now on I'll write more frequently.
Please understand that while we were travelling across we
did nothing but drive interminably and sleep - it was
further than I thought, 3000 miles from South End. Parts of
the journey were splendid, parts boring, parts frightening.
First we drove through Chicago - and got lost and ended
up in a ghetto - where it is positively dangerous for any
white person to be. Chicago is a horrible place, the race
relations are so bad. Even near the centre, shops have signs*

on the doors 'only one person to enter at any time'. So we just did what we had to do there and left fast, admiring the skyline from the rear view mirror. The journey from there was fairly unexciting until we had crossed Minnesota and most of South Dakota. Then we hit the Badlands - an area of completely barren rocks which have eroded into strange shapes, crags and peaks with all the different layers of different coloured rock exposed. Then down to Wounded Knee which I told you about and then to Mount Rushmore to see the faces of the presidents carved into the side of the mountain. That was a truly idiotic detour - pure tourist land and we had our first freak out, it was so hot, there seemed to be such a huge distance to go, lots of mountains and deserts and the car is not exactly eminently trustworthy. In the event it made it here - just - to my immense relief. The following day was one of the best - we crossed a range of mountains in Wyoming at dawn and that was splendid, magnificent - no-one around, cool dawn air, quiet, incredible views over hundreds of miles. Then we went through Yellowstone Park, which is on a plateau about 10,000 feet high, with a huge lake and a volcanic structure which results in enormous turbulent waters under the ground, and huge geysers and hot springs. Dramatic, but over-sold, too many people and tourist signs telling you what and how to enjoy. After that followed more hot, semi-desert country, and the best bits were at the end, when we finally reached Oregon. We had to climb another mountain range, cool and forested with chipmunks running around, really lovely, and suddenly you turn a bend and wham! The Black Crater - a massive expanse of barren, black chunks of lava. Weird. Then over *to the Pacific and down through the Redwoods to San Francisco and Stanford.*

I'll pause the letter there. Did I recognise how she was involving me in her experience? How she was sharing it with me? I don't think so. I think I was filled with envy and jealousy. I was just too young to deal with it.

So that brings you up to date - we are staying at the moment in a really beautiful house in the Los Altos Hill, living in the lap of luxury. But as always, life feels incomplete. I wish you were here because I must admit then life would be pretty perfect. But I'm longing to hear how you are making out in Bath - if indeed that is where you are - I hope there is news from you waiting for me in Stanford. Nothing that I have experienced so far has changed my view that America is really not the place to be for any great length of time - it's fun, there are some interesting people around with fairly weird ideas, but there's something unhealthy about the place. As the foundations upon which the society are based are so ludicrously and horrifically materialist, the reaction formed against it seems in many ways unreal - I think because it's so easy to make out here, the material struggle does not really affect the intellectuals, radicals, etc, so they don't always seem aware that this materialism is what they should be opposing, because they can benefit from it so easily. Run out of space - I'll write again tomorrow. This letter seems a bit impersonal but I did want to tell you what has been happening. All love to you S xxx

It was a great letter. Why and how couldn't I see it that way? What regrets I have.

147

There was no letter the next day. Instead a long silence broken only by the delivery of a devastating telegram. I had been counting the days until her five weeks away came to an end. The telegram told me she was delaying her return by three weeks. I was shocked to my core, felt betrayed. Perhaps it was the seed that led to the destruction of our relationship. I had always trusted Steffe, however challenging her decisions were. But this was one that I felt undermined everything. Why didn't I telegram back, screaming my sense of trust lost, frankly betrayal? Expressing what I truly felt? I was too weak at the time, too ridiculously timid. And I hadn't written the letters that needed to be written. Letters that acknowledged the beautiful descriptions of her travels, her insights into America, letters that said I was really looking forward to sitting down with her on her return talking through what we wanted from our lives together, what we wanted for ourselves. Too young and too confused after over 2 years of an affair.

Los altos Hills
29th August

Roy love,
By now you will have received my telegram and I don't think I underestimate the amount of disappointment it will have caused you. Especially after such a long silence.

'Disappointment' doesn't even get near it. Betrayal would be a better word.

It turns out that I have a lot of explaining to do – but before your spirits drop like lead in the pit of your stomach...

Has she no idea how they have already? Is she that blind to my feelings?

148

Let me forewarn you that this is only to do with me having a good time, wanting to prolong it, feeling that there is much I can yet do here which must be good for my head, and that to cut the stay at this time would not greatly be to anyone's advantage.

Really? Not mine? Not ours?

I'm really sorry that our correspondence had broken down as it has. Naturally I was thinking of all the dire alternatives, such as illnesses lost addresses, parental problems, etc. I didn't really want to keep writing as I didn't know what was happening, either to you or my letters. Then I finally received a letter, addressed here: in which once again you seem to be striving for the ultimate break through your alienation. Oh Roy, I hope you can make it; I have no desire to give you any 'advice', it's your trip. But until you have found a way to stop this problem eating away at your soul, I worry. I feel that I live on such a knife-edge myself, of utter blissful optimism and the other, that if anyone presents me too strongly with the dark side, I rapidly become filled with profound fear and uncertainty myself.

Strange looking back that I presented such a conflicted soul. What I can't work out, even now, is how far that despair came from my ever-demanding relationship with Steffe. Remember I was only just 23. I still felt so immature in some ways, and yet I was embroiled in a deeply adult world.

This has been brought home to me strongly here, as the culture shock and the extraordinary scenes we have got into at times plunged not only me but John into the abyss –

149

*I am not used to having to deal with such crises with J.,
normally a person with such a sure sense of his 'reality',
and found them draining and impossible to help with.*

Again, pain for me. What about me? I don't think Steffe thought for a
moment about how these words might impact on me. She would have
simply felt she was sharing her thoughts and feelings. As she was. I take
no pride in my reaction.

*Fortunately that has passed for him, temporarily at least,
as he has found a most delectable and crazy lady to focus
on and that solves many problems for him. I am really
pleased that this has happened - he has gone through
many changes, all for the better I feel, and I would like to
feel I could leave him less reliant on my companionship.
I will simply supply you with a few concrete details of what
I am talking about. We seem to have dropped into an
extremely stimulating and exciting scene here in the
beautiful Los Altos Hills. We live in an old wooden house
covered in creepers, which sits in the golden hills
overlooking the San Francisco Bay. The life-style is
decadent; much wine and other strange and pleasant
things; waterbeds and stereos in every room.*

I found this just too much. I know she was sharing what she was
experiencing but did she not understand how her description would make
me feel? What if the roles were reversed, would she have felt ok about it
all? And here comes out my insecurity and lack of trust.

*The people are mostly older than us, in their thirties. Have
mostly been through a lot of interesting experiences,
growing up as they did where they did and when -i.e. old
enough to really understand and foreshadow the 1960's*

things. Ken Kesey and the Merry Pranksters were well known here - some of them are still friends of the house. So through them we have rapidly learned to love this aspect of California - the pure joy of living life to the full - hedonism if you like.

I felt I was losing her. How could I compete with this?

There is also, and importantly, an interesting connection with a place called the Village, a commune of maybe 15 or 20 adults and kids in 170 acres of redwood forest some way to the north of California. So far I have only spent a weekend there - but much of my desire to stay longer is that I would like to have at least a full week up there on my own. The people there are largely involved in exploring the land, their natural resources, environmental and spiritual and bodily - they farm, take their water from springs and a river, have no electricity to interfere with that generated by human interaction; do yoga and Tai Chi; chant and do together sensitivity routines, thought, clapping, touching. It is altogether an experience which clearly helps to develop enormous human strength - and has already helped me to deal with situations which otherwise might have quite thrown or demoralised me.

Perhaps I should have simply been connecting with the inner message, what she was communicating. But I was beyond reading it like that.

Often I am asked whether we are into this or that in England - and I can only reply that potentially many, many people are but are totally frustrated by the limitations of land and resources.

So buying into the American dream, eh? Or just struck by Californian dream into reality? But these guys have money.....

For the States, California is a hopelessly overcrowded state - not surprisingly, it attracts an enormous number of people. But besides our ridiculously overpopulated island, there is space yet for people to find themselves - and I am convinced now that the overcrowding and general lack of wealth in Britain is really the reason for its retarded development. We have the will, but ....so I think it's a really unhealthy place.

This was something that worried me about Steffe. Her ability to be swayed and convinced overnight – just a short time before, she had been missing England, talking about America being a sick place, with its obsession with individualism and materialism. Couldn't she see that the wealthy 'hippy' characters she was living with were just trendy cool manifestations of all that we should reject? I felt an unpleasant distance building between us. What else may lure her?

I haven't yet explored Ireland and Scotland so perhaps there is still hope - in terms of space. I only now realise how important this is - we can only escape inwards which is fine but totally insufficient if there is not something external to feed off.
So I have changed the date of my return from next Wednesday to a little over 3 weeks' time, just to give myself a further chance of experiencing all I can here, to give myself some resources which I can hopefully use on my return. Of course I am sorry that you cannot share the experience - the healing properties for you would be enormous. But hopefully we can actually get you into an

environment with similar properties - either by creating it
ourselves somewhere or physically travelling somewhere......
Meanwhile, love to you, Roy, take heart - my thoughts are
with you at this time - Steffe xxxxx

'My thoughts are with you' – rather like 'sorry for your loss' after someone
has died.

Was I being unfair? Almost certainly. But she hadn't consulted me at all,
tried to discuss it with me. I later found out that she had discussed it with
her slick Californian libertines – fat chance they had of understanding the
subtle sensitivities of the soul or of the nature of our relationship. 'Fuck
man, grab the experience! He'll understand'. But I wish I had been wiser.
All this was to prove fatal.

Los Altos
3 September 1975

Dear Roy,
...... As I am about to leave here for a few days in Southern
California, I thought I would write a short letter....
.... Today should have been my departure date - and I
know how let down you must be feeling. But Roy - I don't
know where my head is at the moment. That's why I write
you such impersonal letters. So much has been battering at
my mind and emotions that it takes all my energy just to
keep me head in one place. I always thought California
was over-rated - but it's not. The trouble is, I know this is
not what you want to hear. I should be telling you how
lonely and miserable I am without you - but I am not. I'm
simply not (Well, sometimes I am extremely lonely and
miserable - I just try to pretend it's not so).

Sometimes, Steffe's truthfulness tumbled into insensitivity. There was no need for her to be so very explicit. What she said made me feel very unwanted. Not a hint of love.

My relationship with J. has undergone a radical change. Apart from companionship on odd occasions, I am completely independent of him emotionally (I only wish I had my own car, money, etc, because then I would be able to explore this freedom better). And he is much more independent of me. He is a big hit here, everyone likes him a lot, he fits in well, and because there are no reminders of his past he can develop freely and seems to be blooming. Both of us suffer from identity problems here - one takes so much of one's self-image from one's friends, that when those are not there, and one has to continually assert oneself among new people, identity becomes a precarious item, it has to be self-consciously worked on all the time. So both of us tend to vacillate from highs to lows at an astonishing and unpredictable rate, depending on current feedback. We both need a lot of reassurance I guess. Maybe J. more than me - although I cannot maintain a 'you take me as you find me or fuck you' attitude because I respect the people here and find their evaluation important to me. But before I go on to that, I want to make the point that J. is no longer a barrier between me and anything - we both accept this. Yesterday I was talking to Peggy, one of the women here, about the group of people we are involved with here at La Cresta. At first their behaviour just blew our minds - the totally free sexual relations etc etc - we felt they must be really hard, tough people to handle it all. But it turns out that what was really happening is that many of them have had repressive marriages or repressive jobs or something

154

and in the last 3 - 7 years have broken out of these and having done so, have formed for themselves a world where there are no rules, no repression. And it's hard for them to handle - they get screwed up and fucked over emotionally - but they handle it because they know the value of having this freedom to determine their own lives and relationships. There is a lot to learn from them - they may seem mad, crazy, hedonistic etc - but in fact they are learning themselves all the time, and it is often painful for them, but they do become stronger people for it..... But it does produce an atmosphere where self-reliance becomes tremendously important, and Jesus, I need more of that.

I found this so threatening. What was happening to Steffe? I was scared that she was indulging in sexual freedom. I should have written saying that I really understood that she was having an amazing time but that one thing really bothered me. That I needed to know that she was being faithful to me – that if she assured me of this, that would liberate me. I wish I had. Since I am pretty sure, from later conversations, that nothing did happen.

So that's one part of the fascination of this place. Another is that I feel loved and wanted here. These people are very open with their feelings - and everyone has shown such concern over whether or not I should stay for a while longer and were really pleased when I changed my ticket. In the face of their very convinced arguments that I really had not had time to see and do many things here, I felt that to leave was unnecessary - and that ultimately you would understand.

Well, thanks for including me in the discussion. I am sure you fully filled them in on our relationship! I was growing bitter. Dangerous.

155

I hope that by the time I come back you will have lots of things sorted out. I don't mind at all if you get a job in London - I am feeling that when I return I will want to immerse myself a lot in my London friends, both because I will need them emotionally and because they are very near where people here are at and I shall feel closer to them and want to exchange ideas with them in a way I did not for the last couple of years. Honestly, Roy, England seems so far away - Bath, London, wherever - I just want somewhere I can use my energy, not become flattened - adventure, adventure.

I felt I had really lost her. Not one word about how us embarking on a life together was 'an adventure'. Not one word of love, not one sign of care. And apparently no warmth towards what we had talked about as regards living in Bath. It got worse...

So that will do for now - tomorrow night I shall be in Hollywood - fear and loathing - excitement, danger, the unknown....
I'll write again soon, when I return from my travels.
Take care, take heart, Love Steffe xxx

Los Altos Hills
Thursday 11 September

Dear Roy,
Well, another week seems to have slipped by without writing to you. I returned from my trip to Southern California and Mexico utterly wrecked and wasted, to find two more letters from you - one very depressed one and one to say things

were better on receiving news from me. I read the last one first so was forewarned!

I can tell from how I feel writing that I am still fairly wrecked - feel as though I have got the shakes. I'll tell you about the trip. It was really crazy. One of the group here had to go to the south to do some business and asked if I would like to come along for the ride. I was a little nervous about agreeing, not knowing what my part of the deal was to be, but ultimately it turned out that only my companionship was required, so that was ok. We spent a couple of days in L.A., visited Universal City which is a film studio where tourists in their hundreds are taken in little electric busses round sets, watch stuntmen doing numbers, have screen tests and all that baloney. We also went to Venice, the L.A. beach area where the hippies live, and to some sleazy bars in Sunset Strip. One night we did a whole tank of Nitrous Oxide interspersed with hits of amyl nitrate - Nitrous (laughing gas) is definitely something I must introduce into the British drug culture (unless it's already there) as it really is the original 'gas' - it sends your mind floating off very gently and leaves you feeling very mellow - it's a very dreamy, sensuous number. So it's nicest to do when you feel like getting it on with someone really. (We didn't!)

Then we went to San Bernadino, this guy's hometown, basically drunk a lot, smoked a lot of grass at $10 an ounce (they are very near Mexico there!), took some hearts and went dancing at a really nice Saloon in the mountains, where the band was mainly Mexican and played a lot of Santana. I enjoyed that a lot. Then Mexico for a couple of days. Mexico is basically rather depressing. Possibly because the weather was lousy - overcast - but

157

mainly because of the poverty - the Mexicans really haven't got their shit together. Obviously I only saw a tiny part - the northern extremity - and apparently it's very different in terms of culture in other parts - but poverty prevails throughout. They are really into colour - live in little wooden shacks just thrown together but painted in bright colours, wear colourful clothes …. But it was a bit like being in Brighton on a dull Sunday out of season - we spent most of the time drinking tequila.

I was so jealous. Even if they didn't 'get it on', they were together 24 hours every day, having fun and adventure. And I realised that I was losing trust in Steffe at an alarming rate.

The we went back north to San Diego on the U.S. border - and things started to get out of control. We were boozing heavily; then someone produced some magic mushrooms - raw psilocybin ; we went dancing and after more than 2 hours, no effect so I took some speed and we started drinking again - and yea! The mushrooms hit about 4 hours after chewing and I suddenly realised I was tripping, speeding and drunk. That was heavy. And I thought it was time to get the hell out of it and come home. So they put me on a plane - still hallucinating - and I had the weirdest trip back - it was actually very beautiful. We flew over the fog-covered coastal Range and the sun was shining on the fog with mountain peaks emerging like the backs of dinosaurs and a little further over were the Sierras (the inland mountain range) and beyond that the desert. And you could see this all at once, most of the way up. But now I feel really terrible - weak and weird - and I feel that I never want to see any drug again. I have obviously been on a really escapist trip. A complete Fear and

Loathing. Which tells me that my head is in a bad space - it's probably time I came home.

But I thought this 3 week extension was all about peaceful experience and helping you build your self-identity? So was it all pure hedonism after all? No return visit to the commune you said was a major reason for staying on.

I'm worried about that too - worried about where you and I will be - it may not work you know.

Not now what's happened has happened..... And what she said was so pessimistic. No enthusiasm.

I really need someone to look after me, I don't seem to handle life well at all. I have too many escapist, hedonist and depressive tendencies. We are too alike. But - we'll see. Right now I feel pretty low and not very proud of myself. I hope not too many of my friends will be off on travels - I've been missing them a lot.

Still not a word about missing me.

I'm sorry my not writing sent you down so low - but hopefully that part is past now..... I missed the SLAB youth worker job (in Bristol) as I thought I would. So prepare for the event that I will have to work in London. England seems so far away - to be truthful, I have had doubts about returning, when things have been so high - but I don't think really it's where I should be.

It just got worse and worse. But why didn't I pick up on the last comment?

But I am worried that you are orienting yourself so much around my return - in the sense that I hoped things would have come together for you in my absence. Don't expect me to perform miracles, Roy - I'm only human and very fallible!
Anyway, take care, my love, Steffe xx

Of course her return was central — I had been waiting for two and a half years! But the final letter was awful.

Los Altos Hills
Tuesday

Dear Roy,
Just to give you details of my return.....
I want to get this off to you express so you will get it by the weekend - I should warn you that I am very broken up by having to leave here - I love it so much and the people - England is such a tame environment - how about a big, druggy, orgiastic party SOON ... !!!
Well, I guess that wraps it up after 2 months.... See you soon. Here's looking at you kid....Steffe xxx

I felt completely deflated. Not one word of love, not one expression of looking forward to seeing me. Instead talk of 'having to leave here' and having an 'orgiastic' party. Later, when she talked about the naked swimming parties and licence at La Cresta, I doubted her faithfulness to me. In fact, I had been doubting it for a while. That again was fatal. As was my failure to greet her with love.

THIRTEEN

September 1975

Driving up to meet her at Heathrow, I felt only fear, instead of the joy and hope I would have felt three weeks before. Who would I be meeting?

I stood in the arrivals area and eventually she emerged. She was tanned and fuller of face, perhaps she had put on weight, she was somehow not the same. She spotted me and approached. Brief smiles passed between us but there were no big hugs, just a rather polite kissing of the cheeks. I took her luggage and led her to the car.

We said little as I headed towards, and then on to, the M4. The atmosphere felt cold. I guess I fully contributed to that. She was clearly absolutely exhausted after such a long journey but couldn't she have managed just one loving word? She felt a completely different person to the one to whom I had been so close before she left for America. I felt her head and heart were there, not here.

She spoke a bit – but as I recall mainly to complain about the closed skies of England, in contrast to the vast open skies of California. I talked a bit, trying to tell her that in fact I had established a life in Bath, had fallen into a good scene, had made some good, and interesting, friends. But there was no real communication.

We got back late and she flopped into bed, not even bothering to hold me, tell me anything to suggest she was pleased to see me.

Steffe never said that she was suffering from jet-lag but she must have been. Just as she must have been experiencing culture shock. Waking up the next morning no doubt felt very strange to her, very disorientating. But that was not something I took on board, of that I am sure. I was too locked inside my own feelings, resentments, unspoken complaints. I was still a youth whereas the moment called for a man. What I should have done was to put her first, told her I understood she must feel weird, that I

161

understood, and that I just wanted to do whatever suited her best. She could just rest, we could go for a walk, go to Parsenn Sally – whatever. We didn't need to talk much. Just get used to one another. But I didn't. I was tense, on edge, but not speaking out either. Instead of what should have been a gentle, quiet day, it felt to be a day of nervous distance.

I felt under an obligation to match her Californian lifestyle. So that evening, I took her to Parsenn Sally where we met up with some of my new friends. Overtly it was a good, fun evening but I wasn't at my ease. I felt I was having to perform, indulge her hedonism. Returning to our flat that night, I did not feel happy.

We managed to settle down – to a degree. I continued working at Parsenn Sally and Steffe then joined me as a waitress. We did have fun there and we had many lovely walks around the nearby countryside. But there was still a distance. Why did we not sit down and face up to things, talk through our feelings, work out plans for the future, decide on what we wanted?

Early on, I should have explained my feelings, but I didn't. I could have said:

'You know, Steffe, we really need to talk. I have to tell you that I always trusted you, always believed in your love for me and my love for you, but I've lost that trust. I need to explain. I could, just about, handle you going to America, though you well knew how hard I found it. But when you sent your telegram, when you failed to involve me at all in your decision taking, when you said you were staying for another 3 weeks, something in me broke, it felt such a betrayal. Add to that the fact that your letters became ever more distant, that they reached the point of saying you weren't sure you wanted to return at all, that you didn't miss me, nor once in California did you express any real love or longing for me. So by the time you did come back, I didn't know who was returning. I ask myself now: do you really want to be with me? I have taken our relationship really seriously, and I thought you had too, but now I rather doubt that. And you seem hard in a way that I've never seen before. So I need to hear what

162

you have to say. It's no good me not telling you how I am feeling. I want to talk about where we go from here.'

I wonder what would have happened if I had said this? Unfortunately, I was too young and confused to utter my feelings. I really wish I had. I would have been trying to take control for once and I suspect Steffe would have respected that. Sadly I was weak and it was that very weakness, and how it later manifested itself, that provoked in no small part the tragedy that followed.

And why didn't I seize the opportunity of the moment and excitedly throw out plans for the future? Getting our own flat, me embarking on becoming a lawyer, her looking for social work in Bath or Bristol? Why didn't I take on board what she had said in countless letters that she needed security and support, that she found life very hard and found it difficult to cope on her own? That she needed me to show strength (something I only found afterwards). But I was still just 23. I was who I was. So we didn't have the conversations we needed. It so saddens me.

*

Then a shock. We were at home in Camden Crescent, the post came and there was a letter for Steffe. She opened it and smiled.

'What it is?' I asked.

'I've got a job. Working as a residential social worker at a drug rehab hostel in London called Roma'.

'What? I didn't know you had applied'.

'Oh, I've made a number of applications'.

'But why haven't you told me, talked about it with me?'
She didn't reply.

'So what would it entail?'

'4 days and nights a week at the hostel'.
I was speechless.

'You don't look very pleased for me'.

'Well, I'm not. How could I be? I waited for you for years, you agree to join me in life, then you go off to America and now you're off again. Am I meant to be pleased?'

163

'Oh come on, it's a job. Someone has to be responsible'.

'Oh thanks for your support. Sometimes I think you don't just get it'.

'Well, I think it's great and I'll be taking it'.

This was a hardness I had never encountered before. Where was my Steffe? And where was our relationship if she felt she had to apply for jobs without discussing them with me?

It became a running sore between us. I made my resentment all too clear and rarely asked her about the job once she started it. This was a big, big mistake by me that I only recognised long after.

She was working over Christmas. I felt quite bereft.

Why wasn't Steffe able to understand my feelings? They weren't really so strange, were they? As things panned out, she was only with me two days a week and sometimes those days were during the week when I was at work. If only she had shown she understood my feelings, was kind about them, I think Roma would not have become the issue it became. But she resented my feelings and fought back. I am afraid I feel to this day that she was corrupted by the highly individualist, totally hedonistic and materialist, inward-looking and morally dubious Californians she lived with. It made her hard, impervious to the subtleties of emotion and feelings. It changed her. But I absolutely accept my stupidity in not engaging in proper communication, in getting so locked up in my own feelings, in frankly letting my love become a selfish one.

1975

Over New Year, we managed to go away with three of our Bath friends for a few days renting a cottage in Polperro, Cornwall. It was at times great fun. One day, having smoked some strong grass, we walked down to the beach and along the rocky shoreline. The cliff rose above us and we decided to climb it. It was genuinely pretty vertical but with plenty of footholds. Pete, our Bowie look-alike gay and very camp friend, was wearing Victorian high-heeled lace-up boots. But he somehow managed it to the top. My worst moment was confronting some sea-gulls resting on a rocky outcrop.

But always there lurked the dark cloud of how things were between us. We were not communicating.

So when she came back from her shifts at work, we avoided the discussions we so needed. Instead we still sought out little escapes with our friends. One night, around midnight, a group of us drove up to Beckfords Tower at the top of Lansdown Hill. We were of course all very stoned. Pete was again one of the crew as was Marc, who became my best friend. We started to freak each other out with ghostly tales – the Tower can evoke that. We then drove further into the country. Suddenly, this man emerged from the bushes at the side of the road and just stood there. We were all a bit shocked. He seemed to come from nowhere. We carried on and then, after about 3 minutes rolling along this country road, the man emerged again from the bushes. We all saw him. We all said he was the same man. We were absolutely terrified, a terror that turned into hysterical laughter. So it wasn't all bad.

I was fed up with drifting and finally I decided my best option was to become a lawyer. I successfully applied for articles in a legal aid firm in Bristol.

But the gap between us just seemed to get wider. Looking back, I ask myself again and again why didn't I try to get us to talk properly about things? I can only conclude that I had felt defeated and out of my depth ever since she returned from America.

One evening in March, we went out to eat. Whether the restaurant was actually cold I'm not sure, but the lights were bright and there were very few other customers. Out of the blue, Steffe began talking about all the men she had slept with – an astonishing number. I asked which number I was and when she answered, I realised that there was someone after me. I was dumbfounded.

'I did sleep with someone a little while ago', she said casually, as if describing having met someone on the street.

What was all this about? I once again felt, let's face it, humiliated. I couldn't, in truth, take it in. I was too shocked. It was so disturbing. I didn't even ask who it was. I felt completely lost. I think I began to lose my mind a little from this point on. It became a bit of a nightmare... I felt crushed. I was crushed. How can I have been so weak? Why didn't I express outrage, demand a real talk? It astounds me that I didn't. Our relationship was so unbalanced.

Looking back, I wonder if her intention was to provoke me into ending the relationship there and then. I suspect that's the truth. But I was too overwhelmed to do anything.

So perhaps it wasn't such a surprise when things finally broke irrevocably apart in April... But its manner really did.

FOURTEEN

I was absolutely devastated. I didn't know what to do. It was fortunate I had a demanding job to distract me. I wrote to her and tried to put on a brave face. I guess I was hoping to convince her of something. Why didn't I protest about how we had parted? Challenge her in any way?

Roma
Wednesday evening

Dear Roy,

I got your letter today - you needn't think (again) that I will read it as sounding pompous or self-righteous - because although you do sometimes put things rather formally I do happen to agree with the things you say and understand how you are feeling shock and hurt, but nevertheless self-sufficiency. I don't think I have as wrong an image of you as you sometimes think. I know you've grown and developed a lot recently, I have a lot of respect for you, although you may not realise it. Perhaps in some ways you've grown beyond me - I always used to think you would. I remember saying to you once a long time ago at Waterloo Station that you had a lot of strength inside you - more than me and that one day you would show yourself to be a lot stronger than me. You denied it at the time - reflect on it now.

Not that I think that I am not also strong - but my strength derives more from outside things. I can't offer many explanations for what is going on at the moment - it baffles me as well, you know. Maybe it is simply hedonism and straight selfishness. Or just circumstances. Funnily enough it was you who used to try and make me live in the present, in the here and now, and now I'm doing that and

167

it is rebounding on you. I can't even judge whether I am opting for safety or adventure - it feels like both at once. All I can say is that I can't help my feelings - and they do seem to be taking me away from you at the moment. All I can say is that I need time. But I'm not asking you to wait for me either. That's as pointless as you asking me to break things off and come back before I feel I want to. All we can do is let things follow their natural course. I suppose I am saying 'that's me'. But not without an equal feeling of sorrow, guilt, perplexity, a certain amount of fear. But if this world that I am in now is so alien to me, why am I also happy?

That last sentence hit me so hard. How could she be happy knowing that the youth/man she had loved so intensely was so sad and hurt? Had the roles been reversed, I would have felt mortified to have hurt Steffe so much. I truly believe that. But once again an extraordinary honesty and authenticity.

I do have an earthy, practical side as well as the other more spiritual side - they are equally part of me.

Couldn't she see that was true of me? I was a trainee lawyer but I don't recall her asking about that.

And when it comes to relationships I constantly get caught up in the same conflict. And swing from one to the other. You know that our relationship is the first mature one that I've had in which the spiritual element has been the most important and I've thrived on that - but something must be missing or wrong for me to be doing what I am doing now.

So why didn't you talk to me about it? Why all the subterfuge?

And also it's got a lot to do with having made a bad decision over my marriage, and being determined that I'm not going to be trapped again.
I don't want the old conflict situation back again - it was destroying me. I've got to feel free to move where I want. It does perhaps all add up to selfishness - and a lack of loyalty

Yep.

But I was loyal to J. for a long time and it didn't help either of us
.

Or me, Stephanie, or me. Perhaps you've forgotten that.

So I think it's better that when I feel the impulse to shoot off, I just do it and see what happens.

Jesus, is this the Stephanie I fell in love with? Though, to be fair, wasn't that exactly what she had done when embarking on her affair with me?

I'm sorry - I could write that to the end of my life I should think. But one can't help hurting and being hurt - one just learns how to deal with it, which is what you are doing now. It doesn't destroy your capacity for feeling - in fact, it can make it stronger because you know that you <u>can</u> give your heart and have it rejected without it destroying your life, so you don't need defences. You just enjoy it while it lasts. Intense pain is better than apathy. And intense happiness may follow ... take care, little one, and try to understand. I'll write again soon. My love, Steffe xx

But as always, for all my bitter feelings, there was something about the way she wrote that I couldn't help but respect.

 Looking at the two letters she wrote to me after our separation, realising that she was doing something she had not done for ages, actually communicating, the thought occurs to me that had we kept up our letter writing whilst she was away in London, we might perhaps have broken through the barrier and refound each other.

*

 Before we split up, Steffe had bought as a birthday present for me tickets for us to see a Bowie concert in May. So I needed to find someone to go with. I thought of gorgeous, dangerous, extreme, and totally decadent Patty, married Patty, with the looks of Jane Birkin. She accepted and came.

 I was in a very raw condition. Steffe and I had only been apart a month. I wanted oblivion. Patty and I joined up on Friday night and headed off to the suburbs to pick up a very large bag of coke. Before setting off back to the flat we were using, we tasted the goods. So began a wild, wild weekend. By the time we went to the Bowie concert, we were blown and already pretty wrecked. As we took our seats, I clocked one of Steffe's closest friends sitting just behind us. I so wanted her to clock me and then tell Steffe what a beautiful woman I was with (she was an ex-model). Sad really.

 As the great man performed, singing *Station to Station* ('it's not the side effects of the cocaine'), we sniffed capsule after capsule of amyl nitrate, the smell must have been dreadful. In truth, I was so far gone, I can hardly remember the concert. Just images of this thin white figure bathed in cold light.

 Next day, still having not slept, I fucked her, this beautiful   woman – and it felt like nothing, it was nothing. Was I in an emotional desert? I was.

*

 For a while, I would stay in my room night after night, just thinking. On occasion, when the pain felt unendurable, I would sniff some amyl nitrate to escape reality completely if only for a few minutes, typically listening to

Bowie's Station To Station, a ten minute epic. But amazingly in retrospect, by day I worked hard and conscientiously at my job, despite my overall despair.

Telephone conversations were a disaster. In a letter, I could at least try to lower my passions, restrain my language, seek to be mature and understanding. But when on the 'phone, my raw emotion and desperate pleading poured out. Calls were made from my office to Roma. Hardly conducive to a meaningful interchange.

> C/O Roma
> Thursday evening

Dear Roy,

I should start by apologising for getting stroppy on the phone today - but it's difficult because I have a feeling I know what happens. It's not merely the distance and impotence. It's also the fact that you have to be quick - if the discussion starts getting heavy you can't spend an hour putting it right again, so my reaction is to bonk heaviness on the head, which obviously doesn't go down too well your end. Also the conflicting factor that it is a 2-way means of communication and perhaps in a letter I can put down what I feel without you interrupting before I've finished! Because I read your letter and had to agree with what you wrote about our relationship. It has been the deepest and most intense and in most ways the most fulfilling I have ever known.

So why throw it away?

I will never allow the memory of it to be belittled. It was extraordinarily powerful - my heart still breaks when I remember the total magic of the beginning and the many enchanting periods later on. We _did_ have soul-

171

communication. I put all this in the past tense without really believing all that has gone. The magic has, but not the communication. I doubt if there are many people on this planet who have the power to get through to me the way you did. It's not understanding in the normal sense of the word, because you don't really understand me - not, for example, in the way J. did. He really saw my weaknesses and needs in a real sense.....But he never saw the side of me you did, and if I showed it to him, he would be bewildered and a bit afraid, which was what caused problems between us .... That side of life bewilders me too. If you read Knots by Laing, the last chapter about the inside and the outside, then I am often truly perplexed by my inside and often consider myself empty and wonder what is coming through to the outside that I really have nothing to do with. It's as though I feel that in the mundane world this aspect of me plays no part, but as soon as I get in deep with someone, something is exposed and it must be fairly magnetic but I honestly have no idea what it is and therefore have no control over it. It's at times like this, when I try to explain it to myself or others, that I think I must be literally mad. As I was saying on the phone, there have been 2 times in my life when I have attempted to explore this aspect of myself and relate it to some other-world that I sense is there. But I can't take it. Like acid. First time is magic and then later you start examining the chemical causes. Because it is so hard to accept you are seeing further than you ordinarily do.... I know that now you have a straight job and your feet on the ground - but that's not the point. Which is that we were exploring something beyond this world. On a mundane level we have no more in common that lots of people. Where we worked was somewhere else.

Like magic or acid. But perhaps we reached the limits of this ourselves - or at least perhaps I did. I had got as far as I wanted to on that level, and again I was bewildered and frightened. I don't want security but I do want sanity and reality. Does this make sense? It should do. All through our relationship, until near the end, we were able to make these little flights up to another planet - often through love--making. I will probably never have those experiences again. But towards the end, that was beginning to fade - and that was the substance of our relationship. So Roma came between us, because to me it was very important - I am much more involved in it, doing probably 60 hours a week, and don't think cynically it's just because of David. It's also (sic) because I want to do it, I do like taking things seriously, putting in and getting out as much as I can. Like at LSE, you remember how I worked there? I need that sort of thing. I'm not one for drifting and being on my own - I need the outside world a lot.

She just didn't understand, maybe I hadn't explained it properly, but I wanted her to have work that engaged her. I just wanted it to be local, so we could share our lives. I am sure if she had been patient she would have found work in Bristol. Why didn't she talk to me about her feelings? She really didn't. Never did she acknowledge <u>my</u> feelings, she merely resisted them.

I need people to be close to, and a reason for living. <u>Both</u> - I can't make one person a reason for living. So that may not be self-sufficient - it's the way I've learnt I get most out of my life. I can't take too much introspection - it frightens me. I feel the emptiness and the mystery and feel inadequate. I need to keep proving to myself that I'm a person by responses I get and results I see. I acknowledge *that it's a false way to operate in a sense, but at least the means don't have to be totally selfish - I can kid myself I'm doing my number for the community.*

Such misunderstandings. I really wanted Steffe to find meaningful work. She doesn't recognise this. Again , I can only say I wanted her to work locally so we were really living together. This became the thing that fractured our relationship – plus the fact that I had lost trust and faith in her so I was always wondering if she was screwing someone else when in London – which turned out to be the case.

I don't have many aspirations. You probably think I aspire for too little, and again you may be right. I don't reject the other path, of self-knowledge and knowledge of the universal mysteries - but I don't think I can get much further at this time. I'm not ready. And probably never will be, but perhaps what will occur is a pattern of reaching out and recoiling, and that at the moment I am recoiling.
I am so pleased by what you say in your letter about the way you are handling all this - I prefer to believe what you wrote as against what you said on the phone.

Well, in the letter, I was trying to be 'the together guy', the mature guy….. but what happened on the phone, what I said then, would have been the real truth.

….. As for the relationship ever working again. It could do - there's no doubt I already miss it, just writing it down as the result of thoughts I've had recently makes it clear to me just how precious it was.

So don't throw it away! How many precious things ever happen in our lives?

But I do feel at the moment it has come to saturation point – I don't, can't, get anymore from it now.

So that shut the door in my face. No element of thinking – we need to work on this. Roy is a man I have truly loved. I can't just walk out. This seemed to me to be pure selfishness and not what I thought love was about.

As you know, I always refuse to commit myself for the future as long as it is a question of only being responsible to myself. But as long have no commitments it could always be a possibility. That surely is the case for you as well.

Is it? Have you not betrayed me repeatedly? You appear to have no recognition of that.

If either of us feel the need for it again, feel we could get into that again and the other is willing, it could re-open. But of course things could intervene meanwhile – it's a risk you take.

Did she already suspect the truth?

And perhaps a word about what I'm up to. Without going into details, I have a nice, loving friendship with David and the communication there again is not really at the mundane level, although neither is it at a soul-level. It's purely at the emotional level – we each can give the other the relatively uncomplicated love we both have a need for right now, for different reasons on each side. He has just come through a very emotionally battering divorce after

175

15 years and there's no need to repeat what I've come out of.

What had Stephanie come out of that was, by implication, so terrible? Ah, having an affair with me whilst married, something that she had to recover from? Yes, I felt bitter. And she claims to be in love again? Is she so very fickle and superficial? If things were going badly with me, why not move out for a while, take a breath, and then see where we go from there? Not Stephanie.

I would like to fish my belongings out of the room soon......I will have to fetch the stuff in the van and I would rather do it when you are at work. I don't want a big scene erupting as you watch me move out. If you want to see me, that's another matter but I most certainly don't want it to be in those sorts of circumstances. It would be better one time when you were visiting London.

In view of something that happened when she and David came to Bath, I wish I had just taken the day off work and stayed in our room in the flat. I would like to have confronted them. Asked David if Stephanie had told him the history of our relationship. That we started an affair after she had been married just 9 months. That she was brilliant at lying and subterfuge and that he should be ready for that. After all, hadn't she screwed David whilst living with me? Was it like that in your marriage, David? Knowing what I know now, Stephanie may have hated me for it but I think it's possible it would have so shocked David, the relationship could have been brought to an end. That's just a fantasy, really. It's not how I operate. It would have been a form of violence, a betrayal. But when you are so deeply hurt, deeply sad, profoundly broken, mad actions are attractive.

So I've almost written my arm off and I hope things are clearer for you now. Read between the lines - there's much

condensed thoughts in part of this letter - try to
understand what I am saying.
And meanwhile take the greatest care of yourself. Not too
many drugs.

That's a joke! I frequently sought oblivion through drugs.

Get some women in too.

Oh, please...how very superficial, how demonstrative of her total failure to recognise/face up to, how I felt.

And make the most of your friends. And of our beautiful
Bath which I miss so much. Don't think I'm not painfully
aware of the prospect of London in the summer - it's like a
prison in some ways. I seem to have had so many of them.
But it's where my life is at the moment.
So - that's all,
My love
Steffe xxx

What really shocked me, though, what I found at the time unforgiveable and grossly insensitive, unspeakably hard, what made me want to stop all communication dead, was the fact that when they came to collect her stuff from the flat, the two of them went to Parsenn Sally. How could they, how could she, humiliate me in front of my friends who worked there? That really tore me apart. There was no need for her to grind my nose into the ground. I suspect the possibility of it doing so didn't even cross her mind. At that point, I felt hate.

I was defeated. I never went up to London to see her. What would have been the point? But one day, when I happened to be in London, I searched out the ghastly squat where they were living, and sat in my car a few yards away. I have no idea what I would have done had I seen them. Almost

177

certainly nothing. But I would have stepped out of the car had I seen Stephanie on her own. But I saw no one and drove off feeling both stupid and crushed. And I didn't write. Frankly, I just couldn't face arguing or pleading any more. I had my pride. And I knew I had lost her.

Then came the final, or almost final, shock. She wrote to me to say she was pregnant. I almost felt sick. She also told me her mother had unexpectedly died. I felt no sympathy. I didn't write back. I destroyed her letter.

That summer the weather was glorious, constant blue skies, sunshine – and it made my sadness all the more intense. But I did have my work at which I was very conscientious. And I still did shifts at Parsenn Sally. And I did have friends. But I felt so lonely. In late summer, I moved to a rather lovely flat in Clifton, found through a London friend. Through that flat, I met new people in Bristol and I began to settle into a different life, determined to try to move forward.

And that involved facing up to, really looking at, what had gone wrong in our relationship. I had to accept that I had not recognised so much about Steffe, that I was myself responsible for its breakdown in no small part, that I had become centred only on my own feelings and had not taken on board hers. I tried to avoid blaming myself (although of course I did) by reminding myself that I had been just 23 and she was a much older woman, a very complex woman, in fact a very needy woman, and my immaturity simply did not equip me to sustain the relationship. As I came to appreciate this, my bitterness faded and I felt my love for her returning, despite everything that had happened. I also realised that we had not taken on board the difficulties of moving from a relationship which simply hadn't operated in the outer world, into one existing on a day-to-day basis. We had so much to learn but I am afraid Steffe just didn't see this and nor did I. We should have really sat down and talked things through. Been open about the challenges, reached across to one another. I can't believe we got it so wrong.

Shortly before Christmas, I sent her a card and a message.

29 December 1976

Dear Roy,

Thanks a lot for your Christmas card and nice message - the time has certainly come for a friendly communication from my end....

Well, I am still waiting for the baby to arrive, it is now a few days overdue, which often happens with first babies but it is an incredible drag because you get psyched up for the day and every extra one seems a lifetime. I'll let you know what it is when it finally emerges. I am incredibly huge and uncomfortable and don't believe I will ever recover my former size.

As you can see we are staying with Anthea for the duration as it were - as she decided our derry was not fit for baby habitation (correct, I would say). It's been lovely living in comfort and company again; in retrospect I realise I was getting very depressed on my own all day and every day. I don't know if I told you before but we are hoping to move to Sussex, Hastings, in the New Year sometime. We have found a little house in need of conversion - not your country paradise but at least near the sea and a start. We don't know yet how we shall earn bread down there although we have a few ideas. I'll let you know if we finally do go there.

I should tell you that my divorce came through and David and I were married extremely quietly (just Anthea and Angie to witness) on December 18 so I guess I am G....... now. I don't hear from John anymore - his American girl-friend came over and communication seems to have ceased since.

I later found out that John had been absolutely furious about Steffe getting pregnant and wrote an extremely accusatory and angry letter to her, saying she had absolutely 'fucked him about'. So Steffe wasn't, it turns out, being honest about why communication had ceased.

So I would like to hear how you are getting on now. In retrospect I know I treated you very badly and feel ashamed - but all emotional reactions, one can be very cruel and regret it later but I don't think things could have ended much more gently given the intensity of relationships. I think you handled it all well considering - and I only hope wounds have healed and you have a new life. Let me know and take care,
Love Steffe x

The condition of this letter suggests that my immediate reaction was to screw it up into a ball and chuck it.
Shortly after, she wrote a simple letter saying she had had a son on 3 January. That was a letter I did destroy. It was too painful.
It took me a long time to reply. I had to come to terms with the fact that her baby had obviously been conceived whilst we were still living together, and also with the fact that she had divorced John and then married a guy within eight months of our separating. Also I needed time to write an honest yet kind and loving letter. I made it clear that I was still very hurt, that I still loved her, but that I had learnt a lot and saw just how much I had contributed to us breaking apart. I sought, as it were, to forgive her because I realised that what was most important was for us to remember the wonders that we had enjoyed together. My profound hurt remained but the anger and bitterness had basically gone, though that doesn't mean I never felt them again because I did from time to time. But ultimately I knew what a special woman she was, so authentic though definitely a lot more mixed up than I had realised. I also knew I would

never experience a relationship like this one again. I didn't want it to be tarnished in the minds of either of us. But I knew it was absolutely over.

And so contact ceased. Painful though it was, I knew that Steffe was part of the past. But as the years rolled by, my love for her never died. Sometimes, I would wake up in the morning having dreamt of her and would be overwhelmed with sadness that I would never see her again. My sweet Steffie.

Part Two

The Return

PROLOGUE

From Steffe's dream diary:

3 September 1980
I am in a hall where the exam results are - 3 of my
students have just found out they have failed. I go and try
to cheer them up. Part of the reason I do this is to restore
their faith in me as a teacher. Then we all sit down for tea
and they start criticising another student who has worked
so hard to pass and is so ambitious at the expense of her
family (she has children). I liked the girl and had never
thought of her situation in this way before. She and her
family are at the next table. They get up to leave.
Comments from my table are: 'You see, they are the first to
leave'. I protest that they were the first to come as well, so it
is quite logical they should leave first. I thought I
recognised one of the family - a boy in his twenties. As he
passes the table he notices me and keeps looking round to
check if he does know me. Finally he makes an excuse to
stand by the door and have a really good look. All this
time I have been fiddling with a splinter in my hand - now
I suddenly pull it out - it is very long and my hand feels
better. I mention to a girl on my table about this young
man by the door - we both remember him although in very
different ways - he was a lover of mine some years ago -
Roy.

December 1980

......If I could have balanced relationships but on the 'new' assumptions (as opposed to the 'old' ones) would I have the pain or wouldn't I? To what extent do I cause myself pain by not believing thoroughly enough in my own values of society? This was the way Roy and I used to feel - that even if our relationship disobeyed all the social rules it was obeying a higher much more important rule - that when you find the miracle of love, you had to let that love flourish because it was the most precious thing there could be. And there, at once, the memory floods back and I have to turn my back on it because it is just more pain......I threw it away - that didn't get taken, I threw it away - I can't believe that I did, that I could have done, knowing what I did. Why did I do it? Had I already become so hardened? Was it this - that spiritually with Roy I could grow and prosper but in terms of my emotional needs he could not give me the props I always needed? What a waste.

From Steffe's dream diary

28ᵗʰ May 1981

I met Roy again. We both felt the same about each other as we had always done. He had been so badly hurt by our separation that he had taken himself into a monastery. I was full of remorse and tried to explain to him why I had left, acknowledging that it had been very cruel and heartless, but with my arm around his shoulders I told him that I was sorry, that I knew it must have hurt, but that I loved him again now. We looked at each other with that

amazing recognition and deep understanding and I was
so relieved to have found him again. I made some
reference to the future and how we would be together all
the time now, and he looked agonised and said 'no'. I
could hardly believe what I heard and said that at least
we could see a lot of each other and he said 'not really' -
and I understood that he was going to stay in the
monastery. His feelings had developed towards the
monastery and the monks and he would remain loyal to
them. Tears of hurt and disappointment and frustration
immediately burst from me and woke me up.

From Steffe's dream diary

June 1981
I was at Cambridge University .....standing at a bar
.....then there is a big dinner ....then there are some
congratulations for an engagement - it turns out I am
engaged. Someone says 'When are you getting married?' I
say not for at least five years, if not ten. I am thinking of
my last two marriages and afraid of making another
mistake.
Then I am outside reading a book and suddenly Roy walks
in. He is wearing a funny old mac and I have a surge of
feeling - it is so amazing that he is here. At once I am
afraid to look at him - I know I look so much older and I
don't want to embarrass him - I want to give him time to
watch me and take this in first - then I look up and say
'I've tried so often to get in touch with you'

ONE

23 July 1981

It was a normal Thursday. I had a couple of court appearances that thankfully were out of the way by about 12. I grabbed a sandwich to eat back at the office and drove to Avonmouth, an old, deeply working-class community of Bristol surrounded by the docks and lines of factories stretching north by the Severn. It wasn't far from Lawrence Weston, an out of town 60's development of council housing and flats, now already run down and deprived. My office was set in a row of Victorian terraced houses looking out onto massive concrete buildings with glimpses of cranes in between. I parked my car and walked through the front door. I smiled at my receptionist and secretary. 'All ok?' 'Yes but a few phone messages for you.' She handed them to me. A woman in an abusive relationship wanting reassurance that the injunction against her partner wouldn't make the situation worse, a worried tenant saying his landlord was threatening him, a mother wanting someone to help her son whom the police wanted to speak to about a car theft, the usual stuff. 'I'm going to eat my lunch first, then I'll deal with them. How many appointments this afternoon?' 'Just 3'. 'Starting when?' '2'o'clock'.

I made my way up the stairs to my office. It was at least large if not exactly glamorous, though it had a big old oak desk behind which I settled down to eat my sandwich.

These were exciting times for me. I had just been made a partner of the small legal aid solicitors firm I was working for. I had made it a condition of becoming a partner that I be allowed to open an office in St Pauls where I hoped to develop a criminal practice, which was what I wanted to specialise in some day. There had been a riot there the year before. It was the centre of the black community in Bristol. I felt that there I could establish myself as a radical lawyer, championing black rights and

187

challenging the police and the powers that be. I was at the time searching for premises.

I was looking forward to the weekend. I was going up to London, primarily for a party on Friday night where lots of my London friends would be.

The internal phone rang. I picked it up and my secretary said that there was a call for me from someone called Steffe. Did I want to take it? Steffe. Steffe? Before I had time to think, I said put her through.

'Steffe?' I said.

'Yes, Roy, it is. It wasn't easy finding you'.

'Good Lord. I don't know quite what to say. How are you?'

It was so hard to take this in. I absolutely believed she was part of the past, that I would never hear from her or see her again. And here she was. Hearing her quite unique, beautiful voice melted my heart.

'I am on my own now. Well, I have two sons but I am not with David any more. We're divorced. It all went horribly wrong. But what about you, are you married, involved?'

'Well, no.'

We didn't speak for long but Steffe said:

'Would you like to meet up?'

'Yes, I'd really like that. But when? Do you live in Hastings?'

'I do but David has the boys this weekend in fact and I am going up to London to see my sister, Anthea.'

'As it happens, I'm coming up to London this weekend too. I've got a party on Friday and will be staying at my friend Otto's flat in Notting Hill'.

'So would you like to meet up on Saturday?'

'That would be lovely. Shall I pick you up? Tell me Anthea's address'.

She did.

'So shall I come around lunchtime, sort of 1 to 2 pm? Is that OK?'

We signed off. I just sat there. I couldn't believe it. Coming so out of the blue, I was completely unprepared. Steffe. I was going to see her again. I felt such excitement. There was no doubt in my mind about wanting to see her again.

It was a great drive up to London. At the party I was so happy, smiling, dancing, laughing, talking and smoking a lot of dope. I shared a bed that night with Pippa, a social worker who I had always really liked and got on with really well but with whom a sexual relationship had never happened, even though I found her very attractive. We didn't take off our clothes or do anything. Being the friend she was, I had told her all about Steffe. The year before we were both arrested by the Special Patrol Group when we had been observing a National Front march through the northern part of Notting Hill. We were assaulted by two uniformed thugs and dragged, without any cause at all, into a police van. Thank God we were both acquitted at trial at Highbury Corner Magistrates Court. So we had a close bond. She was really pleased for me.

Saturday arrived. Time for me to set out. I had the most dreadful car, a mustard coloured Austin Allegro, the one with the square steering wheel. I turned on the ignition. Nothing. I tried again and again. Nothing. The battery was flat. I then spotted that I had left the lights on. Christ. When we split up, I was untogether. This would seem like I was still untogether. But I had no choice. I returned to the flat and rang her and told her what had happened. I apologised and suggested she take a taxi.

There were three or four of us in the flat and whilst we idly chatted I paced the floor. I was excited and nervous. It had been a long time.

The doorbell rang. It was a first and second floor flat. Otto went down the stairs to the front door. I waited and then heard Otto's voice and her voice.

Otto came into the living room first and then Steffe. We looked at each other but didn't kiss. She sat down on a sofa. I remained standing. She then gave me her most wonderful wide smile, though rather shyly, lowering her head slightly and looking up. This was an essential element of her beauty. Her lips were full, her teeth perfect. Her cheekbones had become fuller and her smile flowed into them. And as always her dark brown eyes seemed so deep. I was immediately captivated. I smiled back but we didn't speak. We needed to take each other in. Initially I guess I noticed how she looked older, her hair showing streaks of grey, her face a

189

little worn, a little lined. But once again she entranced me. This was the woman to whom my heart had always been given.

'Steffie'.

'Roy'.

My friends melted away, they were so kind and understanding. Otto had told me I had the flat to myself overnight. So we sat down and very gently began to talk.

'My marriage was a disaster. More or less from the beginning. So we separated a year or so ago and now we are divorced.'

'And you have two boys. Tell me about them.'

'Paul's four and Joe's two. In fact, I pretty quickly realised within a year or so of Paul's birth that our marriage was hopeless and that I would have to leave. But I couldn't bear the idea of it being just Paul and me on our own. I felt that would be bad for both of us. So I had Joe'.

'I'm so sorry things have been bad for you. Are you working?'

'Life's a struggle financially. I get virtually nothing from David and what he does give me he resents. But I have jobs. I teach adults at a FE college – sociology mainly. I also teach in a prison. But I am always on the financial edge. But what about you?'

'There's so much to say. But look, the weather's fine, how about going for a walk and then getting some food?'

So out we went. This part of Notting Hill is really lovely. We walked the streets, Ladbroke Grove, Holland Park, and then back towards the restaurants and pubs of Notting Hill Gate. We ambled, and she took my arm as we chatted. It felt so comfortable right from the beginning. There was such a depth of mutual understanding. She had changed, was more reflective, different in a good way I could not yet define. There was the old gentleness back, the soft tenderness. We filled out our respective lives though only in outline. Mainly we just chatted quite randomly and laughed quite a lot.

We decided to eat, early though it was. The sun was now dipping in the blue sky to the west. We found a small, rather charming, pizza restaurant and by the time we walked through the door, we were properly connecting.

We found a table near the window. We ordered food and wine. And then we just looked at each other – it felt magical. We smiled and said nothing for a short while.

'So, Steffie, you rang me. Tell me why. And how did you find me?'

'I had been thinking of contacting you for some time. By the time David finally left last year, my first response was one of pure relief. It had been such an unhappy marriage, one that I had felt so lonely in. But after he went, I felt even more lonely. He has the boys regularly at weekends and I would sometimes not see anyone whilst they were away. I felt I was such a failure, such a bad person. 2 broken marriages. I had never really been on my own for years, in a way ever. I had nowhere to hide. I had to face up to who I was. In August, I decided to see if I could get some psychotherapy and I discovered, through a friend, this marvellous Jungian therapist, Elizabeth. She's very old. Late 70's I guess. She helped me through last winter when I really felt I was hitting rock bottom. Her therapy involves me remembering and writing out my dreams, using them to get deep inside me. It's been revelatory. It's helped me rediscover the spiritual in me. And it brought you back. And I faced up, for the first time, to the tragedy that our separation had been. But I didn't feel I should try and seek you out. Wouldn't I just be being weak, reaching out for help? Yet you stayed with me in my mind. So I went to the post office and read through the telephone directories for Bristol remembering very few of the details of where you had been working 5 years ago. I noted down a couple of numbers but had no real hope of finding you. I thought you would have moved on. So you can imagine my surprise when I rang your office and was told you were at court but should be back by lunchtime. I was excited and very nervous.'

'It was so out of the blue, your call. I couldn't really believe it'.

'Are you ok about me contacting you?'

'Do I not look ok?' I said smiling.

'No, you don't! It's so nice seeing you again.'

191

'And you.'

'So you're not in a relationship?'

'No. I've had two or three but they've never really gone anywhere. The truth is they could never come near what I experienced when I was with you, if I'm honest. I was reconciled to that. Right now, I wonder if I haven't been in a sort of emotional monastery. Instead, work has become my focus. Strange, isn't it, that when we were together I was so unable to find my direction, courting baseless dreams of being a writer, a journalist, whatever, when all along the thing that suited me most was right before my eyes. I love being a lawyer, I mean the kind of lawyer I am. I have real freedom in what I do, I work for the poor and deprived, I love arguing and am good at it, and it's all about fighting back and justice. It ticks just about all the boxes.'

'I'm so glad for you. You do have a real energy about you. It's lovely to see.'

'Whilst I was still a trainee, I developed quite a practice acting for women victims of domestic violence. I became so adept at it that a client may come in at 12 noon and by 5 pm, I would have obtained an ex parte injunction against the violent partner. Ex parte means without giving the man any notice of the application to court. It's an emergency remedy. I have been both moved and made terribly angry by some of the stories I have heard. Often I have had to work hard at getting women to instruct me to take action. They were scared or claimed they still loved their violent partner or maybe just afraid to be alone. So I had the task of trying to empower these women. It was very satisfying.

Steffe looked very involved in what I was saying but also I got the feeling that somehow what I had said had affected her. I moved the conversation on.

'But I want to hear more about you. I know work is very important to you, one of the mistakes I made back in Bath was not recognising this. So tell me more about what you've been doing.'

'it's all been part-time. I have had to juggle things around the boys. David has been singularly unhelpful. Mainly, as I've told you, I've been

192

teaching at an FE college and in a prison. I really love it. I may be shy but I can enthuse before a class. It's pretty challenging teaching prisoners though.'

'I wouldn't be surprised if substantial numbers didn't fall for you. There they are, locked away, and then in you come!'

'Well yes. There was one prisoner who was released, found out where I lived and turned up at my door with a bouquet of flowers asking me out. He was obviously so stricken by me, it wasn't easy letting him down.'

'I don't think you realise how strong your allure can be.'

'That has often been a puzzle to me. I obviously have something but I honestly don't know what it is.'

'No, I can't understand it either! But go on.'

'Well, I realise what I really want to do is therapeutic work. Having psychotherapy has made that clear to me. So I am starting on a counselling course in Brighton in September.'

'Wonderful. A part-time course, I presume?'

'Oh yes. But I am really excited by it'.

'That's great! And inside? How are you feeling there?'

'Battered, bruised, but hopefully working things out, perhaps for the first time. Calling you was part of that.'

So slowly, more came out. We didn't talk about our separation. That would have been a very bad idea. But I felt us getting closer and closer.

The light was fading as we stepped out onto the street and made our slow way back to the flat, my arm around her shoulder, her arm about my waist. We climbed the steps to the front door, opened it and made our way up the stairs to Otto's flat. I turned on low lights in the sitting room and then went across to Otto's record collection.

'So any particular music you are into? I asked.

'I haven't followed music for the last 5 years really, just some Van Morrison and one or two others.'

'OK. Let's see what's here'. I flicked through a few record sleeves and pulled out one of my favourite albums of the time. 'Talking Heads. Excellent. Have you heard of them?'

193

'No.'

'Oh I love them. They are sort of American new wave. This is their third album – *Fear of Music*. Great title. Produced by Brian Eno. Led by a mad genius called David Byrne. Have a listen and I'll roll up a joint'.

'I haven't smoked since we were last together.'

'Really? Well, this will be a treat then. I have lost none of my love of dope'.

I put on side one and we both sat on the sofa, me rolling up and then lighting up. We smoked and listened and slid together. But it wasn't until '*Heaven*' that we began to kiss. And it was just magical. Lyrics touching on the timelessness of physical connection.

As the song ended, I said 'Shall we go up to our room?'

I took her hand and led her up the stairs into the bedroom I had been given. She looked rather shy.

'Shall we get into bed?' I asked as I began to take off my clothes. She looked so warmly and invitingly at me and began to follow suit but said 'I'm keeping my vest on'. It was light green with red stripes. 'I have stretch marks and my breasts are all saggy. I'm not the woman you knew'.

I went across to her, held her and kissed her and led her to the bed. Slowly, in the way only we knew how, we began to make love. There was no sudden urgency, instead a gentle meeting of our bodies, a reintroduction. When we finally came fully together, it felt like ecstasy , like our souls were meeting. That is the truth. I realised that I had screwed a lot of women over the past five years but until now I had not made love. And afterwards, we didn't talk much. We just held each other and drifted off to sleep.

It felt like we woke up at the same time in the morning. I think that both of us were rather taken aback by what had happened, though we were both happy, Steffe in particular. But, for all the joy of reuniting with her, there was a little part of my brain asking if I actually wanted this, could I take the sudden turning of my life upside down, and I had been so hurt before. So as we ate breakfast, Steffe seeming to be, in her rather shy

194

way, absolutely bowled over by events, whilst I, although genuinely going along with her, knew I was holding back to a degree. We agreed to meet for the weekend in 2 weeks' time. I suggested she came to Bristol.

After getting my battery fixed, I drove back to Bristol. It was all so sudden. 72 hours previously I wasn't thinking about her, knew she was part of my past, had come to terms with losing the woman I knew was the love of my life. And now she was back. As always, she made the first move. My heart was full but my head was confused and not a bit uncertain. It was exciting, no doubt about that. And making love had felt like coming home. But I was unprepared. I guess Steffe must have been prepared, if only for it all failing.

I lay on my bed that night, listening as almost always to music. It had been so painful losing her before. The summer of 1976 was the great long summer when the sun shone and shone and it did not rain for months. Those would have been glorious times when we could have strolled around the hills and valleys around Bath, lying under the shade of trees, not talking much, just taking in the beauty of it all. But I was alone so my walks were full of pathos and sadness. I used to think of her in London, happy with her new man. It felt such a dreadfully long summer. At night, I would listen endlessly to music. Sometimes, it needed to be strong and loud. But often I wanted music to soothe and calm me. None achieved this more than Brian Eno's *Another Green World*. That album was one of my saviours. I could close my eyes and drift off feeling the warmth and succour of the music, the softness of the lyrics. *'I'll Come Running'* was a particular favourite, capturing the feeling of lost love and dreaming of a return.

TWO

She came to Bristol and my tiny flat 2 weeks later. When she stepped through the door to enter, it felt as exciting as back in 1973 when I first stayed at her flat. Once again the weather was fine. Photography was a proper hobby of mine at the time, I made up a dark room in the bathroom, developed my own films and then printed them. My camera was second hand but good for the times. I insisted on taking photos of her. They proved to be the happiest photos of her I ever took. Huge smiles but also soulful looks. We drove out to our old Bath haunt of St Catherine's Valley. She was wearing a soft cotton, loosely tailored, red trouser suit with thin shoulder straps.

We found a gently shaded hillside spot and made love. Afterwards, she lay back and I photographed her. Her expression was one of satiation, satisfaction, completeness. It was bliss.

Thought only came later.

Extract from Steffe's journal:

Sunday 9 August

After my weekend with Roy: I want him, I never want to lose him again. I made the wrong choices before and Roy and I could never have survived anyway, the relationship had taken a self-destruct course. But I am lucky enough to be able to make a choice again, and this time I won't mess it up. But it is more than luck - if we had not been so devoted to each other, or addicted to each other, in the first years of our relationship we would each perhaps have found someone else - but I feel we have been waiting for each other - it is such an extraordinary coincidence that we should both be free and still wanting each other.

After her return, she wrote to me.

Monday evening

Dear Roy,

I've just been re-reading a letter you wrote me after Paul was born, i.e. nearly a year after we split up. As in all the best novels, I destroyed all your letters at the end of our relationship - but this one, coming so much later, I kept. It is stunning. In the light of what I now know, and considering it was a reply to my breezy (probably) announcement of Paul's birth - I don't know, Roy. How you were able to retrieve so much of what was good from such a bad situation when the wounds were obviously so fresh (as you say in your letter). It's as if you learned for yourself and understood for yourself about the real meaning of love and suffering - things that have had to be almost

197

explained to me, forced upon my consciousness, you were aware of naturally. You are indeed very much in touch with your feelings, Roy - it was a great letter. I am so lucky to have found you again - this letter of mine cannot express why it needs to be written properly - just that that letter, if I had never met you again, would have been a testament to my own eternal loss of something of enormous value, priceless. Do you understand? What stunned me today reading it was thinking - you were so young, so hurt, and yet you forgave me, forgave yourself, and learned and built on it. And that is _truly_ remarkable. I still have a long way to go, Roy, and the process seems to be quite laborious. I hope I never hurt you again.

.... Since last weekend I feel there has been a really much more solid response in myself - the first meeting left me so absolutely high to the point of confusion, bewilderment and so to anxiety but now I have touched the ground again and I feel certain and good - and strong (well, relatively!). It's a reaffirmation - but everything's different now, what happens from now on is pretty unpredictable, I think it would be a mistake to be complacent. It's exciting. It's very alive.

I'll talk to you soon.

My love

Steffe x

The letter Steffe refers to:

My dear Steffe,

I am sorry I have not written before to thank you for your New Year letter and to congratulate you on the birth of your son. It was good to hear from you.

There is a reason for the delay. Can I be honest? The sad fact is that both your letter and the news of your birth, whilst in part pleasing me, also hurt me quite considerably. They made me realise that I am by no means over you and that my love (addiction) remains.

I have accepted the break, come to terms with it and come to understand so much more about myself, you, our relationship, relationships generally. But why, oh why, do the lessons of life have to be learnt at such expense?

Blame seems to be an absurd thing to try and place anywhere. And so to that extent I really do want to impress on you that you must not feel guilty. I can't say there aren't those emotional times, those weak times, when even now I curse you 'for doing what you did'. But in my calmer, more reflective moments, I realise this is absurd. If anyone is to blame, I guess it's me. But I try not even to blame myself. Just learn from my mistakes. Because I was immature. The end of our relationship seems to have brought on a new-found maturity (as well as a few new-found hang-ups).

It was, I think, a manifestation of my immaturity that led me not to understand your needs or know how to handle them when they asserted themselves. I was, in a profound sense, selfish and paranoid. The irony is that such characteristics actually worked against the continued realisation of the thing that I most wanted — to live with you. Only when you love selflessly do you receive the full bounty of love.... So I have learnt a lot. The trouble is, I am still in love with you.

Maybe, since I had never loved anyone like I loved (and still do love) you, I have to accept that the process of dealing with the end of our relationship is bound to be a very long one. I loved you very deeply and intensely, I gave you my soul, and it's so hard to adjust. I am still very defensive. Remember, being a Cancer, once hurt I tend to retreat into my shell. Hence the fact that I haven't got it together with anyone else in a proper relationship. I genuinely wish I could change loves quickly, and I envy those who can (you?).

Don't get me wrong. In many ways I am content. Not ecstatically happy but ok. I don't seem to be prone to the heavy downers that I used to suffer from. Not that I don't get depressed – I do, just as everyone does. But I think I am now more capable than I was at dealing with them. And so they don't become real downers.

And work is going excellently. Exciting, worthwhile, thoroughly satisfying. Whilst the social scene is not at all bad.

So there we go, Steffie. An attempt at an honest letter. I hope it goes some way to explaining why you haven't heard from me – it's certainly not because I have forgotten you.

I am genuinely pleased that things seem to be going so well for you. That I can truly say. I only wish I didn't at the same time feel so hurt.

Still, one day I will, I trust (I pray!!), fall in love again and perhaps then our relationship will take its proper place in my mind as a wonderful experience, untainted by any residual feelings of pain.

So take care,

My love,
Roy xxx

On the very night she wrote this, I wrote to her.

My dear Steffe,

Lovely though it was, there were occasions over the weekend when I was aware of an anxiety. It's only on getting back home that I've managed to unravel it.

When we were out walking, you asked me if being in contact with you again had upset my equilibrium and brought back the pain of our separation. I said, not wholly truthfully, that it had not. But there is more I need to say.

I was absolutely bowled over by you contacting me and our first weekend together almost overwhelmed me. I felt as if I had never stopped loving you and that we were meant to be together. But I've come back down to earth a bit now.

Whilst the pain I felt 5 years ago is not with me now as such, I realise I am cautious, even though my heart tells me not to be. My head says that I have built a happy and satisfying life for myself and achieved a balance it has taken me a long while to build. I must not jeopardise that. Now I absolutely believe we are potentially capable of giving each other great happiness. I want us to share our lives together. But I also know we are potentially capable of making each other very unhappy. So we need to tread carefully.

I am uneasy about saying this and being so blunt, so please forgive me. But I can't ignore the fact that you have been through two marriages. You can make bad decisions. So I need to be sure that you really are committed to us, that you won't later say to yourself 'another mistake'. You, like me in the past, can be impulsive. I feel you have changed but I need reassurance.

Another thing I worry about is that I recognise in you, as I do in myself, a tendency to act on occasions selfishly, in other words not properly taking on board how our actions may impact on others. Maybe it arises from our mutual love of hedonism and instant gratification. But right now, I need to know there is nothing impulsive about your relationship with me. That you are now clear about what you want.

So all I need is your reassurance that things have changed and that what you decide is genuine, thought through, what you want. Then I will be able to open my arms fully to you and give my whole self to you.

I hope you read this letter with the gentleness with which it has been written. I have great trust in you.

My love,

Roy xxxx

I knew Steffe would find this to be a hard letter to receive so I rang her the next evening. It was clear she was very pleased to hear from me.

That night, I reflected on the fact that the basis of our relationship had changed. Before, Steffe was always ultimately in charge. I had always felt unable to call the shots. This time, I felt we were meeting as equals. It made all the difference. I felt able to be me. She replied.

Dear Roy,

Wednesday's letter didn't get written so let's try this one for Thursday. Today has been really heavenly - partly because - fundamentally because it was such a relief after Wednesday. I have to admit I was really shaken by your letter and gloriously happy to hear your voice last night - but I had already realised there were things to be learned from it in terms of the way I was already sinking into a false sense of security which I wasn't happy with anyway - I was already losing myself in a way I don't want to do anymore. So today I feel I have touched heaven, landed on earth again very suddenly but now have found my feet again and I feel terrific.

....But today has been so special and it's because I am so happy about us that makes it so.....

I had a session with Elizabeth yesterday evening which was really, really good and sorted out a lot of the anxieties and ambivalence I had been feeling which we talked about. She is an amazing woman, so deeply caring. I had felt a strange draining away of my only recently found confidence and faith in myself - you see it's hard to look at the fact that I have been through two marriages and not feel an out and out shit and a totally worthless person - something I have felt a lot during my life: and looking at things in terms of childhood experiences and patterns of behaviour and finding false solutions, really restores or builds for the first time a sense of belief in oneself as making mistakes rather than just acting wickedly - and a faith in oneself is the only tenable starting point for any relationship. I considered (somewhere in myself) that contacting you was a terrible act of weakness and running for cover and that did shake my confidence - and was a false foundation. But now I see it again for what it certainly consciously was - a result of the unending sense of regret that I had lost you - and a very risky impulse to find you again. But although risky I believe it was an important move I had to make at the time - and as it *turns out it has given me an important sense of direction and purpose - I feel I have a tangible aim to work towards. I must simply say again that I understand that for this to work not only do I have to build on what I have started but that nothing that you have built for yourself, which I find so admirable, should be disturbed - as far as possible! In absolutely practical terms, this means I feel quite sure about a few things I am doing: I must continue to work on myself; I should carry through this training in Brighton; and I am never going to marry again. I feel equally sure that your work must continue undisturbed - it is central to your life now. ...... I must admit I am rather full of trepidation at the idea of you spending a few days here with my children - you are going to suffer terrible shell-shock - but we will just have to see. I am terribly conscious of the fact that I am no longer a single unit - it's a case of love me, love my kids - but that is just a consequence of the mistakes I have made and I have to accept it. Mind you, there is no reason on earth why anyone else should. I wonder if my letter will now start off a new chain of anxieties in you - please try not to see it in terms of my trying to map things out or tie you down - believe me, Roy, there can be few people on this earth who have discovered more painfully that people can only live in the way they want to, manipulation is destruction - these are just my thoughts today and I wanted to talk to you. I love you - whatever. Steffe xx*

She was right. Love me, love my children. So that I was determined to do. I went to a bookshop and really enjoyed looking through the books. I settled on *War and Peas* for Paul and *The Little Red Ant* for Joe.

THREE

I was visiting for more or less two weeks. Amazingly, the weather was glorious. It's a long drive to Hastings and it was evening by the time I arrived. The boys were staying overnight with David so we had time to connect. I knocked on the door which Steffe opened. It lead straight into her sitting room. I followed her and pushed the door to behind me. Immediately she held me, kissed me, and showed she wanted me so much. We made love, urgently. Things really were different.

It was an unusual house. Very narrow at the front but broadening out. The ground floor was all one, with a dining area and a kitchen. The garden was surprisingly large, dropping down from the house. There were little staircases leading up through the house. The attic was Steffe's bedroom, accessible only via a loft ladder with a hatch at the top. Going up there for the first time was exciting. It was plain, with a bed on the floor, a fairly ancient record player, candles but it felt like a sanctuary. That first night, we felt such joy. It was like we were in heaven.

Waking in the morning, we made love yet again and then slowly emerged to the reality of the new days. Of course I was nervous, we both were. The plan was to hide myself away when David delivered the boys. He would have reacted badly to my presence. They came, he went. Fortunately, I like young kids, I find them sweet and interesting. So I said hello, smiled and their response was really warm. It was so much easier than I expected. Paul was full of energy, Joe was quietly contemplative. They both had Steffe's dark brown eyes. They both carried her good looks. That was wonderful to see.

We slipped into play. I love the world of childhood, its magic, its playfulness, its conjuring of other worlds and characters, and I plunged into it. They brought to life something important in me.

But I was glad when bedtime came and I could be with my beloved on my own.

We went out every day. It was an easy walk from the house up to East Cliff and views down to the sea below. The Old Town was also nearby, a charming and interesting neighbourhood where many of Steffe's friends lived. Down to the beach and the old fishing huts and boats. Camber sands. Rye. Sitting in the garden in the evening as the sun set.

Maybe for the first time ever I felt truly relaxed and at ease. No longer was there a John or some shadowy other man. I felt an unequivocal love coming from Steffe. No longer was there imbalance between us, so evident when we were together before. No longer did our age difference matter. I had become a man. And I was discovering a new Steffe, or a much more aware Steffe. Perhaps in a way I was also getting to know Steffe properly, as a whole human being, for the first time.

We talked endlessly. That never stopped during the years ahead.

'It's been such a difficult year. My marriage to David was so bad. It really broke me. He now really hates me. Every time we have to meet, he's absolutely horrible to me. It's just impossible to talk to him. When he left last summer, I just felt so desperate, defeated, at sea. I knew I had to do something. Having psychotherapy has helped me begin to understand why I have acted as I have done over the years. One key thing that has come out is something that happened when I was just 3 years old. My family were all going off for a 3 week holiday in France. I was so excited but shortly before we were meant to leave, I became really ill, too ill to travel. So Mum, Dad, Anthea and Lindsay went and I stayed with my grandparents. I missed them so much and kept on asking my grandma how many days it was until their return. Finally the day came. I sat at the window, staring out onto the driveway, listening out for the crunching of their car's tyres on the gravel. I waited and waited but they didn't come. My grandma entered the room and told me they had been delayed and wouldn't be back until the next day. My heart contracted, my eyes welled up, I felt so abandoned. 'Now don't be silly, Stephanie, they'll be here tomorrow'. So I gulped back my pain and desolation, pushed it back down inside. I must 'not be silly'. When they came the next day, I ran into my mother's arms and squeezed her. 'I've missed you so much, Mummy'.

'Well, I'm here now. Let's get the car unpacked. Ah mother. How are you?'
That's an experience that I know now has really scarred me.

   Discovering this memory with Elizabeth was so upsetting, so powerful. I
relived the pain. I came to see how it shaped me. And there have been
other memories revived'.

   It was then she told me about Winnie

From Steffe's journal.

*The experience with Winnie - I loved her and I was so hurt
when I was told my love for her was wicked and disgusting
so I decided to kill my loving feminine side (because to
love a little girl was wrong) and so I became a boy.
I remember going to school that morning - I got there first
and in the classroom I made sure our desks were pushed
together like they always used to be. And waited
desperately anxiously for Winnie to arrive. When she did,
she quite firmly and in a determined way moved her desk
away - she didn't speak to me. My heart was in my mouth. I
tried to say something to her. I said 'Don't move your desk
away. We must stay close together because otherwise the
teachers will think we believe what they say, it'll prove that
we were wrong and they are right'. But she resolutely
moved away and not long afterwards she managed to
swap desks with another girl so she wasn't sitting next to
me at all. It seemed to me like a betrayal, as if she gone
over to the other side. She had abandoned me when they
told me I was wrong and wicked. When Miss Van de L had
told me off I had left thinking - I must find Winnie - when
she hears this she will agree with me that what we were
doing was not bad, she will be on my side. I couldn't
believe it when she left me. I kept hoping she would relent.*

We were cast as the Twins in Peter Pan - I thought at least this will keep us together. But she avoided me all the time - she may even have asked for the casting to be changed. But she wouldn't speak to me.

When we had games lessons after that, the other girls assumed we would want to be on the same team as usual - but Winnie always wanted to be on the other side. So it was as if each time someone new found out about it, it was a new wound, a fresh rejection. What Miss van der L had said to her must have had a terrific impact. I must have filled her with horror. Luckily I didn't realise that, I was just desperately upset because she hurt me so much. I still loved her - I remember she changed her hairstyle, her aunt wanted her to grow her fringe out and wear a slide. I felt even that took her away from me, made her look less like me.

She and her father used to live with her aunt and their family. She also had a little brother, Freddie.

I remember doing Peter Pan was torture - we had to run in holding hands - I think she may even have had that changed. And I hated Miss van de L. But I must have survived it quite well because after that episode. Probably after the summer holidays, I remember having lots of friends and more or less losing interest in Winnie. I know later on her father married again and Winnie hated her step-mother.

How did you feel when Miss van der L spoke to you?
I was shocked, I couldn't quite believe her. Most of all I wanted to find Winnie to make sure she still loved me, that she wasn't going to let this push us apart. So I was in a terrible state of suspense. I think I saw Winnie soon after the same day and she must have been horrible to me

otherwise I wouldn't have been so bothered about moving the desks together the next morning. I can't remember saying anything to Mama and Dada - perhaps I was ashamed to admit to them what had happened. I do remember how I felt when Miss V took the note from me - I think I knew right away that it would be misunderstood - because it was an intrusion into the privacy of the love Winnie and I shared which had nothing to do with the teachers. Certainly all the other teachers had always been very tolerant towards us, more amused than anything else. So how did I feel when I realised Winnie _had_ rejected me? Well, I didn't want to draw attention to myself so I tried not to fuss. I remember later that day, maybe the following day, the other girls talked about it in class - the room was quiet, we were probably meant to be doing some written work on our own and these two girls said in their clear little voices 'What's happened to Winnie and Steph?' 'Winnie's not talking to Steph any more'. 'Have they had a quarrel?' 'Winnie doesn't love her anymore'. All said in that slightly mocking tone - one people often use to describe emotional situations they are not involved in. I sat there, probably trying not to cry - I felt very wretched, dead, unhappy, for a long time. I think I spent a lot of time trying not to cry, trying not to let anyone see me crying. Every occasion like lunchtime or break time was an ordeal - at least in class during lessons one did not have to think about it, there was no attention drawn to the new difference in my life. But breaks and lunch were awful - it emphasised the new aloneness. Everything that belonged to Winnie was important to me - her peg in the cloakroom, her shoes, her clothes - she was very neat, she had a badge

for good posture, and she had a cousin in the class with
bright auburn hair.

And my love was denied - it was rejected and it was called
wicked, bad - and something else, a description I cannot
remember. Implying it was disgusting in some way. It was
as if Winnie had just gradually grown away from me - the
worst thing was that someone else, someone in the outside,
adult world, said it was wrong and she believed them. Not
only believed them, but was horrified at what she had been
told she had done, to the extent that she needed to
absolutely reject me positively - to the extent of being nasty
if necessary. She was very cruel. Perhaps it was something to
do with her mother having died - perhaps her pain at this
loss was turned on me. Because it was not a question of her
saying 'Oh, we'd better stop writing notes and playing this
game' - it was more that she hated me. She must have had
a very hard streak - or a very sensitive, painful area of
feeling that all this had touched. I felt she became less
pretty - after a while she did talk to me again, a little bit if
I asked her a question. I remember so well her fringe
growing out - it must have taken a long time, months, and
I loved her all the time.

So there was all this pain that I felt when I was seven years
old. I coped really bravely at the time. But by bottling up
and covering up my hurt, I killed a part of myself - the
part of myself which loved Winnie, a little seven year old
like me. Probably both of us needed to be loved - neither
of us had enough mother-love - perhaps as seven year
olds we were helping each other find lost little bits of
ourselves. But the attempt was condemned and we both
had to suffer rejection and denial of love. I wonder how
Winnie has developed?

But now I need to find the little seven year old and try to comfort her, maybe reassure her that Winnie would have continued to love her had it not been for the interference of a wicked, twisted teacher. Winnie did not reject me because I was not lovable. I continued to be just as lovable, and Winnie too - she must have been just as badly hurt in her own way. She didn't <u>stop</u> loving me, she was <u>told</u> not to love me. She was told that to love me was bad. It was nothing <u>I</u> had done. So there was no need to reject myself as a lovable little girl, and to try to pretend to be a tough, anonymous little boy instead. Because there was something in my little boy act - the pleasure in it was not being tough, but in being anonymous, unrecognised. If people thought I was a boy, they obviously didn't realise I was Stephanie - well, not the old Stephanie, the little, vulnerable girl - I didn't mind once I had found a new identity and became accepted into a new group of girls. Little seven year old Stephanie - I am so sorry Winnie doesn't love you anymore, I am sorry, it is so hard to bear. All we can do is understand that it is not for yourself that she doesn't love you - you haven't changed, you don't need to change. If you stay just as you are, someone else, lots of people, will love you because you are a lovable person, a lovable little girl - you are loving, you can give love.

Later

Think about how Winnie must have felt after being told her love for me was wrong. She would have had no-one to discuss it with as her mother was dead and I don't think she would have told her aunt, or been well understood if she did. She must have been really bewildered - and have blamed me for her unhappiness and confusion. So there's no need to see her behaviour as a personal rejection. She probably really needed my love and was very hurt at being

213

deprived of it. Also remember I was probably mentally older than she was and understood the situation better. She accepted what Miss V. told her. Have compassion for how Winnie must have felt - and if tears come for either of the little girls, try to sort out who you are weeping for. It is important to try to let the feelings come up again, because then you can feel compassion for the children and not allow the unfelt feelings, the unshed tears, keep you imprisoned in a situation which happened twenty five years ago.

It took a long time for Steffe to talk about this. Such a sad and profound story, showing her desire for love, her sensitivity, and just how brutal, almost perverted, adults can be to young children.

Just like in the past, Steffe was opening up new vistas for me. We talked about Jung, his ideas. We talked of the unconscious, the importance of dreams, the masculine and the feminine. She lead me back to my inner life.

'Steffie, you've mentioned the difficulties you have had with your animus. I'd really like you to explain what the animus is.'

'It was Jung who developed the idea of the animus and the anima. He said the animus is the unconscious masculine side of a woman, and the anima is the unconscious feminine side of a man. Because they are in the unconscious, they can operate on us in ways we don't recognise. With Elizabeth, and through dreams, I have come to begin to know and to understand my own animus. Of course, there is a light and a dark side to any animus, any anima. I have had a very bad connection with mine. I have come to realise that what I have done in the past I is transfer my animus image in my relationships with men. I have projected my animus onto my partner. I have now come to see my animus for what it is and begun to learn how to integrate it into myself, not seek to impose it on the man I am in a relationship with. So I can use the good aspects of the animus, the ability not to be overcome by the emotion and sensitivity that is a central characteristic of the feminine. I'm not boring you, am I?'

'God, no. It's really helping me to understand you and things more. Carry on'.

'It applies just as much to men. The man needs to understand and, be close to, his anima. So he can be intuitive, sensitive, creative, emotional. I reckon you have a very good relationship with yours. I've never met a man like you, to be honest. I really mean that'.

'And I have never met a woman like you. You don't know how much you have helped me become the man I am.'

FOUR

I began to read books Steffe suggested to me, Jung of course, but also books like 'The Moon and the Virgin', 'The Way of all Women', feminist books exploring the inner soul that opened my mind to different ways of seeing things.

It was such a lovely time. We spoke on the phone.

'You know, I realise I'm tired of living on my own. What I've realised is that being on my own was such a blessed relief after living with David, and then was exciting and challenging and gave me the space and time I needed. But since you stayed for a fortnight and I realised with amazement that two adults and two children could share the same living space without endless tensions and arguments and all attendant horrors, indeed that it could be relaxed, happy and easier as well as totally blissful – I don't like being on my own so much.'

Brief extracts from a letter to Steffe

My darling Steffe,

…. Our two weeks together were so lovely – and thank you for being you. I think I know you far more now than I have ever done in the past and as a result my love has grown and deepened….

…But I'm still unsure as to whether I have dealt with all my major problems…. I suppose my biggest fear is that I haven't freed myself of my past possessiveness and tendency to jealousy (which presumably grow from insecurity). Don't get me wrong – I _feel_ very secure and

216

I _feel_ free of possessiveness and jealousy (why on earth should I feel either of them!) but I'm always afraid they may leap out at me – I suppose it's my memory of the past that induces that fear. That's why I continue to call them 'vulnerable areas'. I hope you never test them too much.

..... give my love to dear Paul and Joe and wish them well. As for you, remember I love you enormously.

Full sail,

Roy xxx

'Full sail.' A reference to the Beach Boys song that we played so much, as we did the album LA (Light Album). So emotional, so powerful, so optimistic. And I was hinting at anxieties, at this stage not really defined. We spent another weekend together, but then I fell really ill. My mood, my thoughts, which had been so high and positive, collapsed.

I wrote:

My darling Steffe,

I'm leaning against my bed, an old Santana album is playing, Moroccan smoke hangs in the air, a bottle of wine is open and I feel wonderful.

..... But I wasn't feeling peaceful a couple of weeks ago..... It was all sparked off by my illness. Being on my own for several days on end and feeling that confusion that accompanies fever, my mind travelled to dark places.....

I suffered from the depression of feverish lassitude. It was then, out of my unconscious, I was hit by the memory of losing you before and all the pain that surrounded it. As the memory filled my mind, I, in my state of weakness (feeling intensely the physical distance separating us) suddenly felt fear — fear of losing you again. At times of high fever, as I floated in that strange dream-like state between the worlds of the conscious and the unconscious, all sorts of memories floated before my eyes — the memory of the pain I felt when you told me shortly after Christmas 1975 when we were (sort of) living together that you had slept with someone else was one of them. And then I recalled you saying a few weeks ago that you thought you were 'a bit promiscuous' — other phrases then came to mind. And I felt black. I started to get scared and confused by my own thoughts, taken aback.

As I returned to health, the thoughts all dissipated but I knew they had to be faced up to. They disclosed an anxiety.

My fear of losing you, of you being unfaithful, took me back and worried me. Did I really feel insecure and distrustful? It shook my confidence in myself. I thought I had grown up, cast such feelings aside. Was my strength all a delusion? I actually don't think so.

I travelled back to our past. I was struck by how acutely insecure I felt throughout our time together before. The fact that you stuck with John (and loved him) for so much of the time we were together before did affect me profoundly (and of course you were the first love of my life). I was forced to realise that I couldn't give you all you needed (I didn't really know what you needed) and yet I so wanted you to choose me as your only. And so I felt insecure. From the insecurity grew a jealously of John — yet it was a jealousy that I felt was illegitimate and so I always tried to suppress it. And I was always aware you were sleeping with someone else. That always hurt. I always felt a bit of a lesser person. I got confused — and incredibly touchy and moody. I was always looking for your love and approval and would withdraw into my shell if you spoke warmly about your life away from me. So I didn't recognise or respond to your needs. I guess my love became selfish. I know how unsupportive I was in some ways. What is amazing, looking back, is that despite this, despite the problems you had, we just couldn't bear to be apart. But when we finally lived together, I still carried the consciousness of there being another. I became desperately scared of losing what had taken so long to achieve (that was why I so hated you taking the job at

Roma for it meant that, once again, you were gone —
and so gradually the job exacerbated the problem). I
became ever more possessive, ever more afraid of some
vague person taking you away from me.......
Dwelling on all this makes me realise that any present
insecurity derives purely from my memory of the past.
It's bound to rear its head from time to time. Please be
tolerant. For the fact is I feel so sure about us. I feel safe
in your love and know my love is absolute. But I
wanted to share my thoughts. Let us always be open
with each other.
All my love,
Roy xxx

We spoke on the phone afterwards.
'Roy, I really do need to say that it's not at all about me 'just wanting a
man'. I've been afraid you might think this. It's you I want and love. I really
believe we can be a happy family and I mean permanently'.
*

We had another weekend together. I was keeping my own notebook by
this time. I wrote afterwards on Sunday 11 October 1981:

This weekend has really made me aware of Steffe's
vulnerability and dependence — and her sensitivity. I
never understood this before — I was always the junior
partner, the 'hurt' party requiring care. And so I gave
very little care to her myself — in that sense I was no

220

strength to Steffe at all. She couldn't get simple warmth and understanding when she needed it. If she was hurt, confused or down, I would take it personally – and withdraw expecting her (trying to force her) to come across to me. So I was demanding affection and being selfishly dependent. And further (and this blinded me to Steffe's need for support and love) I almost made her super-human in my consciousness – I really did put her on a pedestal. So there were so many things I didn't give her. But what I always gave her, and she gave me, was love and connection at the most profound level. Before our relationship never existed in the day-to-day world – even when we lived together. Things felt very different now. I had changed, Steffe had changed.

When Steffe was plummeting this afternoon, and I thought she was going to burst into tears, she spoke of how painful life had been with David – before she had described this, but only superficially– today she communicated the pain and isolation, the lovelessness and abuse, very directly. She has suffered – I can so see that. It breaks my heart. I am so full of praise for the way in which she has picked herself up – and this is where Steffe is strong and impressive. She is very vulnerable and sensitive – easily hurt – but she has *such awareness and determination to know herself, to grow and develop. I want to give her the undying love she needs to make her heart and soul warm and comfortable so she can flower – and stop being so hard on herself which she constantly is.*

As I write, tears stream down my face. My poor love. I feel such all-embracing love for her.

..... Steffe said she was afraid of failing me – she obviously thinks I am looking at her with a test-card in my hand and that if she acts in a certain way I will think less of her. But I am now seeing her as a whole person....

Steffe said on Saturday night when we were in bed: 'I so love making love to you. I give myself completely to you. You are the only person to whom I have'.

Steffe held back from telling me the details of the abuse she suffered. Maybe she felt ashamed. Maybe she hated herself for putting herself into that situation in the first place. 'I had made my bed, I had to lie in it'. I was always puzzled by the fact that, feminist as she was, and finding any sort of violence terrifying, she never took any action. Told no one about it. Never seemed to contemplate ringing the police or seeing a lawyer. From my own domestic violence practice, I knew that women normally only came to me as a last resort but I guess I attributed that in part to their class, the culture of 'sticking by your man', the lack of consciousness of the women's movement. But Steffe was highly intelligent, in my experience very determined, acutely aware of issues of gender and inequality. Yet she did nothing. Only later did I come to understand that domestic violence occurs in every class.

I never asked her why she remained silent because I knew it would be too painful for her, too inquisitorial. I didn't want to humiliate her. She carried enough pain and feelings of guilt and inadequacy. I just felt so unspeakably sorry for her.

It made me very determined to attempt to help her get over the trauma, though I don't think she ever really did. Also I knew that I had a big part to play in our original separation. I did not feel guilty about that but I did feel I had a responsibility, that the burden wasn't hers alone. So I didn't poke around raising questions, I just accepted that it had been awful for her, and that the best I could do was simply to love her and support her.

Sadly, David continued to be difficult, indeed horrible, to Steffe. So although they were divorced, it was not possible for her to put the trauma behind her since there were constant echoes of it in the present.
One thing was certain, and rightly so. We would try to do everything possible to protect the boys and allow their relationship with David to continue, whatever the provocations. But that wasn't always easy though we did our very best.

*

As time passed, my visits to Hastings increased to the point where I was going down most weekends, though there was a second visit to Bristol.

At the time, I was now working hard on opening up an office in St Pauls. This meant not only finding premises but making contacts so that there was a potential client base. I really wanted to show Steffe the area in which I would be working so I drove her around and then pulled up in front of a house on the 'Front Line', just yards away from the legendary Black and White café on Grosvenor Road.

'I'm going to take you to see a new friend of mine, Saul, and his wife, Louise. Come on! It will be interesting for you'.

I knocked on the door. Louise opened it and welcomed us in. We were met by a room full of ganja smoke and a smiling Saul sitting on the sofa. He spoke in his rich Jamaican patois, warmly welcoming the two of us.

Louise made some tea and we chatted. Steffe said virtually nothing though spoke a bit to Louise.

On getting back into the car, Steffe said 'How could you understand what Saul was saying? Do you speak his language?'

I really laughed. 'No, that was really pure patois, Jamaican English. To be honest, I could only understand about 40% of what he said but I'm getting better. What did you think of Louise?'

'She seemed really nice. Friendly.'

'I bet that's the first prostitute you've met'.

'What?'

'Well, not now. But I know she worked on the streets for many years. I find it all so interesting. They are both wonderful characters. I've grown very fond of them'.

'So this is where you are going to be working?'

'Well, if all goes to plan. St Pauls is a very disadvantaged community. And there are burning issues as regards race and the police. That's why I want to work here. To be a real radical lawyer. I've been getting out the message to activists and community workers'.

I was so proud of what I was now doing and loved sharing it all with her.

'I cannot tell you how thrilled I am for you.' she said.

*

My darling Roy,

It has crossed my mind many times when we have talked, particularly on the phone, and you have said how happy you are, that there is a real lack of connection between us – somehow I feel I ought to be feeling the same, and feel almost guilty because I can't. Tonight it has struck me terribly and terrifyingly forcibly why there is this lack of congruence which I feel in itself puts you at a distance from me in this respect – not that I would want you to descend to the way I feel and fear, I only want it to be the other way round. But simply you believe in a future for us and I don't. I mean that in the most stupid and fatalistic

224

possible way - that I am convinced this dream of joy will be snatched away - I don't believe it will ever be reality. It is all such a fairy-tale, it has all transpired too perfectly, my unhappy marriage and subsequent divorce, you 'waiting' for me in a sense, and all that we have found together since - it is too perfect, and I don't believe I am going to be permitted such perfection. I deeply believe that something is going to happen to prevent it. I suppose it has something to do with the awfulness of reality as I have found it since I 'grew up' - since having children and finding that I was no longer a spoilt little girl who could have everything her own way - I came to terms so absolutely with the realisation that life was in fact pretty much a struggle, that there was no reason for me to expect it to be 'good', it is really just a series of experiences that have to be lived through and learned from and that some of these experiences will appear to be insuperably hard but one lives through them and carries on - I had just learned all that and really come to terms with it, my absolute aloneness which I felt was my destiny - and like a man clutching at straws I rang you up - just to find contact with someone, I really did expect you to be married or at least involved, in a sense I think I was also trying to burn another boat, to continue all these ghastly clichés, I had to be absolutely certain I was absolutely alone, that I was on the bottom and from there could push myself up again, but in a different way, looking for happiness in different ways, different happiness. And then this fairy-tale began - and I don't believe in it, Roy. I love you desperately, I do absolutely and honestly know that I always loved you, and that I will always love you. And equally I absolutely believe in your love for me. But something is going to prevent it, I

225

know it for a certainty. It has something to do with the children, since if I didn't have the children, we wouldn't be forced to live apart now. Either there will be a catastrophe or, even more likely, I am going to be confronted with a choice, you or the children. Whatever form it comes in, I don't believe we will ever live in Bristol together. It is too beautiful a dream, and dreams like that don't come true. I feel in agony, all I can think of is how I must carry on and cope after the dream has been shattered.

Why do I feel this so strongly, Roy? I terrify myself, I punish myself with unhappiness and despair about something that hasn't even happened. I so long to see you - and yet your rationality terrifies me, your realism is a reminder of the reality I am afraid of. Well, I will see you soon - hopefully this ridiculous mood will have passed.

All my love, for ever, Steffe xxx

Poor Steffe. She paid a very high price for what happened back in 1976. I will do everything I can to give her back her confidence in life.

*

Our first row was very painful for us both. It was on the last Saturday of November. For different reasons, both of us were in rather low spirits. When we finally made our way up to bed, I just wanted to bury myself in love-making. But Steffe, for the first time since we had been back together, just wanted to go to sleep. I grudgingly went along with this. But lying in bed, I kept tossing and turning and finally Steffe protested that I should stop keeping her awake.

'For God's sake, Roy. I just want to be left alone. Can't you just get that?'

'Why are you being so heavy?'

'Sometimes, you are just too demanding'.

'Oh yeah? And I suppose you're not. You don't exactly hold back when you want me to come to you or help you'.

'Oh, so I'm selfish, am I?'

'Well, you seem to want it your way'.

From there, it degenerated. It became frighteningly fierce. Later, we both recognised just how we had been acting. Steffe was being the little girl, stamping her foot and letting out all the frustrations she felt about life. As for me, it all brought back the memory of pain and of being, as I felt it, misunderstood. I did not recognise that the little girl was in control. Instead, I became defensive and in my defence, I attacked. I also drifted into a moan about my own dissatisfactions and projected them onto Steffe. We ended up each looking to the other to be the saviour and both of us proved absolutely incapable of responding to the other. It almost seemed we were hating each other, whilst both being in despair, knowing how strong and important our love was to each other.

It was a wake-up call. We talked it through. Steffe rightly said that when something like this happens, it should be understood that if one of us goes off to be alone (which perhaps she had suggested doing), it should not be interpreted as rejection – that in a situation like that, it is best to be on your own so you can restore an equilibrium, understand the dynamics of the situation apart from each other. I really took this on board.

And I had to recognise my responsibility. My tossing and turning had been a protest, I was not respecting Steffe's own feelings, I was being selfish. And when she reacted, I was defensive, frightened and then nasty. We were both very kind to each other the next day.

*

But I realised I could get angry. It is a demon I have had to grapple with all my life. I hate it when I am overcome by it, it makes me feel I am not in control, I say nasty things I regret. Where does it come from?

FIVE

Our weekends continued full of conversation. I was to meet her father.

'I'm sure he'll like you. You're middle-class, privately educated, well-spoken, a lawyer. And I've warned him to keep off politics. But basically, he's an old fascist'.

'So how do you feel about him?'

'I rather despise him. He was just vile towards Lindsay. He resented him. He went off to the war and there was only my mother, Molly. When he came back, there was this little boy, so close to Molly, and Dad felt he was in the way. There were terrible scenes. My father would watch everything Lindsay did at meal-times. Lindsay was always a nervous boy and my father would chastise him for not eating enough, or for being quiet, or for anything. It became so bad. My father would literally strike Lindsay. There were awful fights'.

'So how did your Mum react?.

'She just stood by'.

'That's awful.'

'I don't think she knew what to do'.

'But didn't she say anything?'

'Not really. I so hated it. I used to try and separate them. Anthea just used to go away and lock herself in her room'.

'I have to say I find your mother's reaction pretty dreadful'.

'I don't think she knew what to do'.

'I don't find that convincing. Of course she could have done something'.

As we talked on I was struck by how defensive of her mother Steffe was. What also now became apparent was just how badly affected Steffe was by her mother's death. It happened very suddenly in July 1976, not long after we split up when she was pregnant. Strangely the truth of just how ill Molly was, how she was riddled with cancer, was kept from Steffe 'so as not to upset her'. So Steffe not only carried the pain of her mother's death but also a feeling of guilt for not having been with her mother enough in the few weeks it took for Molly to die. Now it seemed as if Steffe put her mother on something of a pedestal. She didn't like me criticising Molly.

Yet she recorded this dream she had:

I was terribly unhappy about something and I kept trying to tell my mother about it. But every time we sat down to talk she would read the newspaper. I was getting more and more upset. If we did talk for a little while, she would wait for the first little break in my talking and then try to read the newspaper again. So eventually I said to her 'You keep coming into the room, taking the newspaper off the chair, sitting down and then instead of talking to me, you read the newspaper'. She said in reply 'Has it ever occurred to you that what I might be wanting to do is read the newspaper?' I said no that one automatically picks up a newspaper, whether one wants to read it or not. 'Well, I want to read mine', she replied. I felt this great knot of unhappiness in my chest, I could almost see it, like a great black ball, and I shouted at my mother 'I hate you, I hate you, I keep wanting to love you but you have no love in you at all'. She shrugged and turned away.

As a comment, Steffe wrote:

It is a good thing I can be angry with my mother's animus – I must reject it. It is not my animus and it is not good for me.

I became ever more aware that poor Steffe felt she lacked mother love when she was a young child. I had always been puzzled by the fact that Steffe had seemed unable *not* to be in a relationship, that when we split

229

up, instead of taking a breath, thinking about things, she immediately immersed herself in someone else. Now I began to understand that Steffe had constantly been in search of the love that she was denied by her mother and couldn't bear to be on her own. And then there was the Winnie trauma. But the basic scar was what happened when she was three, when her family went to France, when her mother and father came back a day late.

*

From Steffe's journal

Little girl, I so want to help you and reassure you. You were panicking and there was no-one there to comfort you. But I am back with you now, and I won't leave you again, I will try very hard to be here when you need me. Roy came to see us which was lovely, and I know now that I was leaning on him too much and so were you, my little three year old, which is fine when you are three but not thirty three, as I am. So now I will support you and give you the comfort and security you need. When you next feel anxious and upset and bewildered, I will be there beside you, and I won't be cross with you for feeling like that. And I won't try to push you away, or let you make decisions, because that's not fair, is it, little one, you are too little, you just have your great big needs and great big feelings and it's too hard to sort them out, and you just stand there, frightened and bewildered and scared and needing your Mama, but now she is here with you, and she understands that a little three year old needs someone beside her all the time, to help her through all these big feelings and needs, and take those decisions for you, because she is thirty three and strong enough. And I know how good life can be and how lucky I am to have such a wonderful friend in Roy, and Roy believes in us utterly and is not cross or frightened when the little three year old emerges, because he believes the thirty three year old is in charge, and wants to win through and has strength and determination. And I know he is right. And I know that I don't need to lean on him, that it doesn't make me feel good - what makes me feel good is to feel strong. I can't love him properly when the three year old is in charge. A three year old can't love as a woman loves a lover, she can only love as a little girl loves her Mummy and Daddy who fill her horizon and satisfy so many needs in her. She can make endless demands on them, and they will satisfy them, because she is three and cannot be expected to be independent, she must need people. But thirty three years olds can't need and demand in the same way and find adult love coming back. I know that and I felt it this weekend. I can't experience the real joy of love with Roy until I feel strong and grown myself - as I felt a couple of weeks ago - well, mostly! And like the good mother in me, Roy won't reject the three year old but he'll wait for her to be sorted out so that she can return to him a grown woman. I do believe in us, I do believe in Roy and I, and I know that if I work I will make the dream come true, because it isn't just a dream, it's a real intention; but if I don't work, I may try to let the dream slip through my fingers.

*

My sweet darling,
It's now three days since we were together and I've adapted to being on my own again, to living my life without you, to not holding your warm, soft body

231

through the night, to not experiencing the uniting of our bodies and souls in love, to not emerging of a morning into the world of wakefulness with you — I've adapted to all that, but I so don't want to. I feel something fundamental is missing.

It is true, as you have hinted at, that our constant separations between our times together, times when we give each other so completely to one another, when we feel so totally at one, can feel disturbing. When we part, I feel dreadfully open, as if cold air were rushing in where previously there had only been warmth and intimacy. I used to feel this when we were lovers — we seemed always to be separating. Over the years, it affected me, I felt rather battered and unsure. This increased the feeling of insecurity I felt any rate by virtue of the situation, and that insecurity led to feelings of possessiveness and jealousy. Things are completely different now but even so our separations can spark residual feelings of possessiveness, which I am uncomfortable about.........

You did say at the weekend that you thought I was rather possessive. We were talking, I think, in the context of the children and in response I said I did not think I was. And that is true as far as the children are concerned; I understand and accept their needs, even though I may at times wish those needs weren't quite so demanding! But I do recognise that, even now, I can feel possessive about you. And I am not comfortable with that. Is it just because we spend so much time apart and so will go when we finally live together? I am not in truth sure. And that is when I get a bit worried.

I don't want ever to be possessive because it can be so destructive. I don't like it when I do feel possessive. It makes me crabby, it feels uncomfortable, it harms our relationship. And, of course, it was what blew our relationship before. So I am determined to overcome it. It's something I've tried to work on for years and I do feel I have made real progress. I think I understand something of its dynamics. In truth, I thought I was free of it. But I am not sure I fully am.

Perhaps I am still not able to fully forget the past, or rather, be unaffected by my memories of that past – even though I am absolutely certain of your love for me.

I will continue to work on myself but I would ask for your understanding, not resentment, if it sometimes rears its head, if I ever act stupidly. Believe me, no one could dislike it more than me. I recognise that at times

I do seek reassurance of your love more than is necessary — it's silly but it happens.

My darling, it's because I have such faith in you that I feel I can be frank with you now. It's just that I couldn't bear to lose you again.....

I love you, Steffie, I love you.

Roy

Xxx

It was good that Steffe continued with her therapy because it helped me to look into myself. I was beginning to see that underlying it all was a deeper fear, a fear that went back a long way. A fear of suddenly losing love, of being abandoned, of pain. One weekend, I talked to Steffe about it.

'You know, the way you've identified events in your childhood that have fundamentally affected you — well, it's really led me to think about my own childhood. My Mum may have been quite hopeless at dealing with me as I grew into adulthood, but she was wonderful when I was a child. She gave me so much love and I loved her dearly. I really think that love was a precious gift. Which meant when it was taken away, I collapsed'.

'Why? What happened?'

'It's strange I've never told you. Perhaps that's because for so long, I felt rather ashamed of myself, I felt I was weak. I went to this prep school that was closely linked to a Quaker public school no more than a mile away. Many of my friends and fellow classmates were going there. But something happened which I didn't understand at the time. When I was leaving, the headmaster said 'If you weren't leaving now, I would be demanding you left'. I was shocked. I had been Head of House. His venom was extraordinary. Afterwards, I decided he had found out that a number of us were indulging in mutual masturbation and sexual exploration. His son was one of them. Did he see me as a leader in this? It was horrible.

234

But only then did I fully grasp what my future held for me. I was being sent, as a boarder, to King's College, Taunton. Miles away. It transpired that my headmaster had made it clear to my innocent parents that this was the right place for me. It's clear that he wanted to punish me. I so remember being taken there. The journey in the car lasted for such a long time. They drove into the school. We were rather anonymously met and directed to my house and dormitory. We carried inside my trunk, with my name inked onto the top, and my tuck box, again with my name inked on. We went up some stairs and into the dormitory. We were directed to a group of four beds, partially separated by wooden dividers from the many other beds in the dormitory. I will never forget the smell of fresh, clean wood, but it wasn't pleasant. It felt alien. We unpacked my stuff into the nearby cupboard and drawers. Everything as regards clothes was regimented. My mother had been conscientious in complying with the clothing list. There were no casual clothes at all.

It was then time for them to leave. I can recall so clearly seeing their car drive away. My eyes welled up and tears ran down my face. Gosh, Steffe, this is pretty painful to relate'.

We were sitting at her dining table and, like years before, she reached across and rested her hand on mine.

'I love you, Roy. Carry on'.

'Oh, Steffie, it was so terrible. I remember that first night lying in bed, riven by fear and acute homesickness. This seemed such an alien world. Earlier that evening, the new boys had been called into the housemaster's study. He was far from welcoming and instead read out basic rules. This included him saying that homosexuality was sinful and utterly unacceptable. Was this why my prep school headmaster had sent me here?

I slept fitfully. We were awoken and I nervously put on my uniform and went for breakfast. Why did it seem as if all the other boys were taking it all in their stride?

Classes were very formal, all masters, all wearing gowns. It felt Dickensian. I was afraid of the prefects and found myself calling them

235

'sir'. And I talked to no one and no one talked to me. Day after day, I was locked inside my head. I felt so lost, so abandoned. I missed my home, its warmth, its love, I missed my Mum.

It came to the point when the only time I felt some peace was when we went to chapel. It genuinely gave me some sustenance. But when the service ended, I was back on my own. I remember watching a film on a Saturday night and even that only mildly distracted me – even though it was Hitchcock's North by North West.

I became desperate and managed to claim sickness and entry into the sickness ward. It was a profound relief. Peace. But I couldn't stay there forever. So I decided to escape. The sick block was right by the main road passing the school. There was a front door giving onto a short drive and an open exit. So one morning, when all was quiet, I put on my uniform, left my sick bay, crept down the stairs, desperately fearing discovery, opened the front door and ran to the exit.

Now what? Of course, I had no plan and no money. I walked away from the school towards the city centre. I kept looking around, scared of capture. I hid behind walls. I felt like a fugitive. So I found a phone box, got through to the operator, and asked for a reverse call charge to Bracknell 3440, my parents' number. My Mum answered, immediately sounding anxious.

'Mum, I can't stand it. I just can't. I've run away. I can't go back there. Please just come and fetch me'.

My Mum was lovely but said I needed to go to a police station so they would know where to pick you up.

'But they'll take me back to the school. No.'

'I will tell them not to. We will pick you up'.

I was in the event picked up by two constables. They were very kind and reassuring. So I sat in the police station feeling ashamed, pathetic and also relieved. It took hours but at last they came and back home we went. It felt so comforting. We didn't talk much.

I really did feel ill and retreated to my bed. I stayed there for days. I tried to explain to my parents just what it was like, how I felt, and yet I am not sure I was able properly to articulate my despair. After two weeks, I was sent back but the school, in conversation with my parents, said I could stay in the house of a master and his wife. This, of course, only deepened my loneliness and isolation.

Then things came to a head. The house I was lodged in was large and old. There was a wide, creaky wooden staircase leading up from the centre of the large hallway. There were lots of rooms upstairs and downstairs. One night, the master and his wife said they were going out so I was left on my own in the house. I lay in bed and kept hearing things. I became more and more terrified. By the time they got back, I was beside myself. I rang my parents the next day and they were horrified. They came and fetched me and I never returned to that dreadful place.
But something profound and damaging had happened. I was a mere shadow of my former self, broken, ashamed, wretched. I now wonder if my fear of suddenly losing love, your love, goes back to that traumatic time, when I was taken from a place of love to a place of coldness overnight. I also think it has contributed to my life long suspicion of authority'.

I finally finished. We talked on a bit and then Steffe said 'let's go to bed, my love'.

We climbed the ladder to her attic bedroom and she put on one of our special tracks, *Only with you* from the Beach Boys' album *Holland*.

*

Just before Christmas, Steffe said on the phone:

'I feel I have been waiting ten years, almost all my life, for what we now have. You know, you said a while ago that screwing someone else would be like sacrilege. That's exactly how I feel'.

She came to visit me over the Christmas break whilst the boys were with David. I had really enjoyed getting her presents. I looked until I found things that appealed. In a modern gallery, I bought a piece of modern jewellery, a brooch replicating a kite, made of what appeared to be very high quality thick plastic, upon which colours had been superimposed, and from which dropped two thin plastic tails, with tiny triangles of coloured plastic attached. In a Bath antiques market, I found a beautiful watch fob, silver with a green stone on one side and a brown one on the other. So it could be worn, I also bought a silver chain. In a Peruvian shop, I fell in love with a multicoloured woollen scarf. And of course, I got some music.

I so loved giving these presents to Steffie. She was so touched, affected and moved. Later, I found out that David had never marked birthdays or Christmas with any gift to her beyond some flowers from the local garage. Those two or three days we spent together in Bristol were so special.

A little later I went down to Hastings. Afterwards, Steffe wrote:

My sweet love,
Here are your notes. Even looking at your handwriting makes my heart melt. This is a severe case of love. Thank you for ringing this morning, I was feeling very flat and sad, I did want to hear your dear voice.
Oh love, I miss you. It is now a beautiful sunny day here. It snowed last night so there is a lovely fresh whiteness everywhere.
My darling
Steffe x

SIX

I had been dreaming vividly and noting them down.

- I arrived at my St Pauls office at about 6.30 pm. As I unlocked the front door, I saw two young men sitting on chairs in the reception area. I entered and went behind the reception desk. I looked at the two men, one of whom had a beard, and asked who they were. They said they were from Christian Aid and therefore I assumed they were seeking money for their charity. But I was surprised that they had been inside my locked office and I asked them how they had got in. They said from the first floor. Then they both got up together and approached me. I suddenly realised they intended to rape me. It freaked me out but I did not feel overwhelmed with fear – instead I ran out of the office without panicking and escaped.
- I was travelling in a transit van across St Pauls being driven by a long haired young man. He was driving crazily but I was not scared. We stopped and got out. Some young guys were lying on a nearby grassy bank smoking joints.

Suddenly I realised that the driver of the van was on acid. He was speaking nonsense. I then realised what a risk I had taken travelling in his van.

- I was back in the St Pauls office. It was dark. I was with my best friend's wife and her sister. I looked out of the window onto an area of grass. I saw their mother sitting cross-legged on the ground. She was bathed in white light. She was quite still. At first she was clothed, then unclothed. I left the office and walked up to her. She now wore a white robe. I sat on her left and assumed the same position as her.

I commented:

All the people in the first two dreams are male — do they represent parts of the masculine side of me? All the people in my last dream are female — aspects of my anima? The males are all unknown to me, the females are all known. What do the two rapists represent? Something nasty masquerading as kind? They were evil claiming to be from Christian Aid, i.e. good. They represent destruction — rape is a splitting apart. Does it mean that there is something in my psyche that could be destructive to the point of splitting Steffe and me

*apart? In the second dream, the driver of the van is
(initially unknown to me) under the influence of acid.
On acid, you are out of control. So do these dreams
recognise the destructive dark side of myself and tell
me that they will only be dangerous if I am not in
control, if I am driven by it? The last dream seems to
represent a route out and away. Here I am meeting
aspects of my anima. The mother was imbued with
Sufism and was a deeply spiritual and unusual person.
So she represents to me meditation, calmness,
understanding. It was there I found peace.*

I found it uncomfortable realising that there was an anger that I knew lurked within me and would, over the years ahead, sometimes rear its head. It wasn't until I had psychotherapy in my 60's that I discovered a key experience from my childhood that went a long way to explaining it.

10 January 1982

Back from a weekend in Hastings. When we made love, it reached a new height of intensity and emotion. Steffe said 'I feel that we are one body, that your body is mine, my body is yours. It was always beautiful. Now I see it as holy'.

I gloried in the fact that we were now relating to one another with an intimate mutual understanding of each other, with no barriers, no defences. And that we had such similar approaches to life and the world, politically, spiritually, intellectually , aesthetically. It meant discussions were genuinely exploratory, with basic values and approaches agreed.

And we could talk! Beyond all else, perhaps, I realised that we had such respect for each other and we had found true balance in our relationship. But …. And this is hard. Despite everything, I felt that there was something lurking in the back of my head. Dark and sinister. Still a doubt. It was trust. I still had moments of realising I still had 'trust issues'.

*

From Roy's journal
Monday 18 January

Why am I feeling so angry? I rang up Steffe at 9.20 and she said, rather coldly, 'We're still busy' – she was seeing a client called Nigel. Getting off the phone, I kicked my fire in rage and broke part of it. Why do I feel so jealous, so untrusting? Steffe said yesterday, again, that the one thing she is worried about in me is my possessiveness – and I agree. I _am_ possessive. I almost feel at times I just cannot handle a close relationship because I can't stand the feelings of jealousy and suspicion from which I suffer at times. Why am I letting Steffe's long session with Nigel upset me so? Is it that I am afraid they will get it on? No, that's stupid. Is it that I fear the intimacy – particularly as it's going on in Steffe's house? I think so – then why? Is it that I'm seeking in a woman the total devotion that my mother showed me when I was young? I must find the reason.

*

I wrote this about two hours ago. I had a long telephone conversation with Steffe. I completely disguised my feelings of anger that in any event had dissipated within ten minutes. Thank God, I managed to quell my anger, put it into a box. But it disturbs me so much. What I can't work out is how far my fear and insecurity derives from what happened between us before and how much it's something much deeper. Does it derive from my mother being too doting? Does it come from the trauma I experienced at King's Taunton? I know how deeply in love with me Steffe is. It sometimes makes me wonder if I am so honest in my love. I am devoted to her, I love her absolutely. But is my devotion in part an aspect of my possessiveness, rather than my love? Is my understanding and sympathy for her pain and suffering 100% genuine? I sometimes worry about my authenticity. But it's good that I am questioning everything.

Despite me going down to Hastings many weekends, the writing continued.

Dear Roy,
...... I was telling you earlier on the phone about the memory (buried until recently) of pain that I was too young to cope with at the time and keeps bursting out at inappropriate moments and driving me into situations

*where the fear of pain makes me do things despite myself.
So I have always looked for relationships where there was
no possibility of permanent happiness because the fear of
the pain made me summon up pain-cheating situations so
I could foresee and be prepared for inevitable suffering -
do you follow? And of course that leaves me unable to
really feel true happiness and satisfaction because those
situations are too dangerous - because they might be
followed by pain….So I could cope with my feelings for you
because I was married and when I became free, I became
afraid again - and this is what I don't want to repeat.
And my very fear of reproducing it could reproduce it.
So the struggle continues - and I long to see you again.
My love Steffe xxx*

*

I was learning so much more about Steffe. She would talk about her
family and what it was like when she was a little girl.
She wrote in her journal:

*Once upon a time there was a little girl called Feffie. She
lived with her brother and sister and Mama and Dada in
a big house near the sea. She was the youngest of the
children and so she was often called 'the baby of the
family'. She was rather spoilt and often used to get her own
way, and was her Daddy's pet. This used to annoy her
brother and sister, so when her Mama and Dada were out,
they used to tease her mercilessly until she cried and
screamed 'It's not fair, it's not fair'. She would get herself
into a real rage of fear and frustration and her brother
and sister would be delighted.
At other times she was able to go out alone with her Dada
and visit his family. She would sit on his knee while
everyone admired her. 'So this is your youngest?' they*

244

would ask. 'Oh, yes, she's the baby of the family', her Dada would say and she knew he was very proud of her. 'I bet you spoil her', the relatives would say. Although it was nice to have people admiring her for a change, Feffie used to feel rather uncomfortable about all this, because she didn't really like being the baby, and she knew it was bad to be spoilt. She knew that though the grown-ups might be smiling and admiring, it was not for nice reasons. Yet it was nice to be admired. It was all a bit confusing. Her cousins used to tease her about being spoilt as well, although she used to think they were a lot worse than she was and she knew then that they were just copying the older ones. Still, it was not nice, it hurt her - and yet she wasn't sure what the spoiling was all about. She knew she was Dada' pet, but not Mama's, and certainly the rewards were not worth the teasing and dislike from the other children, She couldn't remember ever having <u>been</u> particularly spoilt.

The only time she felt truly good and admirable was when she was dancing. Sometimes, when her own class was over, she would stand at the back while her elder sister had her class. Often she would try to copy the steps they were doing, as it was boring just watching. Once the teacher, Miss Webb, stopped the class and told the other girls to watch her, Feffie, while she did the Pas de Chat. Feffie felt awful, she knew the older girls would hate being told that Feffie was better than they were, so she deliberately did it badly, and Miss Webb was cross and so was Mama. After that Feffie was more careful about being noticed at dance class. Instead, she used to dance at home in front of the big mirror in the hall - but she didn't like it if anyone saw. She liked it best when she was alone - then she would watch herself in the

mirror. But even then she got into trouble - her brother
and sister used to tell her she was vain. She couldn't really
do anything else.

Sometimes, when she was having her hair brushed in front
of the mirror (her hair was long and curly and got quite
tangled) she would think she looked very pretty and she
knew some of the grown-ups thought so too. But she sucked
her thumb and everyone told her that she would ruin her
mouth and make her teeth stick out like piano keys and so
she used to look at her mouth and it did look a bit funny.
Anyway her brother and sister said it was vain and bad to
look in the mirror and they didn't think she was pretty so
that didn't feel very good.

Sucking her thumb was lovely. She had a card, a piece of
material with a selvage, that she used to wrap around her
fingers. It wasn't allowed and everyone used to go on at
her all the time, but she could do it in bed, in the dark, in
peace and it was lovely. And yet she knew that to suck her
thumb was bad too.

Most of the time Feffie and her sister were enemies. When
they played with the cousins, Feffie paired off with Muffet
and Anthea paired off with Richard, and they played cops
and robbers or cowboys and Indians. Muffet was the
smallest, prettiest and sweetest, so Feffie never felt very good
beside her. When Anthea and Feffie were at home, Anthea
had a friend called Ann. She was invisible but wonderful
and sometimes Anthea would tell Feffie about her.
Sometimes Anthea would play with Feffie - once they put on
blue slides and were friends. Feffie likes playing with
Anthea, they could have good games, but Feffie would
quickly be dropped if an older child turned up, or Anthea
got fed up.

246

Feffie didn't even like her name. It was alright if Mama or Dada used it - it felt nice then, warm and loving. But her brother and sister used to taunt her with it, and amongst the cousins it was a term of derision. They would tease her and taunt her, saying 'Feff-ie, Feff-ie' and then she hated her name. Her Uncle F, who was very large and rather frightening, although everyone else liked him, called her 'Stuffy' which used to make her feel she was no-one at all, because that wasn't her name.

All in all, Feffie didn't seem to get things right. Not many people seemed to like her, lots of children seemed to really hate her and hurt her, and even when people did like her she wasn't sure if it was because she was nice or because she was a vain, spoilt baby. When she eventually went to school, she discovered most people there didn't like her either, so she obviously wasn't very nice. She tried to be nice and good and desperately wanted people to love her, but nothing seemed to work.'

'So you must have felt something of an outsider in your family?' I asked.

'Maybe as a small child but things improved as I entered my teenage years and moved towards adulthood. Although the dreadful fights between my father and brother lived with me. I became close to my brother though ever more distant from my father. Once he said something when I was in the car alone with him. Something about what he said revolted me. It crossed a line. From then on, I maintained a distant relationship with him. My mother, meanwhile, became more important in my life. She took me to all sorts of events. And when as an adult, I messed up, lived wildly, she was always sympathetic and non-judgemental.'

'Rather the opposite in some ways from my experience', I said. 'As I've told you, I never doubted my mother's love for me as a child. But on the other hand, I lived a very isolated childhood. Do you know, I don't think I ever played with another child when I lived in Reigate, in other words up

247

to the age of five? When we moved, and I was sent to school, I had no idea of how to be with the other children. So after one day, I said I wasn't going back. So I moved schools. First to a convent school and then, when 7, to my prep school. As you know, my parents were supportive during my struggles at Taunton so eventually I was able to go to my Quaker public school'.

'My estrangement from my parents and my family began then', I continued. 'Thinking back to when I was young, I remember terrible rows, often involving my elder sister. She would pick up stuff and throw it. She and my mother would scream at each other. My father would say nothing but every now and then he lost it, would shout and swear and on occasion smash stuff himself. One day, when I suspect he was at the end of his tether, he pushed over a display cabinet containing a collection of cut glass. I remember Christmases when my uncle Herbert, my mother's brother, would come with his family. I loved him because he was so boisterous, jovial, funny and also played jazz piano brilliantly. But like his father, he liked to drink. The evenings would always get off to a great start, with humour and parlour games and music – but many was the occasion when, having finally been sent to bed, I would hear the most dreadful row going on below, with my uncle saying appalling things, painful things. This was a characteristic of my family, to lose it and say hideous things. I fear I have that within me now.'

'So how did being at school make a difference?'

'It was in part being outside the family. Being away from it so much and beginning to see how different other families were. In a way, Mum's favourite though I was, I never seemed to be able to influence events being the youngest and being in such a female dominated, choleric family. I became the good little uncomplaining boy. At my Quaker school, I gradually began, tentatively, and over years, to find myself more. Also I learnt to think and feel and to understand concepts and values never discussed at home. By the time I went to Cambridge, I felt very distant from my family.'

'I have found your family pretty terrifying. Do they know about you and me?'

'They do.'

'And?'

'My mother has had the sense not to say anything. After all, I am a 29 year old solicitor and partner in my own firm! But it's clear she's far from happy.'

'You know', I added 'I am sure one of the reasons I have been drawn to you is that you are so unlike my family. You exude a sense of peace and calm, of the contemplative, the inner life. I crave that.'

'But look at where my family life got Anthea. Estranged from the world of emotion, locked into the world of the intellect, prone to mad fixations on unlikely men. And Lindsay, so nervous and fearful, escaping into the world of medieval genealogy. And me, crashing from one mistake to another.'

'But Steffie, you have always engaged with life, not run away from it in the way Anthea and Lindsay appear to have done.'

'Well yes, that's a difference'.

'We both share the need to escape our backgrounds, don't we?'

'But we are what our backgrounds make us.'

'Yes, inevitably to some extent. But you are the one who has made me aware of this and the need to face up to our traumas. It's been really helpful for me. We are travelling, in our own different ways, on journeys into our pasts, into who we are, why we are as we are. And you have shown me, you have shown to yourself, just how important that is to being who we want to be, who we really are'.

'But', she said, 'examining those memories, reliving them, can be so painful'.

'Isn't that the point? That's what you've said'.

'Of course, as Elizabeth says, the pain has to be embraced, accepted, understood. Only that way can we be freed of it. But that doesn't make it easy'.

249

No, and there was a huge pain that I didn't face up to until my 60's when I had proper psychotherapy for the first time. I had eventually told Steffe about it but dismissed its importance, saying that I was very lucky it hadn't affected me. But more than 50 years after it happened, I talked to my therapist Peter about the sexual abuse I experienced at the hands of a teacher at my prep school. At last, it all came out in all its rawness. He got me to describe exactly what went on, the feelings I had had. And he became angry on my behalf and that liberated me – yes, I had all this anger bottled up inside me that I had never recognised was without doubt linked to the abuse of little 11 year old me.

SEVEN

Darling Roy,
Something I found in my dream and work book tonight.
Written just before Christmas 1980. It comes at the end of a
passage about values - that I had come to believe in a new
set of values but didn't know if I had the guts to live by
them.
'......If I could have balanced relationships but on the 'new'
assumptions (as opposed to the 'old' ones) would I have the
pain or wouldn't I? To what extent do I cause myself pain
by not believing thoroughly enough in my own values of
society? This was the way Roy and I used to feel - that even
if our relationship disobeyed all the social rules it was
obeying a higher much more important role - that when
you find the miracle of love, you had to let that love
flourish because it was the most precious thing there could
be. And there, at once, the memory floods back and I have
to turn my back on it because it is just more pain......I
threw it away - that didn't get taken, I threw it away - I
can't believe that I did, that I could have done, knowing
what I did. Why did I do it? Had I already become so
hardened? Was it this - that spiritually with Roy I could
grow and prosper but in terms of my emotional needs he
could not give me the props I always needed? What a
waste.'
Looking through the book I am filled with admiration for
my own courage in facing life through that winter. Things
were so bad, I really did have to reassess everything and
live a lot on faith - faith in the 'new' assumptions. I was

251

discovering, or really rediscovering. As I say in the
passage, I had already discovered them with you and then
thrown it all away. And as I rediscovered them through
Elizabeth, for the first time I fully appreciated the tragedy
of our separation, and the pain was so great, only you can
know how great, that I turned my back on it. But I didn't
really - I think from then onwards you were in my mind (I
would have sent you a Christmas card!).
Darling love - we were so foolish on Friday night - to have
hurt what was most dear to our hearts. Let us not do that
again.
Thank you for your beautiful birthday gifts. Never forget,
my love, that I treasure you most highly, that our love is
the most important thing in my life. I lost you once - now I
have you again, let me never abuse you again.
My love, Steffe xxx

It was a horrible row, the second we had. I was nasty. I hated myself for it. How healing was her letter.

Events were developing. Athelstan Road was on the market and I was looking for a cheap property in Bristol. Steffe and the boys were coming to Bristol. But the timing was uncertain so we continued to live apart, relying on weekends as far as we could.

My darling love,
I've been working on an essay for psychology which involves
reading Erikson, a chapter on play, and in it he talks of
'sex play' in love making - and I am suddenly cast into a
mood of terrible loneliness and love for you - a sudden
terrible realisation of the length of time which separates
us. A little while ago I finished the gateau we made for
supper on Saturday night; the sheet from our bed is now
washed and in the airing cupboard; the marks of our love

252

washed away. The candle we burn when we make love is
standing in its bottle, useless, unlit, with an age of wax
dripping down its sides. Sunday seems so long ago. I've
slept two nights on my own, hugging my hot-water bottle,
and I must spend ten more alone before I can hold you
again - and then so briefly. All the feelings of love I have
for you are associated with feelings of immense joy and
immense pain - Roy, I miss you, I miss you, life loses its
edge, seems to be just marking time, without you. Yet I
enjoy what I am doing, I feel satisfied, stimulated, etc. But
there is nothing to look forward to at the end of the day,
no-one to share my excitement, interest or worries with,
no-one to laugh about the children with, no-one to fill me
and complete me with their love as you do when we lie
together and our bodies and souls meet and create a new
being which transcends us both but which has the power to
nourish us and make us grow. But you are not here. .... I'm
sure Elizabeth would shake her head at this, but when you
have experienced the perfect joy of feeling so completely
and totally one with another as I do with you, the removal
of the other is like taking a precious part of oneself. I can
enjoy and value what I am doing - but I would infinitely
prefer it if I could do it with you, or share it with you after.
Now I shall return to Erikson and sex play which precedes
the final act ..... and love you, and cry for you, and long
for you.
My love, Steffe x

 As always, I made sure I had the space and time before I opened her
letter. They always demanded my total involvement. The letter lay before
me. I read it once, again, and then again. I was so moved, so grateful, so
overwhelmed. This was a love letter like she had never sent before. It
spoke to my very soul. The beauty of her words about our lovemaking,

253

expressing exactly what I feel, and indeed felt back when we were having an affair. What a stroke of fortune that we had found each other again and that we possessed a sexual chemistry that meant we both understood the other and our desires were entirely complimentary. That was central to our love for each other. Sexual language can transcend the rational, it can convey depths of feeling, and beyond all else it can enable union, that indescribable experience of merging into the other so together you become something beyond the individual.

I felt so grateful to have found my love again.

*

We were now actively planning our move and at the top of the agenda was sorting out schools for the boys. One weekend, we were visiting dearest Marc and Susie and talking through options. Susie mentioned that there was a Steiner school in Bristol. It meant nothing to me but Steffe responded positively.

'I know a bit about Steiner education. I'm interested.'

'I've never heard of Steiner. So can you explain a bit?' I asked.

'Well, I only have an impression really, but it seems to adopt an holistic approach, to value the creative, look at the whole child'.

'It's not that different from Montessori', said Susie.

We visited a couple of traditional primary schools and then met with the lead teacher for under 7's at the Bristol Waldorf School. Walking into the kindergarten was quite magical. Walls softly painted in pink, sharp corners made round, natural fabrics, wooden toys, hand-made dolls, no desks, an atmosphere of warmth and peace. We sat and talked to Winny, who became a good friend. The picture she painted of life for the little ones she cared for warmed our hearts and souls.

As we drove back to my flat, we enthused about what we had witnessed and made our decision. It was to prove a turning point, a new focus, for the family life we were about to share.

From Steffe's journal

*A message to my little three year old and any others who
may be feeling troubled at some time.*

*Tonight thirty three year old Steffe feels good and I want to
share it with you. My spirit feels good and calm and strong
- although my body is pretty tired! In the last three days
have felt and watched and been a part of a world of
natural beauty - I have stood on the cliffs and watched the
sea far below, the waves foaming over the rocks like lace,
the sky glowing and radiant over the water, between
heaven and earth, a glorious infinity of light and colour,
clear blue with the golden, piercingly bright rays of the
rising sun. I have felt the wind on my face and through my
hair and against my body, warm beneath thick jumpers,
enjoying the cold, bracing air that quickened the skin on
my hands and face but in no way chilled my soul. I have
breathed in the air, pulled the sharp cold air into my
lungs and felt that nature, the spirit of life, was entering
my body and driving the blood through my veins. And I
have felt every limb of my body respond to the energy of life
around me, and let it run and skip and kneel and sit and
run again like a child, delighting in the feeling of stretch
and pull and release, heaviness and lightness, my
bodyweight and gravity challenged by energy and joy. And
later, on another occasion, I have stood quietly at the top
of a hill surrounded on three sides by sea, river and
countryside lying far below me, and reaching into the
distance, broad horizons hinting at the immensity of
nature and its serenity and eternal beauty; and collected
myself, gathered myself together, allowing the fragmented
and bruised parts to return and exist alongside my strong*

and believing self, knowing they will be loved and accepted and welcomed gently back, safe in the protection of my accepting and respecting strong self; and I have waited quietly for the gathering together, watching the beauty around me, feeling the beauty of the love Roy and I share, feeling the vast peace and agelessness of the natural world. And felt so good, so alive, so joyful and calm, and excited and tranquil and here and now and being - and it was so, it is so, and it will be.

EIGHT

In April 1982, we moved. I had found a house in Montpelier, an alternative part of Bristol, overlooking St Pauls where I had now opened my new office. It was a very narrow house, a stone built Victorian terrace, but it was in a dilapidated condition. We had very little money – purely Steffe's share of the proceeds from Athelstan Road. Our house in Cobourg Road cost us £13,500! Moving into the house was pretty dismal. It had been left in a disgustingly filthy state. It wasn't what I wanted for Steffe. But we were happy to be together and buckled down to some serious cleaning.

But it wasn't all sunshine and roses. I still grappled with feelings of possessiveness and ridiculous jealousy, not that I gave a hint of them. But then we went on holiday to a beautiful cottage in Devon that our neighbour had put us on to. It was attached to another cottage, where the owners lived. They were a lovely couple of ageing artists. The cottage itself looked over a narrow valley, a stream at the bottom. The garden was steeped, with woodland on the left, and terraces below. The lane led down to a stone-built bridge that then rose to climb the far side of the valley. It was blissful.

One evening I was sitting out on the veranda smoking a cigarette and sipping some wine when Steffe came out, having put the boys to bed. She said:

'Maybe I could get married again'.

I was taken aback. I had totally accepted Steffe saying that she would not marry again. And then I realised she was proposing to me.

'Steffie, do you mean that?'

'I do'.

'Oh sweetheart, you cannot know what that means to me. Yes, I would love to marry you. I accept!'.

257

We came together, held each other in the fading light, and just looked into each other's eyes. I had never felt so good. Was this a dream?

'But I want it to be special', she said, 'Not like before. It needs to be somehow blessed. This time I really mean it. I want you as my life-long husband and partner.'

I was so moved, almost speechless. 'So do you have an idea of how we could do it?'

'I want it to be a church wedding. I want it to be spiritual. I want it to have the necessary solemnity.'

'I am so touched. God, I love you'. I hesitated and then said 'But it may not be easy. You know, you being divorced.'

She looked a bit downcast. I thought for a bit.

'Wait a minute, I have an idea! I've got to know the vicar of St Agnes church just around the corner from my office. He's quite the radical and outspoken on issues like race. I'll talk to him'.

'Really? You reckon there's a chance?'

'I can be very persuasive, Steffie, it's my job!'

'How can you be persuasive?'

'I will describe our love. Make it clear to him how special it is, because it is, isn't it? And I know we won't mess it up this time.'

So I spoke to him. I explained who we were, the history of our love, and our belief in it. He agreed to meet us as a couple.

'He's a nice guy, honestly. He knows you're divorced.'

'That I have been divorced twice?'

'Well, no. But why do we need to tell him?'

'I suppose not. But it makes me feel guilty'.

'It really shouldn't. You know that your marriage to John was purely as a result of pressure. You should just have lived together'.

'I know but I still feel so ashamed about my past. I hate even talking about it'.

'But Keith just wants to know that we are serious, that it's not some idle whim. That marrying in his church really matters to us in a deep and meaningful way'.

258

We met him two or three times and he gave us his blessing. But he then told us that he was leaving his parish three weeks later so we had to marry quickly! And marry quickly we did.

It was a miracle that so many of our friends were able to come, granted the shortness of notice. My parents very kindly agreed to hold the reception at their house and to organise, with our help and input, the food and drink – and cake!

We had a rehearsal a couple of days before, taking the boys with us. It was clear that they were pretty uninterested and just wanted to run around. So we asked them if they would prefer to play with our neighbour's children and then come down to the church afterwards and then go on to Bath. They liked the idea.

The day dawned to a clear blue sky and sunshine. A perfect September day. Steffe was wearing a mid-length soft pink skirt, almost gypsy in style, and a similarly rustic white shirt. Around her neck hung a silk pink scarf that she artfully draped over her front. She wore sandals and on her head a beautiful garland of wild flowers. Her hair was carefully cut and, as usual, she wore eye makeup that intensified the depth of her dark brown eyes.

We arrived at the church early. Keith led us to a side chapel, partitioned off from the main church. He spoke softly and warmly to us and then left us alone. We held hands and dwelt on what was about to happen. We could hear people arriving, loud voices at times. But we were alone together and that was very important.

Keith then entered and we followed him into the church itself. We walked across to two chairs set to the side at the bottom of the altar steps. Keith welcomed everyone. The service itself was very much of our own design. None of the readings were from the bible. Christian read from Kahlil Gibran's *The Prophet* on *Marriage*.

Silence fell. Keith asked for us to step forward and we stood with Keith in front of us and the congregation behind us. We then turned to face each other and joined hands . Then, with our eyes never moving from each other, we spoke our vows. We both felt it to be a profound and solemn

259

moment as we sealed our troths by the exchanging of rings. We then held each other and kissed.

Keith then spoke:

'To get married is an act of outrageous faith in disillusioned and cynical times like ours. Faith, because the worthwhileness of the act of commitment is something which will only be able to be assessed at some point in the future, looking back on what has happened over several decades together. Only then will it be possible to fill out the words of the vows, for better for worse, for richer for poorer, in sickness and in health – with real meaning out of personal experience.

If we really knew what it was going to be like, would we have the courage to set out on the journey? Knowing the risk of failure, what makes us believe it's worth it? It is not our ignorance of the journey that propels us but the gift of love.

Love leads us to trust and confide in each other, to want to be committed to stay with each other, irrespective of the risk. The kind of love which leads us to such an act of faith isn't ignorant or blind – but rather realistic about strengths and weaknesses, aspirations and failings. Such love is compassionate and able to forgive when things go wrong – honest about limitations, but always open to the possibilities of change and growth in both the self and the other person.

It is a very different, much deeper kind of love than that which is exalted in popular literature and song, because it makes room for the possibility of sharing suffering and pain as well as joy and hope, in a deep relationship. The shadow of fear constantly falls across the path of life. It sabotages our potential for growth, saps our creative energies and undermines our relationships with each other, as we become preoccupied with mastering the pain fear generates within.

Only the gift of love – the kind of love which creates this dimension of faith between people, is able to cast out fear and enable us to become what we are meant to be. That gift of love is able to fulfil every aspect of our existence. It is something to seek wholeheartedly all our days'.

We were both deeply affected and moved by his words. The ceremony could not have been more perfect. There is a photo of us walking back down the church at the end, holding hands. Steffie has such a happy smile as did I, but there was in that grin also pure satisfaction at having married my true love after such a long journey.

So yes, reader, I married her.

As we came out of the church, the boys ran to us. I took Joe in my arms and Paul held on to Steffe's hand. Photos were taken. I was so proud, so in love with, so delighted by, my new little family. I felt a real adult man. I was dizzy with happiness at the reception as was Steffie. We took time to sit alone together in the garden, terraced and overlooking the city of Bath. Again, there are photos that capture that time – cleverly taken. Pure happiness shone from our faces as we talked, laughed and kissed. It wasn't a grand wedding, with music and dancing into the night. We couldn't have organised that even had we wanted it. But that evening all we sought was to spend time together on our own. So we drove off to the place we were staying in our beloved St Catherine's valley and sank into a rather drunken dream-like state.

Can it really have been just a little over a year ago that Steffe, who I had thought to be just part of my history, had rung me up? And now she was my wife, she had committed herself to me, I knew that, just as I had committed myself to her. Steffe meant every word she had said when taking our vows, that meant everything to me.

It changed things in an entirely good way. I can't say my trust issues completely disappeared overnight, but they basically did. They would just occasionally remind me of their existence, but only mildly. I knew we were going to be together for ever.

Post Script

6 December 2019

We were sitting down for lunch. I had prepared tuna and cucumber sandwiches. We started eating and then I remembered we had received a delivery – a Christmas present for our grandson Marley, our daughter Rosie's second child. I sprang up and went to my study to collect the parcel. I took it back to our dining room, placed it on the table – and then, out of the blue, Steffe collapsed from her chair onto the floor. My first thought was that she had fainted. She had a tendency to. But when I looked at her, her eyes were open and still. I kneeled and immediately realised she wasn't breathing. She had no pulse. I screamed out 'You can't leave me!' and then just acted instinctively. I tried to give her mouth to mouth but got nowhere. I then frantically employed what I knew of CPR. I realise it helped that I was so desperate because I pushed down on her chest repeatedly very hard. And she began, so laboriously, to breathe. Only then did I ring 999. An enlarged ambulance crew arrived within 2 minutes. A paramedic held up her head and asked me if her face looked normal. A stroke test. Yes, the same. I left the dining room. It was so full of people and I was in despair.

I got speaking to one of the crew.

'Look. She's a very ill woman. She has suffered from ME for so many years. She couldn't bear it if she came back from this brain-damaged. Did I do the wrong thing?'

'Does she have an advance directive?'

'Yes she does somewhere. She did it through Dignatis.'

'Well, let's see where we are first, eh?'

He was so kind and understanding. I stood in our front room and was joined by 2 of the paramedics. They responded so empathetically to my turmoil.

Then I heard a voice calling out – 'Roy. Roy'.

I ran to the dining room and knelt down and held her hands, looked into her face. She looked so terrified, confused – my poor love. Her speaking was slurred. I sought to assure her that all was well. She calmed down.

Tests showed all seemed normal again. Everyone relaxed. The emergency was over.

Steffe was placed in the ambulance. 'Can I have a fag before we go?' I asked one of the guys. 'Of course, take your time'

After smoking quickly, I climbed into the ambulance. I took hold of Steffe's hand and started to explain to the crew Steffe's profound health issues. I t told them she had twice been an inpatient at the Romford Hospital CFS unit. I tried to remember the name of the guy who ran it when Steffe said 'Professor Leslie Findlay'. Then I knew her brain was ok.

Into A & E. Steffe had, overtly at least, recovered. Hours passed before she was taken to an admission ward and a room on her own. It all felt so unreal to both of us. What had happened? A doctor came and asked questions but gave no answers. Eventually I left.

I arrived early next morning, going to the ward she had been on only to find she had been moved to the cardiology unit in the Bristol Heart Foundation. I found my way there, an impressive new building funded by the largesse of the last Labour Government – for all its faults, a Government that rebuilt the NHS, PFI deals notwithstanding.
I found her lying in a spacious ward with 6 beds. But I immediately realised it would be so hard for her as a massively disabled victim of severe ME. The others wouldn't understand why she had to lie down so much, and she would not be able to raise her already soft voice across the ward. I sat down and held her hand.
We gently talked. I helped her when needed, like when she shuffled across to the bathroom. The nurses, all from overseas, were so caring, although I almost got caught out one night by a nurse as I was sneaking a sleeping pill to Steffe.

Visits by the junior doctor were rather strange and a bit frustrating. She would repeatedly refer to Steffe's 'fainting' and again and again I had to make it clear that it wasn't a faint – she had died. I pretty quickly realised from my online research that she had suffered a sudden cardiac arrest. Meanwhile, Steffe was fed a cocktail of drugs – all based on possible

268

causes for her unrecognised condition. Blood thinners that meant she began to bleed from her nose …. It all seemed rather haphazard.

Steffe began to find the whole experience traumatic. I was with her all day, every day but a hospital ward is no place for someone with such complex needs that only I understood. She had tests but nothing abnormal was found. It came to the point where the only reason she was remaining in was to have an MRI – but there was a long waiting list and it would take days to happen . So we decided that she should discharge herself. Nothing like that to get the lead consultant to your bedside. He listened but said there was a risk of something happening which could only be dealt with in hospital. Steffe, supported by me, said that the other risk was that her ME would get worse if she remained in hospital as would her mental condition. The consultant said he understood and after 8 days Steffe left hospital. The discharge form said she had suffered from a sudden cardiac arrest – the first time the medics had said this.

*

It was wonderful to have Steffe home. At first, it seemed that she had got through the whole thing unscathed. Weak, battered (bruised ribs from my CPR), disorientated but no apparent brain or body disfunction.

She had an MRI at the end of January. Her heart showed no abnormality. So what caused her SCA? Strangely a question that was not followed up, no more than she was.

But things started to go wrong. She started to misfunction in a myriad of ways. Sleeplessness, acute fatigue, and unusual phenomena like a dry, burning, hot mouth. This just got worse and worse and began to drive poor Steffe crazy. A newly fledged GP from our surgery took Steffe under her wing and would visit regularly and really listen to her. But nothing she tried helped. Steffe just declined.

I searched the internet madly getting anything that might perhaps help, but nothing did.

I had booked us a week during May in an old boathouse by the river Avon near Stratford. We had gone the previous year and had really enjoyed ourselves. But this time, Steffe said 'I am just too ill for this'. We did our best but I knew things were bad.

By now, I had found out a lot about sudden cardiac arrests. How the major organs start shutting down after just 20 seconds. And I asked myself how could a body, so compromised by ill health, recover from such a shock to the system?

Adam Kay, in a footnote from *This is going to Hurt*, writes:
'If your heart stops, you're probably going to die. God is fairly strict on that matter. If you collapse on the street and a bystander starts CPR then your chance of survival is around 8%. In hospital, with trained personnel, drugs and defibrillators, it's only about twice that. People don't realize quite how horrific resuscitation is — undignified, brutal and with a fairly woeful success rate. When discussing Do Not Resuscitate orders, relatives often want 'everything to be done' without really knowing what that means. Really, the form should say, 'If your mother's heart stops, would you like us to break all her ribs and electrocute her?'

Amazingly, Steffe was never electrocuted nor did I actually break any ribs. But …..

Things only got worse. My poor, poor Steffe. For the first time during all her years of illness, I told her, 'I feel my toolbox is empty. I just don't know how to help you.'

No longer were we able to grab those little moments of pleasure and joy.

1 July 2019

We were in our sitting room, Steffe lying on the sofa. She had mentioned how she would like to read some of the letters between her mother, Molly, and father, Eric, during the war years when Eric was away with the RAF in Africa. I told her I had dug them out. She suggested I get them and read them out.

I did. They were extraordinary. Passionate, deeply loving, intense. Steffe was profoundly affected. She had no idea that once the relationship between her parents had such quality.

We felt very close.

2 July 2019

'You know, your mother's letters reminded me so much of yours. A great writer, just like you.'

'I have been really struck by those letters. I never knew. It's good to know.'

'Shall I get out your letters from when our relationship started?'

'Yes, that would be lovely.'

So I read them. It was so lovely to re-experience those days. From time to time, we looked into each other's eyes and smiled. It felt so warm and lovely. Us.

I joined her in bed that night and held her in my arms until she fell to sleep. Then I crept out to get into my own separate bed in the front room. We had been forced to sleep separately many years before because her disabilities meant she needed to be able to use the whole double bed.

3 July 2019

I woke at about 7.15 and went into Steffe's room. I gasped in horror. She was dead. Grey and as if covered in ice. I could hardly approach her. My love, my love.

What should I do? I googled and found I needed to ring 999 who put me through to the police. That surprised me.

'It's my wife. She's died in the night.'

'A knife?' he replied.

'No! During the night'.

I was told a policeman would come round. He came just before an ambulance with 2 paramedics. They were hopelessly carrying an oxygen cylinder and mask. The policeman was very kind. He chatted to me as I stood in the kitchen, tears running down my face. A female paramedic came in, confirming Steffe's death.

'How do I tell my daughter? She lives nearby.'

271

'How about texting her, asking her to come round?'

I did but immediately Rosie rang. She knew straightaway.

So she came, followed by her partner Arran. We sat quietly in the sitting room until the paramedics and the policeman left. We were to wait for the coroner to collect Steffe's body. We didn't watch them take her away. Words are inadequate.

*

Later on, when alone again, I went to her bedroom and found an envelope addressed to me. I opened it and saw it was a birthday card from Steffe to me, my birthday being the 6th.

My darling love
Roy

Here is the special
card we have been
saving for you!
Hope you have a
very Happy Birthday

my love
   forever
      and ever

Steffe x x x x

Thank you for the
life you have given
me and above all,
the LOVE. I love
you so much x x x

The children were wonderful. Paul flew over from Prague and stayed for a long time. He was such a support. Rose and Joe were so understanding of my pain.

We came together planning Steffe's funeral. We had already bought plots, side by side, at the Memorial Woodlands, north of Bristol. Acres of woodland, orchards and grassland. We had both decided we wanted to be buried.

Rosie came with me to meet the funeral director. We said we wanted no celebrant, that we wanted to run the service ourselves. He assured us he would do all he could to facilitate that. We chose a wicker coffin, saying that we would arrange the flowers. Rosie asked a fishponds local grower to provide seasonal, cottage garden flowers, for the coffin and in little jars to put around the reception area.

Paul agreed to design and produce the order of service. It was beautiful. It incorporated the music I had chosen to play. We were going to give Steffe a wonderful funeral.

On Thursday 16 July, Rosie and I went to meet Steffe in her open coffin. I approached nervously but then saw her, beautiful, at peace, and wearing the clothes we had chosen. I placed my hand on her cold one, lent forward and talked to her. I was strangely cheerful. Somehow I wanted to say things would be ok. But I was so, so sad. My beloved. It felt like I had lost half of my soul, of what made me who I am. I left the room allowing Rosie to have her own time with her Mum.

22 July 2019

We rose early and Paul and I loaded the car with booze, stopping off to collect the flowers. We drove to the Woodlands. All was so peaceful. They only allow one funeral a day, so you have the whole place to yourself, the beamed reception rooms, fronted by a large pool with water lilies, carp and large goldfish, all the grounds – and, for us, the chapel.

275

We went in and saw Steffe's coffin resting at the front. All religious elements had been taken away, as requested. We carried the flowers for her coffin and laid them on top. We both just stood there.

People arrived and at noon we all entered the chapel. A group of Rosie's friends sang softly and beautifully.

Jeff Buckley's 'Corpus Christi Carol' was played.

Then I, directing my words to Steffe in her coffin, read my last letter to her:

My darling love,

Letters were for a time such an important part of our relationship. Since you died, I have reread your letters so many times. They were so beautiful, so rich, so full of meaning. And seeing your gorgeous handwriting makes my heart melt. So let me write one more letter to you, my sweet love.

How I remember getting to know you after we first met in 1972. How I remember finding you unspeakably beautiful, intriguing, fascinating, sensuous, graceful, deep, complex and intelligent. Our coming together, when it came, was magically powerful. I was just 20. In one of your earliest letters, you wrote:

'Do you realise that I'm nearly 5 years older than you? Have you tried following that thought around?
Here's looking at you kid'

Do you remember the night when it all properly started? I had been coming round to where you lived with increasing frequency. Do you remember how one stoned night, I rushed back to my lodgings to fetch this amazing album by a new band, Roxy Music? I put it on your turntable and I was so thrilled by you being so knocked out by it. That first album became the sound track of our early days. You will hear a shortened version of If There is Something at the end of this ceremony. But the night so deeply etched in our memories was at a party when I wanted nothing more than for us to come together. I was standing still when I felt a finger run itself from the base of my spine to its top and hearing the voice I have always loved so much say 'I'm crazy about you'. The joy, the joy.

So why did we fall in love? Right from the beginning, we sensed some fundamental soul-like connection that we never lost. How I loved hearing about your days in the late 60's, how you embraced the counter-culture of those radical times in all its aspects, exploring new ideas, alternative values, different ways of looking at the world – not to mention the liberating hedonism that was central to that counter-culture. You were there at the famous Grosvenor Square demonstration against the Vietnam war in 1968, for goodness sake! And your time at Durham university sounded such fun.

When I came up to Cambridge, I was yearning to discover and enter the counter culture that had so entranced me from the age of 15. At school, I had overtly been the star pupil, the Oxbridge candidate, the head boy – living up to the expectations of others but I felt there were whole aspects of myself that I had not been able explore. Coming to Cambridge seemed at last to give me the chance of real freedom. You were absolutely key to this. I know that by the time you came to live in the city, you had lost some of the dynamism and spirit of rebellion, of alternative values, of inner exploration and spirituality. And I know that I somehow reignited your fire and what a journey of discovery we then had.

It is pointless to ignore how drugs were also part of the picture. But in those heady days, they were used by us to enhance experience, indulge in some astonishing music, and to open up new doors of perception. How we would open our hearts, minds and souls to each other! And what books you led me to, be it Hermann Hesse, the anti-psychiatrist R.D. Laing, Tom Wolfe's Electric Kool Aid Acid Test and so many others. And of course, crucially what music! How I miss the many evenings we spent throughout

277

our lives together listening to an amazingly wide range of music. From Dylan, Cohen, Jefferson Airplane through to Nick Cave, Laura Marling, Imogen Heap, Radiohead and so much more.

But beyond else, we felt our souls touching and that our love somehow was becoming bigger than any ordinary love. What a crazy passionate affair we had. We constantly separated purely because you tried so hard to do the right thing. But the mutual yearning never faded. And during those times of separation, your lovely letters were such a balm. And again and again we came back together because we just couldn't bear to be apart.

Dear Ivo, who sadly cannot be here today, wrote after I told him of your death "It is so long since I saw her so I will always remember her in all her splendour at Cambridge – how ethereally beautiful she was with a wry humour". I thought you would like that. And so true – your sheer beauty was overwhelming.

But all the while, you were determined to advance yourself, so for 3 years from 1972 to 1975 you worked so hard to obtain an exceptional degree from the LSE in social policy. Meanwhile, as you will recall all so well, I, along with quite a few friends, did basically no work for much of our second and third years. I had lost all interest in the desiccated Cambridge law course and instead thought there were much better things to apply myself to. Night after night, talking with friends till 5 in the morning. Do you remember when my day inverted? Sleep from 8am until 4 or 5pm, and then the day/night starting. And always you were in my thoughts and heart all the time.

Then, after 3 years, things went wrong. I think this is when our age difference mattered. I was immature, just 23 and frankly all over the place, you were 28. So we separated for 5 years. I never stopped loving you and thinking about you but never thought I would hear from you again.

Then, in 1981, I was sitting in my office having been at court and my secretary buzzed me to say there was someone called Steffe on the phone. I couldn't believe it and hearing your voice was pure joy. I learnt that things had gone badly for you with the sole exception of now having 2 wonderful boys, Paul and Joe. We met in London 2 days later and wasn't that a magical time we had. It was like, as it proved to be, neither of us had stopped loving the other and it felt like 2 souls were reuniting again.

You wrote shortly after "The first meeting left me so absolutely high to the point of confusion, bewilderment and so to anxiety". Later, you wrote "I love you desperately; I do absolutely and honestly know that I always loved you and that I always will love you. And equally I absolutely believe in your love for me". And so began our new, lifelong, life affirming, adventure.

As before, we returned to exploring the inner meaning of life. You led me to the writings of Carl Jung, spiritual feminist works like The Moon and the Virgin, The Way of All Women, and so on.

You were so nervous about me meeting the boys. Would it be OK? I stayed with you all for a fortnight and it was just splendid. The best summer holiday ever. I love little kids and the boys awoke the child-like in me and we played endlessly. You wrote afterwards how it was 'blissful'. 9 months later you all moved to Bristol and we became a family. And what precious fabulous letters you wrote over those 9 months. I treasure every one.

In one letter, written soon after we got back together, you said you would never marry again. After you moved to Bristol, we took a holiday in a lovely cottage in Devon that we returned to many times. I remember sitting out on the veranda one evening and you coming out and saying in a typically low key way 'maybe I could get married again'. I was being proposed to! Though neither of us is religious as such, we both felt that a register office just wouldn't do justice to what our marrying represented. We wanted to marry in church but there was the problem of you being divorced. It was only in 2002 that the Church of England said divorced people could marry in church. I had started working in St Pauls and got to know the vicar of St Agnes church, Keith Kimber. So I spoke to him and explained our wishes. He met you and me over a period of time and he said he knew it was the right thing to do to let us marry in church. He was quite the radical. But then he explained that he was leaving his post in 3 weeks time so we had to marry quickly. And we did. My darling, the photos from that day really do capture our unadulterated happiness.

So our life together in Bristol began. Through you, we discovered the Bristol Waldorf School and the educational theories and practices of Rudolf Steiner. All our children received a Steiner education. How you and then me embraced the spirit of the school. You became so involved in the school community and together we learnt a whole different approach to family life. You were brilliant at weaving the seasons and the festivals of the year into our home life. You were so typically diligent at making our house a place of beauty.

Meanwhile, you were looking ahead at what you wanted to do. Having done social work and teaching, you undertook a course in counselling and always had as your aim becoming a psychotherapist. Sadly, because of your devastating illness, you were never able to achieve this ambition. That makes me so sad. You were so empathic, so understanding, so wise, so clear headed, so intrigued by deep psychology, so in touch with your soul life – you would undoubtedly have been an amazing psychotherapist.

And then, of course, your political activism – a passion we both shared. In the early '80s, with cruise missiles being deployed at Greenham Common, weren't we genuinely terrified by the prospect of nuclear annihilation, terrified for Paul and Joe? You became so active in the fight back, going to Greenham, going to Newbury Magistrates Court to support those arrested,

280

and forming with others your peace group, Women for Life and Peace. Your commitment to a better world never faltered. Though unable to participate directly, in recent years you recognised the climate emergency as the number one threat and, like me, thought constantly of our grandchildren.

You then became pregnant and our joy was boundless. On the very morning of your own birthday, a beautiful sunny morning, you gave birth to our beloved daughter Rose. By this time, we were both following Steiner's wisdom so for 7 days you were with Rose in the candle lit room where she was born so that for one week she was never exposed to brightness, since you wanted to ease her passage from the womb to the harshness of the world.

1987 arrived. We enjoyed a wonderful, really active holiday in France. But in October, you fell ill to the illness that in so many ways robbed you of the life you could and should have had. My darling, I don't want to dwell on the years that followed. But you proved yourself to be such a brave, uncomplaining and stoical woman. And our love never faltered. We grabbed what pleasures we could and we made ourselves a life. Books and music became central to our lives and we saw our children grow up and become grandparents. What grandchildren we have. Your closeness to Marley and Elijah in particular gave you, I know, such warmth. It is so sad you will not see them all grow and mature.

Sweetheart, I miss you, I miss you. My love for you will remain with me all my life. You are now in my heart and in my soul. At least I can tell myself you are free of the suffering you endured these last few months. But I miss you.

All my love, now and forever.

Music: 'Only With You' by the Beach Boys.

Then Rosie spoke:

Dear Mum,

There is so much to say, too much for this moment and much of which cannot even be shaped into words – and yet I know you will know it all.

But if I can capture just a little bit of it here, what would I say? I would like to talk about the great gifts you have given me. There is so much to take from all that you were and all that you are. If I were to pull on that, if I were to let that be my guide, how would I choose to live my life? What things would I call in?

I think of your bravery. Your enormous bravery in life and in the face of so much challenge – I would like to call in that courage and let it fill my heart.

I think of your sense of adventure' I have learnt so much through reading through your old letters and journals and by the amazing stories you shared. So I would like to call in your sense of adventure – to drink it in, to say YES, to grasp every opportunity with both hands, to let adventure be part of the everyday.

I think of your boldness and your fabulous first letter to Dad, so I hear you say 'be bold', be upfront in who you are and what you want and ignite that boldness in others.

I welcome in your sense of quiet – the beauty that can be found in silence and stillness, in peaceful observation and reflection.

I welcome in your sense of belief, conviction and passion – your desire to make a difference. I want to act on that, to stand up for what matters and do it boldly and beautifully.

I welcome in your sense of the feminine – the powerful, heartfelt spiritual woman who seeks to nurture and who can and will make a difference.

I think of your wisdom and intelligence – your incredibly sharp and perceptive mind and your journey of inner growth.

I remember those moments when I used to read to you and I am grateful for the books you introduced me to, and the love of literature and language you helped to instil.

I think of your dry humour, wit and smiley eyes.

I think of your gentle connection with our children, your heart so close and your love so deep for them.

I think of your beauty and spirit – and call upon that spirit to walk in and with me.

And finally, when I think of you – and you and Dad – I think of the gift of great love. The power, beauty, truth, rarity and preciousness of love. The gift of bravery and belief to dive into love and keep returning to it again and again. To let love in and to trust in love – and give that gift out to the world.

And so I would like to end with what the vicar said at Mum and Dad's wedding. Theirs was a marriage which really summed up the meaning of true, eternal love.

And yours, Mum, was a heart so full of love.

Music: 'Heaven' by Talking Heads.

Then Paul spoke:

I so wish I had clearer recall of Mum in the days of my childhood, before she got ill. But there was nothing, then, to tell us that Dartmoor rambles and Cornish beaches and long bicycle rides in Brittany would soon become a thing of the past.

But I do remember. Mostly small memories, inconsequential, like the mystery of Mum ordering her crepes "beurre sucre" when she could have had them with a proper filling like chocolate ice cream.

I remember mum's fear that we would live to see a global nuclear war, and her fierce determination to make our future safer. I remember Rainbow Warrior stickers and CND badges everywhere. I remember going to visit mum at Greenham Peace Camp. How cool is that?

I remember a party when us kids all got face and body paint. I wanted a Native American warrior with a spear on my front. Mum being Mum – the anti-war activist – she painted the spear point down to show he came in peace. Kids being kids, I decided it was to make the spear quicker to throw at an enemy. Sorry, Mum.

I remember Mum's dreadful Italian lover, Luigi. Ah, Luigi! Roy had these characters he played to make us laugh, and Luigi was one of them. He would show up any time we had Italian food to try to seduce mum in the most outrageous ways he could think of, running kisses up her arm and leering appallingly while she struggled to fight him off in laughing horror. Such small memories, but they add up to one big memory: a memory of being surrounded by a huge, unquestioning love.

Children begin by loving their parents, then after a time they find them a screaming embarrassment. It's a part of growing up, like horrible taste in music and unwise haircuts. Which, as it happens, was a topic close to my

284

mother's heart. It still brings a glow to my cheeks to remember the hairbrush of humiliation at the school gates. Later she'd wonder endlessly how I could see with that fringe over my eyes, and tried to convince me that an Alice band would make me look like Axel Rose. Yeah, right, Mum. Almost everything changed after Mum became ill. Never her love and loyalty, of course. And never the thing with the hair, either. Even when I was in my twenties, every time I visited she had The List of things she needed to talk to me about – and number one was always The Hair.

To a child, Mum is just Mum. A child's vision doesn't have room for a whole grown-up person with their own life and history and needs and loves. So it was really as an adult that I got to know Mum not just as my Mum but as a friend.

We bonded over Dylan and Cohen, and I learned bits of her past. And I realise that damn, she was cool! I went to Reclaim the Streets demos. She was at Grosvenor Square! I hitched to the Reading Festival. She hitchhiked across America and took mescaline! I saw the Levellers. She saw Jimi Hendrix play at the Roundhouse! It was fun. I still boast about how cool my Mum was!

Any yet these were also the decades of the illness that stole so much of her life and robbed her of so many joys. She felt a tremendous sadness at how it prevented her from being a "proper mother" – and, later, grandmother. But she was a wonderful mother. And she was my friend.

She also became an ally, a comrade-in-arms in the long battles we both fought against mental illness – which for her was one of the effects of ME. Mental illness, at its heart, is about ways of thinking and feeling and acting that don't give way to reason. Everyone who suffers mental illness has known that point when others' empathy gives way to frustration. One precious secret Mum and I shared was that we could go that step further, *truly understanding each other even when our reactions were obviously broken. I'm grateful for that.*

That illness though. My Mum was a hell of a fighter. It was awesome. She fought her illness in every way she knew, Roy at her side as her constant ally and support.

It would be absurd to say her courage never faltered.

Again and again she won small and hard-fought victories, clawing part of her life back through sheer effort and determination, only to have her achievements snuffed out by yet another relapse. She frequently despaired. The erosion of her strength, her increasing isolation, the sheer inevitability of her illness – how could she not?

And yet. And yet.

Over the last few years, Mum and Roy launched perhaps the most magnificent, most inspiring of their challenges to M.E. They decided that they would seize hold of small joys and revel in them, accepting the cost. They were small joys indeed, like listening to music together on a Saturday evening, with a glass of wine. Or making very brief trips to beautiful places like Birdcage Walk. They even went on some short holidays. The rediscovery of taking joy in such things – it was truly wonderful. I cannot begin to say how much these things meant to Mum.

The cardiac arrest at the beginning of the year was a final, terrible denial of every one of her victories. It left her broken in body and despairing in spirit. Her passing, now, was undoubtedly a freeing, but I am so thankful that she stayed with us those last few months. It gave us time for a final bonding, a long farewell.

We spoke often on the phone, long calls that gave us both comfort. And the last times I visited I read to her, sharing some of my favourite stories. I sat in peace with her, held her hand, shared acceptance and a deep love. That's a beautiful thing to hold on to at the end.

286

Music: 'Shelter from the Storm' by Bob Dylan

The Joe spoke:

Thank you Paul, Rose and Roy for your wonderful words.

I would like to talk about how Mum inspired me intellectually, and in my relationship.

We were brought up to be empathic and inquiring. We discussed politics at the supper table. So we were intellectually interested in the world - but also caring to change it.

I was inspired to follow Mum's footsteps to study social sciences at university, and to live in Brighton where she had lived as a girl - I even took some of her old sociology books with me.

While I followed her subject, I couldn't quite live up to her hedonistic approach to university life.

Later also followed her into the LSE – treading the same corridors, lecture theatres, even discovered I had one of the same tutors as she had had in the 70s.

While I was there I spoke to Mum about my latest essay in the morning, before going in to my interview at the IPPR – then used all our ideas in the interview. That meant I was able to escape the civil service that was not allowing me to express that sense of inquiry and empathy.

Radio was her window onto the outside world and she would always tell me when one of my tutors or colleagues had been on, keeping tapes for me to listen to or sending me iPlayer references (and then checking that I had listened).

I hope she got some satisfaction from my following in her footsteps, and I hope I can stay true to those values of inquiry and empathy.

But I also know for a fact that whatever pride she might have felt in a degree certificate or a new job was nothing compared to her relief, and then delight, when at the age of 20 I finally brought home my first girlfriend, Claire.

Mum & Roy's love was an inspiration for me – and it was clearly very important to her that we found love in our lives.

Mum and Roy's love was also an inspiration to us as a couple - their love for each other as well as shared love for nature, beauty, music, art and literature and for ideas.

Mum was a source of wisdom for Claire and me as we developed our relationship, our career and our travels, and then in our own parenting.

We already miss her wisdom, but we are lucky to have known it and even luckier to have discovered in the past few days a jewel that she left us.

Claire and I finally got married in 2008, a couple of years after Mum had given up asking me when I was going to propose. One of the biggest worries for us was whether Mum could be there with us when we got married.

But she decided to make a trip of a lifetime (in Lindsey's Quirky Campervan) to come to Sussex, having not been further than Nailsea dental surgery for about 10 years, and not seen more than 10 people at once for even longer.

It was such a huge undertaking that, like Scott of the Antarctic, she kept a diary of her adventure, on an audio recorder. And in the last weeks, we discovered these recordings and found they contain such beautiful, eloquent, inspiring and wise reflections, that spoke to us in this time of mourning and celebrating our love for Mum.

288

So this is Steffe, this is Mum's voice if you can bear to imagine her lying in the van while the rain hammered down on the wedding outside:

'Having thought about it some more, I think the effect of having been practically a recluse to suddenly being in amongst this enormous group of people had this effect on me:

When you are just with one or two people you are just exchanging emotional energy with them, it's not too complicated, and that's what I've been doing for the last god knows how many years. Never more than five or six or at the most ten people at once. So this is what happened.

When I got into the church and I looked around, I saw lots of faces that I knew, from all different stages of my life, really from babyhood through to just now. And it was as if all the different mes, all the different stages of my life became overlapping each other and adding to each other, and I was exchanging this emotional energy with this very big crowd of people. And that almost overwhelmed me, and for a couple of minutes I nearly became overwhelmed literally, and was just going to sit and weep.

And then I remembered Joe and Claire, and I realised that all these versions of me that I had been glimpsing had all arrived at this 60 year old woman who was watching her son getting married and I actually managed to come back to my centre, and be that woman. And reengage with exactly what was happening before my eyes.

And the other thing that was happening was that these two people, Joe and Claire, were having a peak experience. When I say a peak experience I mean they were living in every cell of their emotional and spiritual and physical bodies in that moment, they were so there, so communicating to each other and so demonstrating the depth of their love for each other , that they really did give off this physical buzz that made everybody buzz. That's what made it such an intense experience, and made it so wonderful. And it became a peak experience for me and for Roy, and we've talked

289

about it and we really do feel this. It's been a truly, truly special and unique day.'

When we listen back to Mum's beautiful voice it feels like she is speaking to us again, sharing her wisdom, her spirituality, her love. We can all carry that with us in our hearts forever.

So as we all sit in this chapel today remembering Mum/ Steffe, let us remember all our different Steffes, all her different mes and stages of her life. Allow them to overlap and add to each other, and exchange that overwhelming emotional energy together.

Then let us also come back to our centre and engage with this moment as a peak experience to celebrate the love that we feel for Steffe in every cell of our emotional and spiritual and physical bodies in this moment. Let's try and feel the buzz of our love and her love.

Music: 'Suzanne' by Leonard Cohen.

There was there a period of peaceful reflection when two of her old friends spontaneously shered some of their experience of Steffe. Then 'If there is Something' by Roxy Music began to play. Paul, Joe, Claire, Rosie, her partner Arran and I then rose and assembled around the coffin. Under direction, we took hold of the rope handles and lifted it on to our shoulders. We then slowly walked down the central aisle and exited the double doors st the back. There was a dais waiting and her coffin was placed on it. It was pushed along a gravel drive, us beside it, guests following. We came to the pear and apple orchard where she was to be buried. We went to the graveside and the coffin was placed on a pedestal with leather straps underneath. Rosie's friends again sung, very softly and gently. Rosie read a poem as did I.

290

We then took hold of the leather straps, lifted her coffin and lowered her into her grave.
Flowers were tossed and we slowly returned to the reception area.

Stephanie Claire Douglas
6.3.1948 - 3.7.2019
Deeply loving
Deeply loved
SP88-86

Roy Douglas is a retired criminal defence solicitor and university lecturer in law. He has 3 children and 6 grandchildren. He lives in Bristol.

Printed in Great Britain
by Amazon